HTML
THIRD EDITION – ILLUSTRATED

INTRODUCTORY

HTML
THIRD EDITION – ILLUSTRATED

INTRODUCTORY

Vicki L. Cox
Elizabeth Eisner Reding
Lynn Wermers

COURSE TECHNOLOGY
CENGAGE Learning

Australia • Brazil • Japan • Korea • Mexico • Singapore • Spain • United Kingdom • United States

COURSE TECHNOLOGY
CENGAGE Learning™

HTML, Third Edition — Illustrated Introductory
Vicki L. Cox, Elizabeth Eisner Reding, Lynn Wermers

Managing Editor: Marjorie Hunt

Senior Product Manager: Christina Kling Garrett

Associate Product Manager: Shana Rosenthal

Editorial Assistant: Janine Tangney

Senior Production Editor: Catherine G. DiMassa

Developmental Editor: Barbara Clemens

Marketing Manager: Joy Stark

Marketing Coordinator: Melissa Marcoux

QA Manuscript Reviewers: John Freitas,
    Susan Whalen, Ashlee Welz

Text Designer: Joseph Lee, Black Fish Design

Composition House: GEX Publishing Services

For product information and technology assistance, contact us at
Cengage Learning Customer & Sales Support, 1-800-354-9706
For permission to use material from this text or product, submit all requests online at **www.cengage.com/permissions**
Further permissions questions can be emailed to
permissionrequest@cengage.com

ISBN-13: 978-0-619-26845-9

ISBN-10: 0-619-26845-X

Course Technology
20 Channel Center Street
Boston, MA 02210
USA

Cengage Learning is a leading provider of customized learning solutions with office locations around the globe, including Singapore, the United Kingdom, Australia, Mexico, Brazil, and Japan. Locate your local office at:
international.cengage.com/region

Cengage Learning products are represented in Canada by Nelson Education, Ltd.

To learn more about Course Technology, visit **www.cengage.com/coursetechnology**

To learn more about Cengage Learning, visit **www.cengage.com.**

Purchase any of our products at your local college store or at our preferred online store **www.ichapters.com**

Steve Jobs photo courtesy of Al Luckow; New Media Architect

Web site permissions courtesy of Laramie County Community College; Town of Estes Park, Colorado; Tomahawk Resort; Google; comScore; and Macromedia.

Trademarks:
Some of the product names and company names used in this book have been used for identification purposes only and may be trademarks or registered trademarks of their respective manufacturers and sellers.

Printed in the United States of America
5 6 7 8 9 10

The Illustrated Series Vision

Teaching and writing about computer applications can be extremely rewarding and challenging. How do we engage students and keep their interest? How do we teach them skills that they can easily apply on the job? As we set out to write this book, our goals were to develop a textbook that

- works for a beginning student
- provides varied, flexible, and meaningful exercises and projects to reinforce skills
- serves as a reference tool
- makes your job as an educator easier, by providing resources above and beyond the textbook to help you teach your course

Our popular, streamlined format is based on advice from instructional designers and customers. This flexible design presents each lesson on a two-page spread, with step-by-step instructions on the left, and screen illustrations on the right. This signature style, coupled with high-caliber content, provides a comprehensive yet manageable introduction to HTML—it is a teaching package for the instructor and a learning experience for the student.

Acknowledgments

I want to thank all the people at Course Technology who helped bring this project together. Many thanks to managing editor Marjorie Hunt for giving me the opportunity to write this book. My gratitude also goes to product managers Christina Kling-Garrett and Jennifer Muroff, who skillfully guided this project from concept to completion; and production editor Catherine DiMassa, who put it all together. Quality assurance tester John Freitas helped us immeasurably. My special thanks go to my developmental editor, Barbara Clemens, who worked so hard to guide me through the painful process of learning to author textbooks. I also want to thank my loving husband and best friend, Rick, whose gentle patience kept me going, and my children, who love me enough to nag, "Mom, get some sleep!"

Vicki L. Cox

I would like to thank Barbara Clemens for her insightful contributions, great humor, and patience.

Lynn Wermers

Preface

Welcome to *HTML, Third Edition–Illustrated Introductory*. Each lesson in this book contains elements pictured to the right.

How is the book organized?

This book is organized into eight units covering essential HTML skills, including creating, linking, and formatting HTML documents, as well as adding tables and forms, and working with Cascading Style Sheets. A glossary and appendix provide supplemental reference information.

What kinds of assignments are included in the book? At what level of difficulty?

The lessons use Paradise Mountain Family Resort, a fictional resort in the Rocky Mountains, as a case study. The assignments on the light blue pages at the end of each unit increase in difficulty. Data files and case studies, with international examples, provide a variety of engaging and relevant Web development possibilities. Continuing cases at the end of each unit include site development for: a local water district promoting water conservation, a startup company in the timeshare vacation rental business, and an established computer sales and service business. Students also have the chance to research Web accessibility and usage issues. Assignments include:

- **Concepts Reviews** include screen identification, matching, and multiple-choice questions.

- **Skills Reviews** provide additional hands-on, step-by-step reinforcement.

- **Independent Challenges** feature case projects requiring critical thinking and application of the unit skills. The Independent Challenges increase in difficulty, with the first one in each unit being the easiest (most step-by-step with detailed instructions). Subsequent Independent Challenges

---

Each 2-page spread focuses on a single skill.

Concise text introduces the basic principles in the lesson and integrates a real-world case study.

UNIT A HTML

Importing Web Content

You have learned that content added to the body section appears in the browser window. However, it is not necessary for you to type in all the page content. You will often discover that the content you need is already saved in digital format, such as a word-processed document, for another purpose. You can easily **import**, or bring in, that content instead of retyping it. To avoid retyping company information, you decide to use a rich text file (.rtf) you obtained from the Public Relations Department as the main content on your new page.

STEPS

TROUBLE
Do not select the closing body (</body>) or closing HTML (</html>) tags, or the "Page modified by" paragraph.

1. **Click before the first opening paragraph tag (<p>), drag to select all of the content through and including the second closing paragraph tag (</p>), then press [Delete] to remove the page content**

2. **Start Microsoft Word or another word-processing program, then open the document htm_a-1.rtf from the location where you store your Data Files**

3. **Click before the word Located in the first paragraph below the page heading in the htm_a-1.rtf document, then drag to select all the remaining text**

TROUBLE
If you accidentally copied and pasted the page heading from the RTF file, delete it now.

4. **Click Edit on the menu bar, click Copy, then click the text editor program button on the taskbar**
   You copied the text and returned to the index.htm file that is open in your text editor.

5. **Click in the line below the level-one heading, click Edit on the menu bar, then click Paste**
   You pasted the copied text into the content area of the index.htm file. Your file should now resemble Figure A-9.

6. **Close the rtf file, then save your work**
   Although you are not finished, it is time to preview your new page in a browser. Saving your work ensures that your recent changes will appear in your browser.

7. **Start your browser, then cancel any dial-up operations**
   The procedure for opening the page may vary, depending on your browser.

TROUBLE
If you are warned that Windows security settings will not allow you to open a local file from the browser, find the file in My Computer, then double-click it to open it in a browser.

8. **Click File on the menu bar, click Open or Open Page, click Browse or Choose File**

9. **Navigate to and then click the file index.htm in your paradise site folder, click Open, then click Open or OK**
   Compare your page with Figure A-10. The level-one page heading appears in boldface type and is larger than the rest of the text. See Table A-3 for a list of heading levels you can use with text. The paragraph text runs together because it is not marked with paragraph tags; the browser does not read blank lines and other white space typed into the HTML code of a document.

Clues to Use

Viewing Web page source code

An excellent way of learning what other designers are doing is to view the source code of other pages on the World Wide Web. To view a page's source code in Internet Explorer, click View on the menu bar, then click Source. The page opens in Notepad. In Navigator, click View on the menu bar, then click Page Source. The code is not editable, but you can copy and paste it into a Notepad document. It is acceptable to copy the HTML code itself, but it is not acceptable to copy and use someone else's content, including text, graphics, or logos. All Web content is considered copyrighted and using someone else's content without permission is a violation of copyright laws.

HTML A-10 CREATING AN HTML DOCUMENT

Hints, as well as troubleshooting advice, are located right where you need them—next to the step itself.

Clues to Use boxes provide concise information that either expands on the major lesson skill or describes an independent task that in some way relates to the major lesson skill.

Every lesson features large, full-color representations of what the screen should look like as students complete the numbered steps.

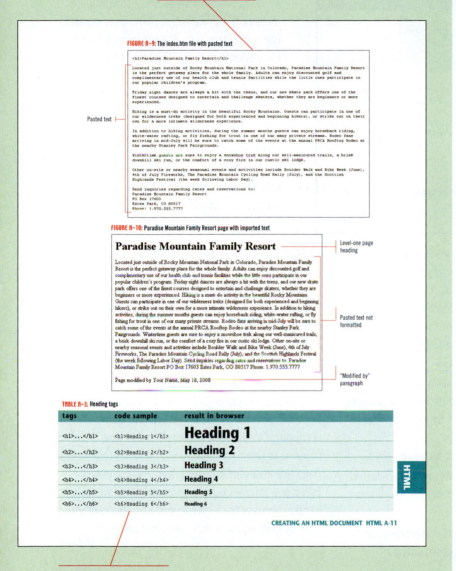

FIGURE A-9: The index.htm file with pasted text

```
<h1>Paradise Mountain Family Resort</h1>

Located just outside of Rocky Mountain National Park in Colorado, Paradise Mountain Family Resort
is the perfect getaway place for the whole family. Adults can enjoy discounted golf and
complimentary use of our health club and tennis facilities while the little ones participate in
our popular children's program.

Friday night dances are always a hit with the teens, and our new skate park offers one of the
finest courses designed to entertain and challenge skaters, whether they are beginners or more
experienced.

Hiking is a must-do activity in the beautiful Rocky Mountains. Guests can participate in one of
our wilderness treks (designed for both experienced and beginning hikers), or strike out on their
own for a more intimate wilderness experience.

In addition to hiking activities, during the summer months guests can enjoy horseback riding,
white-water rafting, or fly fishing for trout in one of our many private streams. Rodeo fans
arriving in mid-July will be sure to catch some of the events at the annual PRCA Rooftop Rodeo at
the nearby Stanley Park Fairgrounds.

Wintertime guests are sure to enjoy a snowshoe trek along our well-manicured trails, a brisk
downhill ski run, or the comfort of a cozy fire in our rustic ski lodge.

Other on-site or nearby seasonal events and activities include Boulder Walk and Bike Week (June),
4th of July Fireworks, The Paradise Mountain Cycling Road Rally (July), and the Scottish
Highlands Festival (the week following Labor Day).

Send inquiries regarding rates and reservations to:
Paradise Mountain Family Resort
PO Box 17603
Estes Park, CO 80517
Phone: 1.970.555.7777
```

Pasted text

FIGURE A-10: Paradise Mountain Family Resort page with imported text

Paradise Mountain Family Resort — Level-one page heading

Located just outside of Rocky Mountain National Park in Colorado, Paradise Mountain Family Resort is the perfect getaway place for the whole family. Adults can enjoy discounted golf and complimentary use of our health club and tennis facilities while the little ones participate in our popular children's program. Friday night dances are always a hit with the teens, and our new skate park offers one of the finest courses designed to entertain and challenge skaters, whether they are beginners or more experienced. Hiking is a must-do activity in the beautiful Rocky Mountains. Guests can participate in one of our wilderness treks (designed for both experienced and beginning hikers), or strike out on their own for a more intimate wilderness experience. In addition to hiking activities, during the summer months guests can enjoy horseback riding, white-water rafting, or fly fishing for trout in one of our many private streams. Rodeo fans arriving in mid-July will be sure to catch some of the events at the annual PRCA Rooftop Rodeo at the nearby Stanley Park Fairgrounds. Wintertime guests are sure to enjoy a snowshoe trek along our well-manicured trails, a brisk downhill ski run, or the comfort of a cozy fire in our rustic ski lodge. Other on-site or nearby seasonal events and activities include Boulder Walk and Bike Week (June), 4th of July Fireworks, The Paradise Mountain Cycling Road Rally (July), and the Scottish Highlands Festival (the week following Labor Day). Send inquiries regarding rates and reservations to: Paradise Mountain Family Resort PO Box 17603 Estes Park, CO 80517 Phone: 1.970.555.7777 — Pasted text not formatted

Page modified by Your Name, May 18, 2008 — "Modified by" paragraph

TABLE A-3: Heading tags

tags	code sample	result in browser
<h1>...</h1>	<h1>Heading 1</h1>	# Heading 1
<h2>...</h2>	<h2>Heading 2</h2>	## Heading 2
<h3>...</h3>	<h3>Heading 3</h3>	### Heading 3
<h4>...</h4>	<h4>Heading 4</h4>	#### Heading 4
<h5>...</h5>	<h5>Heading 5</h5>	##### Heading 5
<h6>...</h6>	<h6>Heading 6</h6>	###### Heading 6

HTML

CREATING AN HTML DOCUMENT HTML A-11

Tables provide quickly accessible summaries of key terms, toolbar buttons, or keyboard alternatives connected with the lesson material. Students can refer easily to this information when working on their own projects at a later time.

become increasingly open-ended, requiring more independent problem solving.

• **E-Quest Independent Challenges** are case projects with a Web focus. E-Quests require the use of the World Wide Web to conduct research to complete the project. The E-Quests in this text focus on real-world Web accessibility issues associated with the subject matter of each unit.

• **Your Site Independent Challenges** give students the greatest degree of flexibility as they develop their own Web sites. Students who complete these challenges will develop a business or personal site of their choice, which they complete as they work through the text.

• **Advanced Challenge Exercises** set within the Independent Challenges provide optional steps for more advanced students.

• **Visual Workshops** are practical projects that require independent problem solving and critical thinking skills. Students are shown layout sketches or completed Web pages and, based on the skills they gained in the unit, are asked to create the pages.

Instructor Resources

The Instructor Resources CD is Course Technology's way of putting the resources and information needed to teach and learn effectively into your hands. We believe that with an integrated array of teaching and learning tools that offers you and your students a broad range of technology-based instructional options, this CD represents the highest quality and most cutting edge resources available to instructors today. Many of these resources are available at www.course.com. The resources available with this book are:

- **Data Files for Students**—To complete most of the units in this book, your students will need Data Files. Put them on a file server for students to copy. The Data Files are available on the Instructor Resources CD-ROM and the Review Pack, and can also be downloaded from www.course.com.

Instruct students to use the **Data Files List** located at the back of this book, on the Review Pack and the Instructor Resources CD. This list gives instructions on copying and organizing files.

- **Solutions to Exercises**—Solutions to Exercises contains every file students are asked to create or modify in the lessons and End-of-Unit material. A Help file on the Instructor Resource CD includes information for using the Solution Files. There is also a document outlining the solutions for the End-of-Unit Concepts Review, Skills Review, and Independent Challenges.

- **PowerPoint Presentations**—Each unit has a corresponding PowerPoint presentation that you can use in lecture, distribute to your students, or customize to suit your course.

- **Instructor's Manual**—Available as an electronic file, the Instructor's Manual is quality-assurance tested and includes unit overviews and detailed lecture topics with teaching tips for each unit.

- **Sample Syllabus**—Prepare and customize your course easily using this sample course outline.

- **Figure Files**—The figures in the text are provided on the Instructor Resources CD to help you illustrate key topics or concepts. You can create traditional overhead transparencies by printing the figure files. Or you can create electronic slide shows by using the figures in a presentation program such as PowerPoint.

- **ExamView**—ExamView is a powerful testing software package that allows you to create and administer printed, computer (LAN-based), and Internet exams. ExamView includes hundreds of questions that correspond to the topics covered in this text, enabling students to generate detailed study guides that include page references for further review. The computer-based and Internet testing components allow students to take exams at their computers, and also save you time by grading each exam automatically.

Brief Contents

Contents

| HTML | Formatting Page Elements with HTML | C-1 |

| HTML | Adding Graphics and Multimedia | D-1 |

| HTML | Formatting with Cascading Style Sheets | E-1 |

| HTML | Working with Tables | F-1 |

Project Files List   1

Glossary   4

Index   11

Read This Before You Begin

Software Information and Required Installation
In order to use this book, you will need:

Hardware and Software

- **An IBM or compatible** computer with at least a Pentium processor, 16 MB of RAM and a Windows 98 or higher operating system or **a Macintosh computer** with similar memory, color, graphics, and video capabilities.
- **A text editor program** such as Notepad or the Macintosh equivalent.
- **A Web browser:** This book is to be non-browser specific, and was tested using several browsers including Netscape Navigator, Microsoft Internet Explorer, Opera, and Mozilla Firefox. While you need only one browser installed to use this book, establish you should test Web pages in different browsers to ensure that your pages appear as desired. Some security options may prevent files from appearing as expected. To correct this, choose Internet Options from the Tools menu, click the Advanced tab, scroll to the Security options, then check "Allow active content to run in files on My Computer". Netscape settings may have to be adjusted as well.
- **Access to the Internet**.
- **E-mail software** that will support attachments such as Microsoft Outlook, or one of the free e-mail services available through providers such as Hotmail or Yahoo, or your online course e-mail interface.
- **An FTP client software program** (if using FTP to transfer files to a remote directory).
- **An external media storage device** such as a Zip disk, a "thumb" (USB) drive, or other external storage device. If you use floppy disks, be aware that even though Web documents are small, Web support files might not fit on a floppy disk.
- **Some type of graphics-editing software** is helpful, but not required. Students without graphics-editing capabilities can use graphics in the student Data Files or download them from links on the Student Online Companion or can surf the Web.

FTP Configuration: This text provides instructions on transferring files to a server using FTP Commander by InternetSoft, which can be downloaded for free of charge by clicking the FTP Commander link in the Student Online Companion. Links to download sites and instructions for using other FTP Client programs are also available there. Students who are not transferring files can complete the course by following guidelines set by their instructor.

Data Files: To complete the units in this book, you need to use Data Files. A Data File contains a partially completed document that allows you to focus on the core lesson material without losing valuable time typing all the information in the document yourself. Your instructor will either provide you with copies of the Data Files or ask you to make your own copies. Your instructor can give you instructions on how to organize your files, as well as a complete file listing. You can also find the list and instructions for organizing files in the Review Pack.

Saving your files

The author assumes no specific location for the Data Files you are provided or site files you create. Whatever location you use, carefully organize your files by case project. If you are using floppy disks, it is recommended that you have at least one floppy disk per site. Some case studies can become large and require more than one floppy disk.

Why is my screen different from the book?

Your desktop components and some dialog box options might be different if you are using an operating system other than Windows XP. Depending on your computer hardware and the Display settings on your computer, you may notice the following differences:

- Your screen may look larger or smaller because of your screen resolution (the height and width of your screen).
- Your title bars and dialog boxes may not display file extensions. To display file extensions, right-click the Start button on the taskbar, click Explore, click Folder Options on the View menu, click the View tab in the Folder Options dialog box, click Hide extensions for known file types to deselect it, then click OK. Your dialog boxes and title bars should then display file extensions
- Your browser may display different menu and toolbar choices than those shown.

Creating an HTML Document

OBJECTIVES

Understand Web concepts
Plan an HTML document
Write an HTML document
Understand W3C coding standards
Import Web content
Mark up Web page content
Print an HTML document
Understand file transfer methods
Transfer files with FTP Commander

The **World Wide Web** (also referred to as simply the **Web**) is information contained on the vast **network** of interconnected computers known as the **Internet**. **Web sites** are related collections of files stored on those computers. Web files can be documents called Web pages; they can also be images or other files that are accessible through a Web browser program. Although navigating the World Wide Web with a browser is a useful skill, mastering just a few more basic concepts enables you to create and publish your own Web pages. You can create Web pages by learning Hypertext Markup Language (HTML), the language upon which all Web pages are based. Before you begin, you must plan your Web site and write its contents so that it conforms to specific standards. You can then publish those pages on the Web so others can view them. You work in the Information Technology (IT) Department at Paradise Mountain Family Resort, a family vacation destination specializing in "something for everyone." The resort owners have decided they need a Web site to publicize their goods and services, and you have been given the job of creating the Web site.

Understanding Web Concepts

HTML, which stands for **Hypertext Markup Language**, is the authoring language used to create pages for the World Wide Web (WWW). HTML allows various computer systems to interpret Web information in the same way. Web pages, also called **HTML documents** or **HTML files**, are text files made up of text and HTML instructions. Each of these instructions is called a **tag**. Together these tags and text make up the document's **source code**, often called the **source** or the **code**. You need to design and create a Web site that is easy to use, so vacation-bound families can easily find information about Paradise Mountain Family Resort. Before you begin, however, you review some basic Web terms and concepts.

DETAILS

Some basic Web terms and concepts are:

- **Web page**

  Also known as a Web document, a **Web page** is a single text file that has been **marked up** (annotated) with HTML tags so it is viewable on any operating system using any browser.

- **Tags**

  HTML includes many tags that allow you to describe how you want each of your Web page elements to appear in browsers. Although most HTML tags are part of a **tag set** that contains an opening and a closing tag, it is proper, and easier, to refer to the set as simply a tag. For example, you can refer to <p>...</p> as a **paragraph tag set** or as a **paragraph tag**. Sometimes tags with no closing counterparts are referred to as **open tags**.

- **Web browser**

  A **Web browser** is a software program installed on your computer that allows you to view Web pages. Some popular browsers are Microsoft Internet Explorer, Netscape Navigator, Mozilla Firefox, and Opera, which was created by a European consortium research project. Figure A-1 shows a Web page displayed in Microsoft Internet Explorer.

- **Web site**

  A **Web site** is a collection of related Web pages and other files housed in the same directory on a Web server. Pages in a Web site are connected by hyperlinks that visitors can click to navigate from one page to another.

- **Hyperlinks**

  Commonly called links, **hyperlinks** are specially-formatted text or graphics users click to move from one file to another on the World Wide Web. Hyperlinks give users an easy way to pursue information they find useful or interesting.

- **Web server**

  A **Web server**, or **server**, is a computer that is connected to the Internet and accessible to anyone with an Internet connection and a Web browser. Each server has its own four-part numeric address, called an **Internet Protocol (IP) address**, such as 1.160.10.40, that makes it possible for Web users to find site information.

- **URL**

  A **uniform resource locator (URL)** is the exact Internet address of a Web file. Figure A-2 shows the parts of a URL.

- **Search engine**

  A **search engine** is a Web-based program that helps you locate information on the Web. To use a search engine, type a word or phrase into a blank area called a **search box**, then click a **search button**. Some popular search engines are Google and Yahoo.

- **World Wide Web Consortium (W3C)**

  The **World Wide Web Consortium (W3C)** is an independent industry consortium that develops common protocols and sets new Web standards to promote WWW evolution and ensure interoperability among products and platforms.

FIGURE A-1: Web page with hyperlinks

Hyperlinks

URL

FIGURE A-2: Parts of a URL

http://www.paradisemountain.com/spa/wraps.htm

- Protocol
- Server (machine) name
- Domain name
- Directory
- File name
- File extension

Clues to Use

Understanding URLs

Each URL consists of several parts including the **protocol**—a standardized format for sending and receiving data, the machine or server name, the domain name, and the file name. The protocol for delivering Web documents is `http://`—**Hypertext Transfer Protocol**— or `https://`—**Hypertext Transfer Protocol Secure**. The **Web server name** or **machine name** is assigned by the server administrator and can be almost any combination of characters but is often "www, " for World Wide Web. A **domain name** is a unique name chosen by the site's owner. It represents a group of computers at the same Internet address. Each domain name contains a suffix, such as .com, representing a top-level domain, the highest category in the Internet naming system. A top-level domain can indicate the site's function or its country of origin. Common top-level domains include: commercial (.com), educational (.edu), governmental (.gov), nonprofit organizational (.org), network (.net), United States (.us), Canada (.ca), or Thailand (.ta). The last part of a URL is the file path, which consists of the directory, file name, and extension. Figure A-2 shows the parts of a URL.

HTML

Planning an HTML Document

Before writing an HTML document, you should have a preliminary idea of how you want your final Web page to look. Although you'll inevitably modify your initial page format as you go along, a master plan helps keep you focused on the information you want to convey. ░░░░ You decide to use the Web to research the process of creating an HTML document and to find a list of suggested steps for planning and creating a Web page.

Follow these steps to plan and create a Web page:

- **Sketch your Web page**

  Create a rough sketch showing the desired appearance of your final Web page. The goal of this process—which is called **storyboarding**—is to show the elements you want to include and how you want them arranged on the Web page. You then can make sure you know how to use the necessary tags for each element, and you can research those that you haven't used before. Figure A-3 presents a **storyboard layout sketch**, or **storyboard**, showing the first few elements you want to add to the Paradise Mountain Family Resort home page.

- **Enter structuring tags for the file**

  Every Web page begins with an opening HTML tag and ends with a closing HTML tag. These beginning and ending HTML tags identify the file as an HTML document and provide basic information about it to the browser. A Web page also contains tags that divide it into two main structural sections, the head and body sections, which hold section-specific content. See Figure A-4 for examples of these tags.

- **Enter the head section elements**

  The **head section** contains identifying and descriptive information. It can contain **meta tags**, which add information that helps search engines identify and describe your page content. The most commonly-used metatags are the **keywords** meta tag, which allows you to list words users might type into a search engine, and **description**, which lets you give more detail about your page content. Other head section elements can include **scripts**, lists of commands that run automatically on the Web page to provide extra information to the user or to track user movements. The head section also often contains some page formatting information. Although many different head section elements *can* be included in a Web page, only one element, the page title, is recommended for every Web page. **Page title** information does not appear in the browser window; instead, it appears in the title bar at the top of the browser window, as shown in Figure A-5. All content of a Web page's head section is coded between the opening and closing head tags (<head>...</head>). Your Paradise Mountain page will include a title and a keyword meta tag. (For more information on meta tags, see the appendix.)

- **Enter each Web page body element**

  Web page content, the information that appears in the browser window, is contained within the **body section** of the Web page and falls between the opening and closing body tags (<body> and </body>). The most common Web page elements are heading and paragraph elements and tags containing source references used to display graphics and multimedia elements on a Web page. You can enter tags to add special formatting to text, to create tables, or to add links to other Web pages. It is generally best to add one new element at a time, and then preview the Web page. If the page doesn't appear as you expect, you then have a good idea of which HTML tag or tag set is likely to contain the error. Figure A-4 shows the source code for a basic Web page.

- **Preview the Web page**

  As you create your page, you should preview it often in a Web browser. Figure A-5 shows the output from the code shown in Figure A-4. Such previews allow you to notice any elements that don't appear as you intended. Correcting errors often can be as simple as adding or editing an HTML tag. Because different Web browsers, such as Microsoft Internet Explorer or Netscape Navigator, sometimes display the same code differently, it is best to preview your work in multiple browsers to ensure that it appears as you planned for all users.

- **Test links**

  If your document contains links to other Web pages, preview your page in a Web browser and test each link by clicking it. If clicking a link does not open the Web page you intended as the target, you can edit the code.

FIGURE A-3: Storyboard for Paradise Mountain Web page

FIGURE A-4: Web page source code

HTML tag set

Head tag set

Body tag set

Opening and closing title tags (title tag set)

Content in body section with level-one heading and paragraph tags

FIGURE A-5: Web page preview in browser

Page title

Level-one heading

Paragraph output

HTML

Writing an HTML Document

Once you've planned how you want your document to look, you can start creating its structure and adding page elements. You can create an HTML document in any application that allows you to enter and save text. Notepad, a text editor program installed with Windows, and the Macintosh Text Editor, are popular tools for writing HTML code. These applications include simple methods of saving a document in text format without the additional formatting added by some word processors. You decide to create your first HTML document using Notepad and begin coding the Paradise Mountain home page by entering the structuring tags and adding some basic page elements.

STEPS

QUICK TIP

Use a plain text editor instead of a word processor to ensure results like those found in these lessons.

1. **Click the Start button ⊞ start on the taskbar**

2. **Point to All Programs, point to Accessories, click Notepad, then maximize the Notepad window, if necessary**
   A blank Notepad document opens.

QUICK TIP

Be sure you do *not* use the Save As HTML command if you are creating your HTML document in a word processor.

3. **Click File on the menu bar, then click Save**
   The Save As dialog box opens.

4. **Click the Save in list arrow, then navigate to the location where you want to store your site files**

5. **Click the Create New Folder icon 🗁, type paradise as the new folder name, then double-click the paradise folder to open it**
   It is important to organize your Web files as you create them. The paradise folder will serve as the home or **root folder,** which is the top-level folder for your Web site.

6. **Click the Save as type arrow, then click All Files**
   Choosing All Files when you save your HTML file prevents your file from being saved with the .txt extension appended to the filename such as index.htm.txt.

TROUBLE

Make sure to type a period followed by htm after the file name. Otherwise, your text editor will automatically add the .txt extension to your filename when you save it. Double-check your filename to make sure it ends with .htm.

7. **Click in the File name text box, type index.htm, compare your dialog box with Figure A-6, then click Save**
   On most servers, the default file name for a home page or the main page in a Web folder is index.htm or index.html. However, other default filenames exist. Check with your instructor or webmaster to determine the default name for your server and name your page accordingly.

8. **Click in the blank area of the text editor, type <html>, then press [Enter]**
   Every HTML document begins with the <html> tag and ends with a closing </html> tag. Table A-1 lists commonly used HTML tags. A browser can interpret HTML tags that are in either uppercase or lowercase. However, because of new W3C Web standards, it is best to consistently use all lowercase characters.

9. **Type the remaining tags, as shown in Figure A-7, using extra return characters after each tag and your own name and the current date in the "Modified by" paragraph, click File on the menu bar, then click Save**
   You typed a level-one heading and three paragraphs. Because browsers do not recognize extra spaces, hard returns, or tabs in most HTML code, pressing [Enter] twice after each line to create extra white space makes your HTML code easier to read without affecting its appearance as a Web page.

FIGURE A-6: Notepad Save As dialog box

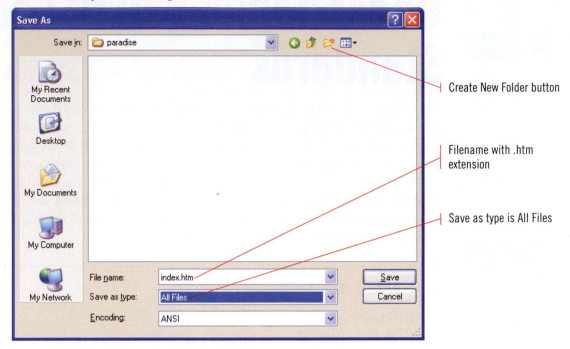

Create New Folder button

Filename with .htm extension

Save as type is All Files

FIGURE A-7: Paradise Mountain Family Resort HTML code

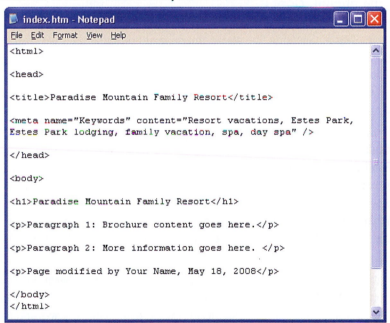

TABLE A-1: HTML tag sets

tag set	purpose
`<html>...</html>`	Identifies the file as an HTML document to the program opening it
`<head>...</head>`	Identifies the document's head area, where you can code information about your document, including its title
`<title>...</title>`	Formats the document title, which appears in the browser's title bar; search engines use information found in the title to help identify page content and rank pages for search queries
`<body>...</body>`	Identifies the document's body area, which contains the Web page contents that appear in the browser window
`<p>...</p>`	Defines a paragraph, the basic content unit for Web text

Understanding W3C Coding Standards

In the early days of HTML, designers used a hodgepodge of personal styles when coding or marking up a Web document. For example, some used all capital letters to specify their tag names. Others used all capital letters for opening tags and lowercase type for their closing tags. Still others discovered that they could use shortcut methods of coding by leaving out the closing tags of some tag sets. As a result, many Web documents were extremely untidy with code that was difficult to read. However, as newer Web technologies make their presence felt, Web coding standards are tightening. Before coding any more of the Paradise Mountain Web site, you review the W3C coding standards so that you will be in a better position to tackle newer technologies as your Web site grows and matures.

DETAILS

Some W3C coding standards are:

- **Use lowercase letters**

  Because many newer Web technologies such as **DHTML** (dynamic HTML) and **XML** (extensible markup language)—often used for creating database connections—are case sensitive, the W3C recommends using all lowercase letters for HTML documents.

- **If you open it, close it**

  Most HTML tags are part of a tag set, except for open tags which, as you learned earlier, have no closing counterpart. Tags representing line breaks, images, and horizontal rules are open tags. These open elements are now closed by inserting a single space followed by the closing slash (/) after the tag name (if no **attributes**—additional instructions inside the opening tag that change the appearance or behavior of the affected element—are applied). You will further explore the proper method of closing tags in Unit D. A list of old and new tag elements is shown in Table A-2.

- **No spaces in folders or file names**

  From the time that Microsoft introduced the first Windows 9*x* system with support for long file names, computer users began to learn that they could place spaces in folders or file names to make their file names easier to understand. This practice is not accepted on the Web. In fact, giving HTML documents and other Web files names with spaces can cause linking, display, and scripting problems down the road. If you must use more than one word to identify a file, combine words with an underscore character (file_name.htm) or run both words together, but capitalize the second word of the file name (fileName.htm).

- **Keep it neat**

  When a browser reads the code of a Web document, it starts at the beginning and reads the document straight through to the end, paying no heed, in most cases, to line breaks, tabs, and extra spaces that occur within the code. However, code that does not include extra carriage returns, spaces and/or tabs is extremely difficult to read for humans. Sloppily coded pages are much more likely to contain coding errors than are pages to which "code-beautification tactics" such as extra carriage returns, spaces, and/or tabs have been applied.

- **Put everything in its place**

  Stacked tags are tags that are closed before the next tag begins or are opened after the previous tag has ended. **Nested tags** are tags that are fully contained within another tag. There is a proper tag nesting and stacking standard for HTML documents and, with XML standards in mind, it is important to adhere to the standard. According to the standard, when stacking tags, the opening tag of a subsequent HTML element must not be inserted into a document until the closing tag of the previous tag element has been inserted. With nested tags the rule is that the first element opened is the last element closed. Figure A-8 shows an example of a Web page with stacked and nested HTML elements.

FIGURE A-8: Stacked and nested tags

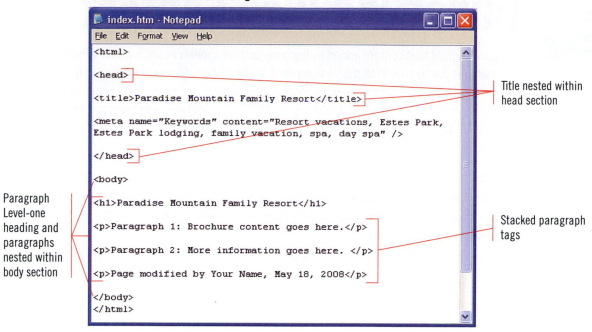

Title nested within head section

Paragraph Level-one heading and paragraphs nested within body section

Stacked paragraph tags

TABLE A-2: Coding to W3C standards

tag	old style	new style
Paragraph	`<P>...</P>` or `<p>`	`<p>...</p>`
META	`<META Description="...">`	`<meta description="..." />`
Line break	` ` or ` `	` `
Horizontal rule	`<hr>` or `<HR>`	`<hr />`
Image	`<img src="filename.jpg">`	`<img src="filename.jpg" />`
List item	`<li>List item`	`<li>List item</li>`

Clues to Use

Using a text editor versus a word processor or other program

Many word processors and desktop publishing programs, such as Microsoft Word or Microsoft Publisher, offer a Save as HTML command on the File menu. This feature allows you to create and format a document using word-processing features with which you are familiar, and then automatically create a Web page that contains the same information and layout. Such a feature makes Web page authoring possible even for people who don't know anything about HTML. However, this automated method has its drawbacks. In some cases, page elements do not appear in a Web browser exactly as they did in the word processor. Also, the generated code is usually full of extra formatting information and making any change to the Web page requires regenerating the HTML code from the word processor. Creating pages by entering the HTML tags yourself—known as **hand coding**—gives you more precise control over the exact appearance of your Web pages. You can fine-tune a page's appearance by making direct and specific changes to the HTML code. Because you are studying HTML, you should use a plain text editor such as Notepad (for Windows) or SimpleText (for MAC systems) to complete these lessons. If you choose to use a word processor instead, be sure to save each file in text format with an .htm extension. Do not use the word processor's **native format** (.doc or .wpd) or its HTML document type.

Importing Web Content

You have learned that content added to the body section appears in the browser window. However, it is not necessary for you to type in all the page content. You will often discover that the content you need is already saved in digital format, such as a word-processed document, for another purpose. You can easily **import**, or bring in, that content instead of retyping it. To avoid retyping company information, you decide to use a rich text file (.rtf) you obtained from the Public Relations Department as the main content on your new page.

STEPS

TROUBLE
Do not select the closing body (</body>) or closing HTML (</html>) tags, or the "Page modified by" paragraph.

1. **Click before the first opening paragraph tag (<p>), drag to select all of the content through and including the second closing paragraph tag (</p>), then press [Delete] to remove the page content**

2. **Start Microsoft Word or another word-processing program, then open the document htm_a-1.rtf from the location where you store your Data Files**

3. **Click before the word Located in the first paragraph below the page heading in the htm_a-1.rtf document, then drag to select all the remaining text**

4. **Click Edit on the menu bar, click Copy, then click the text editor program button on the taskbar**

   You copied the text and returned to the index.htm file that is open in your text editor.

TROUBLE
If you accidentally copied and pasted the page heading from the RTF file, delete it now.

5. **Click in the line below the level-one heading, click Edit on the menu bar, then click Paste**

   You pasted the copied text into the content area of the index.htm file. Your file should now resemble Figure A-9.

6. **Close the rtf file, then save your work**

   Although you are not finished, it is time to preview your new page in a browser. Saving your work ensures that your recent changes will appear in your browser.

7. **Start your browser, then cancel any dial-up operations**

   The procedure for opening the page may vary, depending on your browser.

8. **Click File on the menu bar, click Open or Open Page, then click Browse or Choose File**

TROUBLE
If you are warned that Windows security settings will not allow you to open a local file from the browser, find the file in My Computer, then double-click it to open it in a browser.

9. **Navigate to and then click the file index.htm in your paradise site folder, click Open, then click Open or OK**

   Compare your page with Figure A-10. The level-one page heading appears in boldface type and is larger than the rest of the text. See Table A-3 for a list of heading levels you can use with text. The paragraph text runs together because it is not marked with paragraph tags; the browser does not read blank lines and other white space typed into the HTML code of a document.

Clues to Use

Viewing Web page source code

An excellent way of learning what other designers are doing is to view the source code of other pages on the World Wide Web. To view a page's source code in Internet Explorer, click View on the menu bar, then click Source. The page opens in Notepad. In Navigator, click View on the menu bar, then click Page Source. The code is not editable, but you can copy and paste it into a Notepad document. It is acceptable to copy the HTML code itself, but it is not acceptable to copy and use someone else's content, including text, graphics, or logos. All Web content is considered copyrighted and using someone else's content without permission is a violation of copyright laws.

```
<h1>Paradise Mountain Family Resort</h1>

Located just outside of Rocky Mountain National Park in Colorado, Paradise Mountain Family Resort
is the perfect getaway place for the whole family. Adults can enjoy discounted golf and
complimentary use of our health club and tennis facilities while the little ones participate in
our popular children's program.

Friday night dances are always a hit with the teens, and our new skate park offers one of the
finest courses designed to entertain and challenge skaters, whether they are beginners or more
experienced.

Hiking is a must-do activity in the beautiful Rocky Mountains. Guests can participate in one of
our wilderness treks (designed for both experienced and beginning hikers), or strike out on their
own for a more intimate wilderness experience.

In addition to hiking activities, during the summer months guests can enjoy horseback riding,
white-water rafting, or fly fishing for trout in one of our many private streams. Rodeo fans
arriving in mid-July will be sure to catch some of the events at the annual PRCA Rooftop Rodeo at
the nearby Stanley Park Fairgrounds.

Wintertime guests are sure to enjoy a snowshoe trek along our well-manicured trails, a brisk
downhill ski run, or the comfort of a cozy fire in our rustic ski lodge.

Other on-site or nearby seasonal events and activities include Boulder Walk and Bike Week (June),
4th of July Fireworks, The Paradise Mountain Cycling Road Rally (July), and the Scottish
Highlands Festival (the week following Labor Day).

Send inquiries regarding rates and reservations to:
Paradise Mountain Family Resort
PO Box 17603
Estes Park, CO 80517
Phone: 1.970.555.7777
```

Pasted text

FIGURE A-10: Paradise Mountain Family Resort page with imported text

Paradise Mountain Family Resort

Located just outside of Rocky Mountain National Park in Colorado, Paradise Mountain Family Resort is the perfect getaway place for the whole family. Adults can enjoy discounted golf and complimentary use of our health club and tennis facilities while the little ones participate in our popular children's program. Friday night dances are always a hit with the teens, and our new skate park offers one of the finest courses designed to entertain and challenge skaters, whether they are beginners or more experienced. Hiking is a must-do activity in the beautiful Rocky Mountains. Guests can participate in one of our wilderness treks (designed for both experienced and beginning hikers), or strike out on their own for a more intimate wilderness experience. In addition to hiking activities, during the summer months guests can enjoy horseback riding, white-water rafting, or fly fishing for trout in one of our many private streams. Rodeo fans arriving in mid-July will be sure to catch some of the events at the annual PRCA Rooftop Rodeo at the nearby Stanley Park Fairgrounds. Wintertime guests are sure to enjoy a snowshoe trek along our well-manicured trails, a brisk downhill ski run, or the comfort of a cozy fire in our rustic ski lodge. Other on-site or nearby seasonal events and activities include Boulder Walk and Bike Week (June), 4th of July Fireworks, The Paradise Mountain Cycling Road Rally (July), and the Scottish Highlands Festival (the week following Labor Day). Send inquiries regarding rates and reservations to: Paradise Mountain Family Resort PO Box 17603 Estes Park, CO 80517 Phone: 1.970.555.7777

Page modified by Your Name, May 18, 2008

Level-one page heading

Pasted text not formatted

"Modified by" paragraph

TABLE A-3: Heading tags

tags	code sample	result in browser
<h1>...</h1>	<h1>Heading 1</h1>	# Heading 1
<h2>...</h2>	<h2>Heading 2</h2>	## Heading 2
<h3>...</h3>	<h3>Heading 3</h3>	### Heading 3
<h4>...</h4>	<h4>Heading 4</h4>	#### Heading 4
<h5>...</h5>	<h5>Heading 5</h5>	##### Heading 5
<h6>...</h6>	<h6>Heading 6</h6>	###### Heading 6

HTML

Marking up Web Page Content

Two basic tags, the line break <br /> and the paragraph tag <p>...</p>, allow you to control the space between lines of text and to determine where those lines break on the screen. Other tags allow you to apply special formatting styles to Web content. For example, heading tags, which come in a range from h1 (the largest) to h6 (the smallest) act like paragraph tags in that they cause extra white space to appear above the tag; however, unlike paragraph tags, heading tags also cause their content to appear as boldface type in the browser window. Table A-4 shows the descriptions and samples of paragraph and line break tags. It is important to note that text formatted with heading tags appears with slight differences in different Web browsers. The best way to make sure your Web page appears as you intended is to preview it in all of the most common Web browsers. To make your page appear as expected, you want to format it as a Web page by using HTML markup tags.

STEPS

1. Click the **text editor program button** on the taskbar, click before the word Located, type **<p>**, click in the white space after "program." at the end of the paragraph, then type **</p>**

2. Add opening and closing paragraph tags at the beginning and end of each paragraph, like the tags shown in Figure A-11, then save your work

QUICK TIP
In Internet Explorer, you can press F5 as a keyboard shortcut for the Refresh button.

3. Click the **browser program button** ☐ Paradise Moun... on the taskbar, then click your browser's **Reload** or **Refresh button**

The browser displays the new version of your Web page, in which the paragraphs are displayed as separate blocks of text. However, because the browser recognizes only *coded* line breaks—those that are forced by using the HTML line break tag—the contact information at the bottom of the page runs together, as shown in Figure A-12.

QUICK TIP
Be sure to type a space between the "br" and the slash.

4. Click the **text editor program button** on the taskbar, click after the line that reads, Send inquiries regarding rates and reservations to:, then type **
**.

5. Type a line break at the end of the next three lines, as shown in Figure A-13, then save your work

6. Return to the browser window, then click the browser's **Reload** or **Refresh button**

The browser opens the most recently saved version of the Web page showing that the line break tags you entered produced a hard line return at the end of each line, but, unlike the paragraph tag, did not produce any extra white space, as shown in Figure A-13.

TABLE A-4: Basic HTML text tags

tag	description	sample	result in browser
 	Adds a line break; this open tag has no closing counterpart and so the closing slash is placed within the opening following a single space after the tag name (br)	line 1 line 2	line 1 line 2
<p>...</p>	Adds a blank line before and after the current paragraph; does require a closing tag	<p>paragraph 1</p> <p>paragraph 2</p>	paragraph 1 paragraph 2

FIGURE A-11: Text marked up with paragraph tags

Opening and closing paragraph tags surround paragraph sections

Add opening and closing paragraph tags to the next four paragraphs

```
<h1>Paradise Mountain Family Resort</h1>

<p>Located just outside of Rocky Mountain National Park in Colorado,
Paradise Mountain Family Resort is the perfect getaway place for the whole
family. Adults can enjoy discounted golf and complimentary use of our health
club and tennis facilities while the little ones participate in our popular
children's program.</p>

<p>Friday night dances are always a hit with the teens, and our new skate
park offers one of the finest courses designed to entertain and challenge
skaters, whether they are beginners or more experienced.</p>

<p>Hiking is a must-do activity in the beautiful Rocky Mountains. Guests can
participate in one of our wilderness treks (designed for both experienced
and beginning hikers), or strike out on their own for a more intimate
wilderness experience.</p>

<p>In addition to hiking activities, during the summer months guests can
enjoy horseback riding, white-water rafting, or fly fishing for trout in one
of our many private streams. Rodeo fans arriving in mid-July will be sure to
catch some of the events at the annual PRCA Rooftop Rodeo at the nearby
Stanley Park Fairgrounds.</p>

<p>Wintertime guests are sure to enjoy a snowshoe trek along our
well-manicured trails, a brisk downhill ski run, or the comfort of a cozy
fire in our rustic ski lodge. </p>

<p>Other on-site or nearby seasonal events and activities include Boulder
Walk and Bike Week (June), 4th of July Fireworks, The Paradise Mountain
```

FIGURE A-12: Reloaded page after paragraph markup

Friday night dances are always a hit with the teens, and our new skate park offers one of the finest courses designed to entertain and challenge skaters, whether they are beginners or more experienced.

Hiking is a must-do activity in the beautiful Rocky Mountains. Guests can participate in one of our wilderness treks (designed for both experienced and beginning hikers), or strike out on their own for a more intimate wilderness experience.

In addition to hiking activities, during the summer months guests can enjoy horseback riding, white-water rafting, or fly fishing for trout in one of our many private streams. Rodeo fans arriving in mid-July will be sure to catch some of the events at the annual PRCA Rooftop Rodeo at the nearby Stanley Park Fairgrounds.

Wintertime guests are sure to enjoy a snowshoe trek along our well-manicured trails, a brisk downhill ski run, or the comfort of a cozy fire in our rustic ski lodge.

Other on-site or nearby seasonal events and activities include Boulder Walk and Bike Week (June), 4th of July Fireworks, The Paradise Mountain Cycling Road Rally (July), and the Scottish Highlands Festival (the week following Labor Day).

Send inquiries regarding rates and reservations to: Paradise Mountain Family Resort PO Box 17603 Estes Park, CO 80517 Phone: 1.970.555.7777

Page modified by Your Name, May 18, 2008

Added paragraph tags create white space between paragraphs

Address elements on same line because there are only paragraph marks between them in source code

FIGURE A-13: Coded line breaks and output

Hiking is a
our wildern
their own f

In addition
white-wate
arriving in
Rodeo at t

```
<p>Send inquiries regarding rates and reservations to:<br />
Paradise Mountain Family Resort<br />
PO Box 17603 <br />
Estes Park, CO 80517<br />
Phone: 1.970.555.7777 </p>

<p>Page modified by Your Name, May 18, 2008</p>

</body>
</html>
```


 tags added to force line breaks in output

Wintertime guests are sure to enjoy a snowshoe trek along our well-manicured trails, a brisk downhill ski run, or the comfort of a cozy fire in our rustic ski lodge.

Other on-site or nearby seasonal events and activities include Boulder Bike Week (June), 4th of July Fireworks, The Paradise Mountain Cycling Road Rally (July), and the Scottish Highlands Festival (the week following Labor Day).

Contact paragraph output with coded line breaks

Send inquiries regarding rates and reservations to:
Paradise Mountain Family Resort
PO Box 17603
Estes Park, CO 80517
Phone: 1.970.555.7777

Page modified by Your Name, May 18, 2008

Printing an HTML Document

Even though HTML documents are designed to facilitate information exchange over the Internet, sometimes you need to print hard copies. You can print the HTML source code for your pages using the same text editor you used to create them. For a fully developed Web page, the source code can span many printed pages, so you might want to print only selected pages if you are checking specific lines of code. Web browsers also allow you to print your Web pages as they appear in the browser window. You want to present your preliminary work on the Paradise Mountain Family Resort Web page at your design team meeting later today. You will print both the HTML source code and the Web browser display.

STEPS

1. **Click the text editor button on the taskbar, click File on the menu bar, then click Print**

   The Print dialog box opens, allowing you to select your printer. Your dialog box should resemble the one shown in Figure A-14, although your printer may display different options.

2. **Verify that your preferred printer is selected, then click Print**

   The text editor prints a single copy of the source code, as shown in Figure A-15. By default, the filename prints at the top of each page, and the page number at the bottom.

3. **Click the browser program button on the taskbar**

4. **Click the Print button 🖨 on the browser toolbar, then, if necessary, click OK**

   Figure A-15 displays the page printed from the browser window. Notice that the page title appears at the top of the page and the file path or URL appears at the bottom of the page.

5. **Click the browser window Close button**

6. **If necessary, click the text editor program button on the taskbar, then click the text editor window Close button**

Clues to Use

Changing browser headers and footers

When you print a Web page from a browser, the output includes information about the Web page, such as its location and the page title, as shown in Figure A-15. Both Netscape Navigator and Microsoft Internet Explorer Web browsers allow you to customize the information that prints, whether you created the Web page or not. In both browsers, you click File, then click Page Setup to change header and footer information. In Navigator, the Header and Footer sections include list arrows that allow you to select or deselect header and footer items. The default selections print the Title and URL at the top of the page, and the Page number, date, and time at the bottom. Instead of list arrows, Internet Explorer uses codes consisting of an ampersand (&) and a letter, such as &u for the URL and &p for the page number as shown in Figure A-16. Although using codes takes a bit more work, Internet Explorer offers more choices of what you can show in the header and the footer, and also allows you to choose the order of the elements. You can also enter text before or after the codes. To display an index of the Internet Explorer codes and their meanings, click in the Header or Footer text box, then press F1.

FIGURE A-16: Internet Explorer Page Setup options

Page Setup

Paper
Size: Letter
Source: Auto Select

Headers and Footers
Header
Codes → `&w&bPage &p of &P`
Footer
`&u&b&d`

Orientation
⦿ Portrait
○ Landscape

Margins (inches)
Left: 0.75   Right: 0.75
Top: 0.75   Bottom: 0.75

OK   Cancel   Printer...

FIGURE A-14: Notepad print dialog box

Depending on your printer and printer choices, your options may differ

FIGURE A-15: Paradise Mountian home page printouts from Notepad and from Internet Explorer

File name

Page title

Page number

File path or URL

HTML

Understanding File Transfer Methods

While you usually create and save Web sites on a desktop computer, you can never really be sure exactly how your pages will appear to users until you **upload** (transfer) them to a Web server and view the "live" site using one or more Web browsers. This way, you can find and fix display problems stemming from improperly constructed link and source paths early on in the development cycle. Before you post files to a server, you must obtain permission to do so from the server administrator; this is called having **write access** to the server. You must also have a **user ID** (a unique identifying name) and a valid password, also assigned by your server administrator. The most common methods of transferring files to a Web server include File Transfer Protocol (FTP), Secure File Transfer Protocol (SFTP), direct file transfer through a mapped network drive, and file publishing through a Web development software application's publishing interface. You are eager to begin transferring Paradise Mountain's Web pages to the Web server so you can see how they look in a live setting. You set up a meeting with your network manager to review the various methods of transferring files and determine which one is best for you.

DETAILS

- ### File Transfer Protocol (FTP)

   File Transfer Protocol (FTP) is one of the most common methods of transferring files to a server. You can use DOS command-line FTP instructions to transfer files, but most people find it easier to use a special program called an FTP client. **FTP client** programs, such as InternetSoft FTP Commander, Ipswitch WS_FTP, and Fetch Softworks Fetch (for Macintosh users), let you transfer files without having to remember a list of command-line FTP instructions. Instead, most FTP client programs use a graphical user interface, which uses windows, icons, pointers, and the like, to navigate among folders and subfolders in much the same way that you do with your computer's file system. Figure A-16 shows the FTP Commander interface.

- ### Secure File Transfer Protocol (SFTP)

   Secure File Transfer Protocol (SFTP) works like FTP, except that files transferred with SFTP are encrypted for additional security. If your file transfers must be secure, it is important that you choose an FTP client application that supports SFTP.

- ### Mapped Network Drive

   Direct transfer through a mapped drive is as easy as copying or moving files on your own computer. You simply drag files from your local disk to the desired server location. However, this method is also the most dangerous because it can alter file path integrity. For example, files transferred in this manner often end up with drive letters and file designators such as file:///C:/mydirectory/myfile.htm in their file paths. If you test your remote files from your development station after transferring them in this manner, file-path problems will not be evident because your local files and "live" files have access to the same mapped and local drives. To prevent this type of error, examine your source code before transferring files to ensure that there are no drive-letter references in your file paths.

- ### Web Site Development Program Publishing Interface

   Web development software packages, such as Macromedia Dreamweaver (now owned by Adobe Systems), and Microsoft FrontPage utilize their own publishing interfaces to transfer files. In fact, some sites developed with these applications are **extension specific**, meaning that they do not perform properly unless specific files, called extensions, are stored on the Web server and unless the sites are published and updated using the application's publishing interface. Hand coded sites are not extension dependent and so have no need of a program-specific publishing interface.

FIGURE A-16: FTP Commander interface

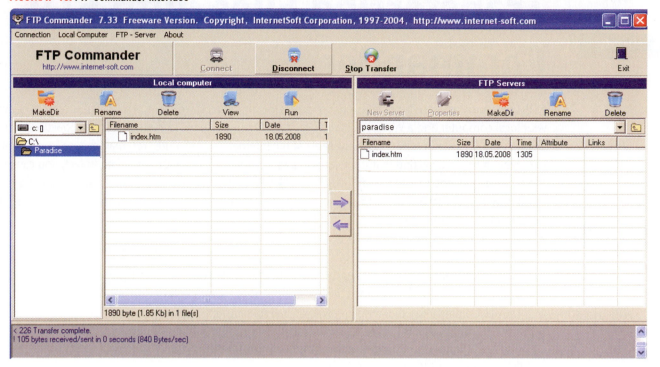

Clues to Use

Downloading FTP Commander

Although you can use any FTP client program to transfer your files, the freeware program, FTP Commander, is easy to install and to use. Complete the steps below to download and install FTP Commander. (These steps describe the download process from Internet Explorer; your browser steps may differ.)

1. Open your browser, then go to the InternetSoft Web site: Go to the Student Online Companion for this book and find the links for Unit A.
2. Click the DOWNLOAD link in the navigation bar near the top of the page.
3. On the Download page, click the Download link next to FTP Commander. (Notice that there is no charge for this program.)
4. If the Windows File Download - Security Warning dialog box displays the message, "Do you want to run or save this file?" click Run. (If you are on a very slow connection, you might want to save the file first and run it later.)

Wait a few moments while the small FTP Commander Install file downloads to your Temporary folder.

5. Click Run when the Internet Explorer - Security Warning dialog box displays the message: "The publisher could not be verified. Are you sure you want to run this software?"
6. After reading the FTP Commander License Agreement, click to select the check box indicating that you agree with the license terms.
7. Click Next.
8. When the FTP Commander Destination Directory dialog box appears, click Browse to select a different storage location or

click Start to accept the default destination. FTP Commander unpacks and installs the necessary files.

9. When the files are installed, make sure that the Run Installed Application box is checked, then click OK. You are now ready to begin using FTP Commander. The first time you run the application, a Windows Security Alert dialog box may warn you that Windows Firewall has blocked some features of this program. If this happens, click Unblock, as shown in Figure A-17.

For information on using WS_FTP Home for Windows or Fetch for MAC operating systems, see Using Other FTP Programs in the appendix of this text or in the FTP Resources section of the Student Online Companion.

FIGURE A-17: Windows Security Alert dialog box

Transferring Files with FTP Commander

FTP Commander is an FTP client program created by InternetSoft that lets you easily transfer files between your local computer and a Web server. The program is **freeware**, meaning that you can download it at no charge from the Internet; it is readily available at the Internet-Soft Web site. You may choose to use another FTP client; if so, you will find that it operates in a similar manner to FTP Commander. In fact, you can apply the same basic steps to almost any FTP client. Now that you have a basic understanding of file transfer methods, you are eager to see how your site will appear on a "live" server and decide to use FTP Commander to transfer them there.

STEPS

TROUBLE

If FTP Commander is not installed on your computer, you need to download and install it. To do so, complete the steps in the Clues to Use in the previous lesson. You will also need access to a server directory with an assigned username and password that grants your permission to control files in that directory.

1. **If FTP Commander is not already running, click the Start button** start **on the taskbar, point to All Programs, point to FTP Commander, then click FTP Commander**

   The FTP Commander window opens to display the contents of the FTP Commander folder in the local directory (left pane) and a list of servers on the remote site in the right pane. These servers are public access FTP sites where you can go to download information. Before transferring files to and from a server, you must first define your local and remote directories.

2. **Click the Browse local drives list arrow shown in Figure A-18, then navigate to the location where you store your site files**

   Any available folders in your selected drive are displayed in the Folders pane. When a folder is selected, the folder content, which could include other folders as well as files, is displayed in the Folder content pane. You need to define the path to your remote server.

3. **Click New Server under FTP- servers**

   The FTP Server Properties box appears.

QUICK TIP

If you need to change your Server Definition Properties again later, select the server name in the SERVER LIST pane, and then click the Modify FTP server properties Properties button.

4. **Type your information as described in Table A-5, then click Save**

   FTP Commander Server Properties settings may change over time. If necessary, go to the Student Online Companion for this text and unit, then click the FTP Resources link to see an updated table.

5. **In the SERVER LIST pane, double-click the name of the server you just defined to open an FTP connection to your server**

   Your remote site content appears in the server pane. If you have not yet transferred any files to your remote site, your files list contains no items.

6. **Click index.htm in the Folder content pane of the Local computer window, then click the Upload files to FTP - server button** ➡ **to start the file transfer to the server**

   The paradise home page file is copied to the FTP server, as shown in Figure A-18.

7. **Start your Internet browser, type your remote URL in the browser's Address box, then click Go or press [Enter]**

   Your remote page is displayed in the browser window. Your remote URL is usually a combination of your FTP server name plus any subdirectory and filename (with extension). However, on occasion, some FTP servers use an FTP alias that is not the same as your URL. Check with your instructor or server administrator to make sure you have the correct URL.

8. **Close your browser and your text editor**

FIGURE A-18: Transferring a file using FTP Commander

Browse local drives button

Click to select local file

Folders pane

Folder content pane

File appears in server file listing

Click Upload Files to FTP Server button

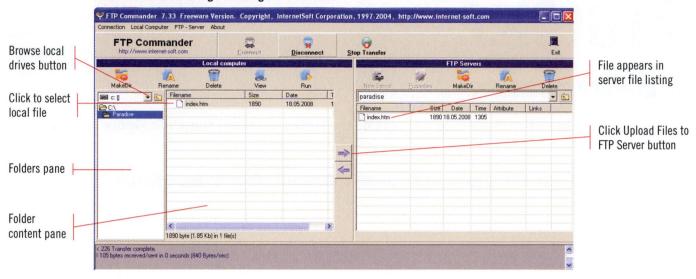

TABLE A-5: FTP Commander Server Properties settings

section	property	value
Server	Name	An identifying name for your site
Server	FTP Server	Use the FTP server name, including any subdirectory paths, as assigned by your instructor or server administrator. Do not include any protocol designation such as ftp:// or http://.
Server	FTP Port	21 (unless otherwise instructed)
User	User ID	Obtain from your instructor or server administrator
User	Password	Obtain from your instructor or server administrator
User	Save Password	If computer is your own, leave checked; if computer is shared, do not check this box
User	Mask Password	Checked
User	Passive Mode	Unchecked unless otherwise instructed
User	Anonymous Login	Unchecked unless otherwise instructed
User	E-Mail	Leave blank unless otherwise instructed
Additional Options	Use "/" as initial directory on FTP server	Unchecked unless otherwise instructed
Additional Options	Shared virtual host	Unchecked unless otherwise instructed
Additional Options	Use relative pathname	Unchecked unless otherwise instructed
FTP Server response type	Drop-down menu	Obtain from your instructor or server administrator. For Microsoft servers, choose the current Windows server version; for UNIX servers, choose Default.

Practice

▼ CONCEPTS REVIEW

Name the function of each marked element of the Notepad screen shown in Figure A-19.

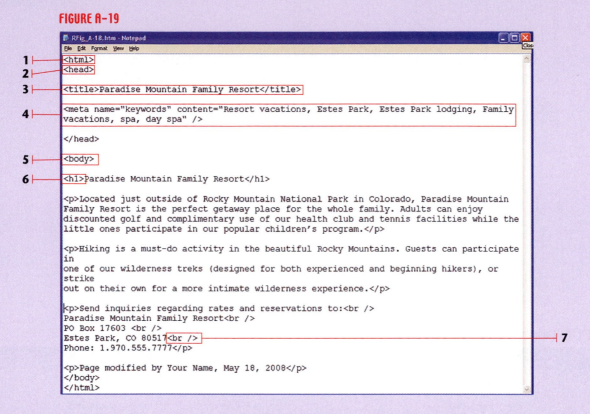

FIGURE A-19

Match each term with the statement that best describes it.

8. **Tag**	**a.** A Web-based program that helps you find information you are seeking
9. `<title>...</title>`	**b.** An instruction in HTML
10. **Web site**	**c.** Tag set surrounding Web page contents that appear in the browser window
11. **Search engine**	**d.** Tag set for text to appear in the browser's title bar
12. `<body>...</body>`	**e.** A collection of related Web pages
13. **Source code**	**f.** The HTML code used to create a Web page

Select the best answer from the list of choices.

14. **If you wanted to reduce the text size of a level four heading, which tag set would you use?**

  a. `<head>...</head>`   **c.** `<h5>...</h5>`

  b. `<h3>...</h3>`   **d.** `<br>...</br>`

15. **In the URL http://www.paradisemountain.com/spa/wraps.htm, paradisemountain.com is the:**

  a. Machine name.   **c.** Directory name.

  b. Domain name.   **d.** Protocol.

16. **Which is the proper method of coding a line break?**

  a. `<BR>`   **c.** `<br />`

  b. `<break>`   **d.** `<lb>`

▼ SKILLS REVIEW

1. **Plan an HTML document.**
   a. Consider a Web page you might create for Paradise Mountain's spa. Assume it will have a page title, a level-one heading, a subheading, and two text paragraphs.
   b. Create a sketch of how the page will eventually look.
   c. On your sketch, identify each heading and/or subheading.
   d. On your sketch, identify your page content area.
   e. On your sketch, use boxes to identify areas that will eventually contain images.

2. **Write an HTML document.**
   a. Locate and open the paradise folder in the directory where you store your site files.
   b. Create a subfolder in your paradise folder called **spa**.
   c. Start your text editor with a blank document.
   d. Save your new file as **index.htm** inside your spa folder. (*Note*: Be careful *not* to save the new file in your paradise folder. Be sure to type the .htm extension and use the All Files file type.)
   e. Enter the HTML code shown in Figure A-20.
   f. Format the text "Paradise Garden Day Spa" in the body section as a level-one heading.
   g. Format the text "Your Eden in the Rockies" in the body section as a level-two heading, then save your document.

3. **Import Web content.**
   a. Open the file **htm_a-2.rtf** in your word processor and copy all of the text.

FIGURE A-20

   b. In the index.htm document, click to place the insertion point after the closing tag for the subheading, "Your Eden in the Rockies" and press [Enter] to add a new line.
   c. Paste the copied text into the document, then save the file.
   d. Close the RTF file, then preview the index.htm file in your browser.

4. **Mark up Web page content.**
   a. Return to the source code and surround each of the paragraph sections with opening and closing paragraph tags.
   b. Click after phone: in the second to the last paragraph, then add a line break.
   c. Update the "modified by" paragraph with your name and the current date.
   d. Save your work.
   e. Reload the page in your browser to display the latest version of the document.

5. **Print an HTML document.**
   a. In your text editor, print the source code for the spa/index.htm file.
   b. In your browser program, print the Web page.
   c. Close the browser window.
   d. If necessary, close the text editor program.

6. **Transfer an HTML document.**
   a. Start FTP Commander (or whichever FTP program you are using).
   b. Find the server definition you created during your FTP lesson and double-click it to establish a connection to your remote directory.
   c. Double-click your remote paradise folder to open it on the server.
   d. Use the Browse local drives list arrow to browse to the directory where you save your site files.
   e. Single-click the spa folder to select it, then click the Upload files to FTP server button to transfer the folder and its contents to your server.
   f. Open a browser window and type the URL to your remote file in the browser Address bar. (*Hint*: Don't forget to add the folder and file name to the remote path.)
   g. In the browser program, print the spa/index.htm file from its remote location.

▼ INDEPENDENT CHALLENGE 1

You have recently started a vacation resort rental agency called Star Vacations that brokers rentals of time-share properties in the United States, Canada, and the Bahamas. It is a priority for you to provide a Web site so potential clients can research your available services. Using the skills you learned in this unit, plan and create a Web page for your agency. Use a text editor to write your HTML tags, then use your browser to view the finished page. Your page should include at least two headings, as well as some placeholder text and contact information for your company.

    a. Create a sketch of your Web page, including a page title, a heading, and at least one paragraph of descriptive text.

    b. On your sketch, define which HTML tags you will use for each page element.

    c. Start your text editor and enter the structuring tags for the page, along with the title and heading elements; be sure to add a "Modified by" paragraph at the bottom of the page with your name and current date.

    d. Create a new folder called **vacations** in the location where you store your site files. (*Hint*: Do not create the new folder inside your paradise folder.)

    e. Save your work inside your vacations folder as **index.htm**.

    f. Preview your page in your Web browser, then edit the source code, if necessary, to format the page as you want it to appear.

    g. Print the document in your text editor and in your browser.

    h. Transfer your new folder and its contents to your remote server directory, then view the remote file in your browser.

    i. Print your remote vacations/index.htm file from the browser.

▼ INDEPENDENT CHALLENGE 2

You are the Water Resources Manager at Metro Water, the local water department, and have volunteered to help create a Web site for your employer. Your priority is to create an information source about your community's water resources and to encourage water conservation. Because you are familiar with the topic of water resources in your area, you will also gather additional information to include in the site.

    a. Create a sketch that includes the items you want to include on your Web page.

    b. Add notations about the HTML elements and the code needed to create each element.

    c. Create a new folder called **water** in the directory where you save your site files.

    d. Start your text editor and enter the structuring tags for the page, along with the title and the heading elements, add some general page heading and paragraph placeholder content, then save your file as **index.htm** in your water folder.

    e. Preview your page in your browser, edit the source, if necessary, to format the page as you want it to appear, then save your page.

    f. Edit the page by adding the following contact information paragraph, making sure to insert a line break after each colon (:): **For more information, contact: Your Name, Water Resources Manager at: (303) 555-4H2O (555-4426)**.

    g. Save your work and preview it; print the document in your text editor and in your browser, then close your source code file.

    h. Transfer your new folder and its contents to your remote server directory, then view the remote file in your browser.

    i. Print the remote file from your browser window.

Advanced Challenge Exercises

    ■ You want to start creating a page with links to online resources. Open your text editor, start a new document, and add basic page formatting elements with a page title.

    ■ Connect to the Internet and use your favorite search engine to find at least 5 sites that contain information on water resources and water conservation that you can include in a list of linked resources.

    ■ Copy the complete URLs of each of your resources, then paste each URL into your document, pressing [Enter] once after each one, and adding a short description of the site below it.

    ■ Press [Enter] twice after each description, then paste the next URL into the document.

    ■ Save your file as **resources.htm** in your water folder.

    ■ Add a level-two or level-three heading with the text **Water Conservation Resources** above your list of URLs.

    ■ Separate each item from the others by enclosing each URL and its description in an opening and closing paragraph tag.

    ■ Add line breaks to the end of each URL to force its description to the next line.

    ■ Save and preview your page and then transfer your water directory to the server.

    ■ View your new page in your browser from the remote location, then print the page and close all programs.

▼ INDEPENDENT CHALLENGE 3

In this unit you have practiced using basic HTML tags to create some of the fundamental elements of a Web page. As you learn more tags and their functions, you will be able to add different elements and formats to your Web pages. The Web itself can be one of the most useful tools for learning more about HTML. Try it out by seeing what you can find on the Web about a tag or a tag set that you haven't used yet.

    a. Use your favorite search engine to locate one of the following online HTML references: W3C, Webmonkey, or WebReference, or go to the Student Online Companion for this book and see the Unit A links.

    b. Click the link for HTML if you see one, then use the site's search utility to find information about one of the following tag sets:

    `<em>...</em>`, `<i>...</i>`, `<ol>...</ol>`, or `<ul>...</ul>`

    c. If you're using Internet Explorer, enter your name in the header section of the Page Setup dialog box, after any codes you see there.

    d. Print at least two pages that discuss what the selected tag does and how you use it in Web page code. (If you are using a browser that doesn't allow you to add text to the header, write your name on the printout.)

    e. Write a paragraph about your selected tag. Include the following information:

      • Its name (what the letters in the tag stand for)

      • What feature(s) it adds to a Web page

      • An example of where in Web page design you think the selected tag would be useful

▼ INDEPENDENT CHALLENGE 4

You have decided to create your own Web site. Because it is your site, you can use your imagination in determining a site theme and topic. Your site can be a business site, an informational site, a fan site, or a personal site. One of the most basic sources of design ideas is published Web pages. After determining your site subject, use a search engine to find good examples of similar sites. Analyze the sites to determine what makes them effective. Then create a basic Web page as the initial home page for your Web site.

    a. Use your favorite search engine such as Google, Alta Vista, or Yahoo to find Web pages similar to the site you want to create. If you have trouble locating a search engine, go to the Student Online Companion for this book, and use the links for Unit A as a starting point.

    b. Add your name to the footer, then print the home page from the site you like the best.

    c. On your printout, indicate familiar elements (such as titles, headings, empty lines, and paragraphs of text) and indicate the tag you think was used to create each element.

    d. List at least two design aspects that you think make the page functional, such as placement of elements, colors, and text phrasing. List at least one aspect that could be improved. Write a paragraph describing how you would improve the design of each Web page.

    e. Sketch your own page design using boxes to indicate the items you want to include, such as images, page navigation elements, headings, and paragraph content, then add your name at the top.

    f. Create a basic home page for your site with at least a page title, a page heading, and placeholder paragraphs describing what you will eventually include on your site, as well as a paragraph containing your contact information.

    g. Save your page as **index.htm** in a folder you create and designate as your site folder, then transfer the folder to your remote site.

Advanced Challenge Exercises

    ■ View and print the page source for the site you critiqued.

    ■ Compare your speculations with the actual code used to create the page you viewed. Then consider the following: How close did you come to guessing the code tags? List up to three tags that you do not recognize.

    ■ Search the Web for information on one of the tags that is new to you.

    ■ Write one or two paragraphs about that tag and its purpose.

▼ VISUAL WORKSHOP

You work for a local computer store called Bits and PCs, which is celebrating its 20th year in business. Your employer has asked you to design a Web site to promote the store's anniversary celebration and to highlight its advertised specials. You sketched a storyboard of page ideas and want to use it for reference as you add the basic elements for your home page. Create a folder in the place where you store your site files, called **bitspcs**. Then, using the skills you have learned, create a page based on the lay-out sketch shown in Figure A-21. Save it as index.htm in your bitspcs folder, then transfer the folder to your remote directory.

FIGURE A-21

Creating Links to Web Pages and Other Files

OBJECTIVES

Plan a Web Site

Create internal links

Create links to other directories

Create external links

Create e-mail links

Create jump links

Open links in new windows

Add link titles

What makes the Web so useful is its ability to present **non-linear content**—content that need not be read in any particular order—through hyperlinking. **Hyperlinking** is the ability to jump from one content point to another by clicking on **hypertext links**—text or graphics that, when clicked, direct site visitors to other information. The ability to link one page to another allows you, the site designer, to make it easier for site visitors to find the information they are seeking. Using hyperlinks, Web site visitors can jump from place to place within a page, from file to file within a site, or across cyberspace to a file in another site. You can also create links that launch external e-mail programs for sending messages or that cause linked files to open in a new window. You have a lot of information to present and want to organize it into sections that you can link to your home page. You also want to create links to external information you think will interest your site visitors.

Planning a Web Site

Before you start creating your Web site, you need to plan it. Decide what type of site you want to create, identify your target audience, determine your content sources, and define your site's purpose and goals. In addition, you should organize your content into logical divisions and create a site structure chart. You decide to meet with the Paradise Mountain Family Resort owners and their Public Relations Director to plan the site structure and content and to identify its target audience.

Steps to planning a Web site include:

QUICK TIP

Business sites often start out as brochure sites, then later add interactive features such as shopping carts, payment processing, and order-tracking pages.

• **Determine your site type**

Before you start creating your site pages, you need to determine your site type and define the content for each page. Three common Web site categories are business, support, and personal. **Business sites** are divided into two main categories: **brochure sites**, which display information similar to that found in a printed brochure; and **e-commerce sites**, which contain catalog information and order-processing elements such as shopping carts and order-tracking pages. Brochure sites are not designed to sell a product, but may contain links to e-commerce sites where products and services are sold. **Support sites** often contain downloadable user manuals, forms, and software drivers. **Personal sites** offer the greatest degree of flexibility in design; they can be used to communicate with friends, post professional résumés or portfolios, or honor a favorite public figure. You determine that the Paradise Mountain site will be a brochure site.

QUICK TIP

When available, always list your business address including your city and state, and your contact information, including your area code and phone number.

• **Define the site's purpose**

Is the purpose of your site to sell goods, provide general information, or showcase your own talents? Answering this question helps determine the type of content to include on your pages. Paradise Mountain's site will deliver information about the resort and provide a listing of resort and area activities.

• **Identify the target audience**

Your **target audience** is the group or groups of people you are trying to attract. Are they young or middle-aged? Are they male or female? What is their income level? What technology do they have available? Knowing your target audience enables you to design pages that include content, features, and colors attractive to them. Paradise Mountain Family Resort caters to families who are attracted to "the Great Outdoors," so you decide to use primarily blues and greens to represent clear skies and trees.

QUICK TIP

All information posted on the Internet is copyrighted. Taking information from one Web site and using it on your own without written permission is a violation of federal copyright law.

• **Identify content sources**

If you are starting a new business or developing a personal site, you will probably create your own original content. However, for an existing business or organization, you will probably find that you can repurpose existing information such as company brochures, mission statements, and catalogs, for use on the Web. Remember that you must have permission to use any information you collect. Paradise Mountain's Marketing Department already has many documents that you can repurpose for use on the company's Web site.

• **Organize your site content**

To make your content accessible to site visitors, organize it by subject matter into sections and pages, then create navigation elements to help your site visitors find the information they need. You decide to include pages with general information about the resort, as well as two content sections—one for the resort's spa and one for resort and area activities.

• **Create a site storyboard**

Once you have determined your site categories, you can further organize your site structure by creating a diagram called a **site storyboard** or **site map**, which can help you design your site navigation elements. Figures B-1 and B-2 show common site structures, a **net structure** (also called a Web structure), where all pages are linked to one another, and a **hierarchical** structure, in which information is organized in content sections, moving from general to more specific. Net structure is effective for organizing very small sites; hierarchical structure is perfect for organizing large sites or sites with potential for fast growth. Figure B-2 shows the hierarchical structure you will use for the Paradise resort site.

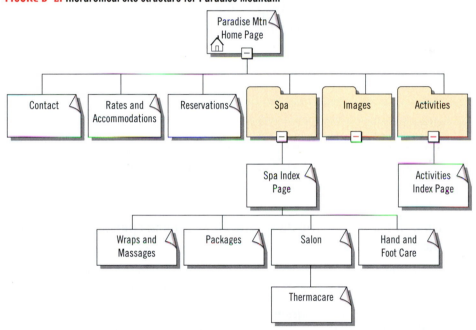

Clues to Use

Designing for company intranet sites

Intranet sites are private Web sites available only to authorized users who log in with special credentials. These sites often contain links to company support materials and allow employees to upload and download company documents and to access shared databases.

Intranet sites offer a greater flexibility in design because you can develop pages based on technology known to be available to company employees.

HTML

Creating Internal Links

Once you have information stored in two or more pages (files), it is important that you link those pages to make all site information accessible. In a link, the **anchor tag** (<a>...</a>), also known as a **link tag**, surrounds information that users click to navigate to another location. By itself, the anchor tag is useless. To function, the opening anchor tag must contain an **attribute,** (feature), and a **value** that specifies or changes the tag's behavior or function. Values modify attributes in the same way that adjectives modify nouns. The required attribute for a link is **href**—which stands for hypertext reference. The href value used to create most types of links is the URL—the file path and name—as shown in Figure B-3. Links to files within the same site are called **internal links**. Internal links are usually **relative links**, because the link URL traces a path to the desired file *relative to* the file from which the link originates. The easiest type of relative link to create is one to a page in the same directory. For an internal link in the same directory, the href value is the name of the target file as follows: `<a href="file.htm">View the file</a>` Because both files are in the same directory, no folder path is necessary. You have created an additional page for your site and want to give visitors access to this information. You decide to add a site navigation bar to link your pages.

STEPS

1. **Using your file management system, locate and open the folder where you store your Unit B Data Files, click to select contact.htm, click Edit on the menu bar, then click Copy**

   The contact.htm file is copied to the clipboard

TROUBLE
If you did not complete the Skills Review in Unit A, the spa folder will not be part of your directory structure. If it is not, you may copy the spa folder from your Data Files into the paradise folder at this time.

2. **Locate and click to select the paradise folder in the directory where you save your site files, click Edit on the menu bar, then click Paste**

   The contact.htm file is copied to your folder as shown in Figure B-4. In the following step, and in all HTML code you type, make sure that your text editor or word processor does not have the smart quote feature turned on; you must use straight quotation marks or the links will not work correctly.

3. **Open the paradise\index.htm file in your text editor from the place where you save your site files, click after the </h1> tag, then press [Enter] twice**

4. **Type `<p>|<a href="index.htm">Home</a>|`, press [Spacebar], type `|<a href="contact.htm">Contact Us</a>|</p>`, then save your work**

   You have created links to your home and contact pages. These links are the first part of your site navigation bar.

5. **Drag to select the navigation bar code (including opening and closing paragraph tags), then copy it**

6. **Open the paradise\contact.htm file in your text editor, click after </h1>, press [Enter] twice, paste the code, update the "modified by" paragraph, then save the file**

7. **Start your browser program, click File on the menu bar, click Open, click Browse, navigate to the index.htm file in your paradise folder, double-click index.htm, then click OK to open it in the browser**

8. **Move the mouse pointer over the links**

   As you rest the mouse pointer over each link, the linked file's URL appears in the browser status bar and the mouse pointer turns into a hand pointer 🖑, indicating that the link is active.

9. **Click the Contact Us link, then from the contact.htm file, click the Home link**

   When you click the Contact Us link, the target page appears in the browser window. Clicking the Home link from the contact.htm page returns you to the index.htm file. Figure B-5 shows a completed navigation bar. Notice the single space between the links.

FIGURE B-3: Parts of a hyperlink

Opening anchor tag
Tag name   href attribute   URL   Linked text
Closing anchor tag

`<a href="http://www.course.com/contact.cfm"> Course Technology contact page </a>`

FIGURE B-4: Files copied to paradise folder

Paradise folder (your path may differ)

Imported files (your view may differ)

FIGURE B-5: Site navigation with target URL displayed in navigation bar

Linked text

Single space between links

Target URL (your path may differ)

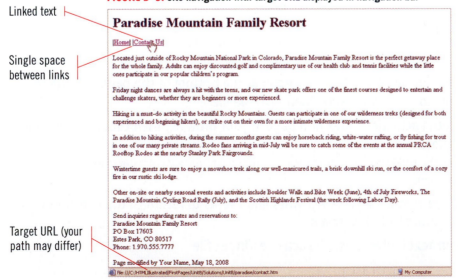

Paradise Mountain Family Resort

|Home| |Contact Us|

Located just outside of Rocky Mountain National Park in Colorado, Paradise Mountain Family Resort is the perfect getaway place for the whole family. Adults can enjoy discounted golf and complimentary use of our health club and tennis facilities while the little ones participate in our popular children's program.

Friday night dances are always a hit with the teens, and our new skate park offers one of the finest courses designed to entertain and challenge skaters, whether they are beginners or more experienced.

Hiking is a must-do activity in the beautiful Rocky Mountains. Guests can participate in one of our wilderness treks (designed for both experienced and beginning hikers), or strike out on their own for a more intimate wilderness experience.

In addition to hiking activities, during the summer months guests can enjoy horseback riding, white-water rafting, or fly fishing for trout in one of our many private streams. Rodeo fans arriving in mid-July will be sure to catch some of the events at the annual PRCA Rooftop Rodeo at the nearby Stanley Park Fairgrounds.

Wintertime guests are sure to enjoy a snowshoe trek along our well-manicured trails, a brisk downhill ski run, or the comfort of a cozy fire in our rustic ski lodge.

Other on-site or nearby seasonal events and activities include Boulder Walk and Bike Week (June), 4th of July Fireworks, The Paradise Mountain Cycling Road Rally (July), and the Scottish Highlands Festival (the week following Labor Day).

Send inquiries regarding rates and reservations to:
Paradise Mountain Family Resort
PO Box 17603
Estes Park, CO 80517
Phone: 1.970.555.7777

Page modified by Your Name, May 18, 2008

Creating Links to Other Directories

As your site grows and matures, you will likely need to organize some of your content into subdirectories. Creating relative links to files in other directories is easy once you understand relative file paths. As shown in Figure B-6, to direct the browser to move from one directory to another, use **dot-slash notation**, a combination of dots and forward slashes that serve as path designators from one folder to another up and down the directory tree. A pair of dots followed by a slash direct the browser to move one level up the directory tree before seeking the linked file. A folder name followed by a slash tells the browser that the file is one directory-level down in the designated folder. 🎨 The owners of Paradise Mountain Family Resort have asked you to develop a set of pages to promote the resort's activities center and to link it to the Paradise Mountain home page.

STEPS

1. **Using your file management system, copy the activities folder and its contents from the location where you store your Unit B Data Files, then paste it into your paradise folder in the location where you save your site files**

QUICK TIP

Although system folder paths are designated using backslashes (\), Web paths are always specified with forward slashes (/). You might see backslashes in file paths when a local file is displayed in the browser, but *do not* use backslashes in your file paths.

2. **Open your paradise\index.htm file in your text editor, click just before the </p> in the navigation bar code, press [Spacebar], type |<a href="activities/index.htm">Activities and Events</a>|, then save the file**

   The Activities link directs the browser down from the root folder to the activities folder and finds the activities/index.htm file.

3. **Drag to select the modified navigation bar, click Edit on the menu bar, then click Copy**

4. **Open your paradise\activities\index.htm file in your text editor, click after </h1>, press [Enter] twice, click Edit on the menu bar, then click Paste**

   The navigation bar code you just pasted from your site home page must be modified so that the links will work from the activities directory.

5. **Locate the Home link, click between the first quotation mark and the file name index.htm, then type ../**

6. **Click between the first quotation mark and the file or folder name in each of the other URLs and the two other links, type ../, then save the file**

   By adding ../ to the beginning of each root-level page link and to the sub-folder link, as shown in Figure B-7, you instruct the browser to move to the parent directory before searching for the root- or sub-level file, creating a universal navigation bar that will work from any page in a first-level sub directory. Because the structure of this site has only one sublevel, the root directory is the parent directory for your subfolders.

7. **Locate the "modified by" paragraph at the bottom of the page, change the text "Your Name" to your own name, then save the file**

TROUBLE

If the linked files do not display as expected, check your code to ensure that ../ precedes each link path and that each href value is enclosed in straight quotes.

8. **Open the activities/index.htm page in your browser, then click Activities and Events to test the link**

   Because the HREF value points to the index.htm file in the activities directory, the file is reloaded when you click the link.

9. **Click the Home link, click Activities and Events to return to the Activities page, then click the Contact Us link to test it**

10. **In your text editor, close the activities/index file**

FIGURE B-6: Relative file paths

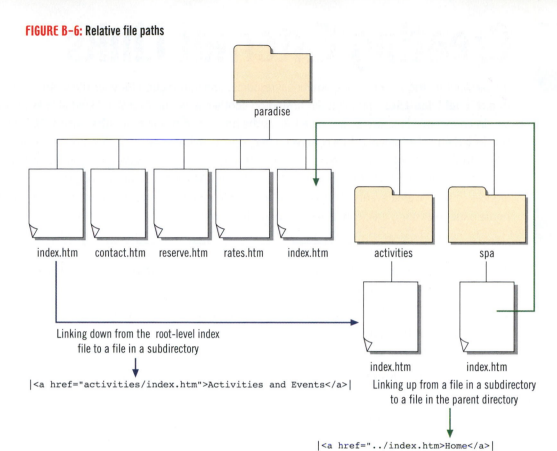

Linking down from the root-level index file to a file in a subdirectory

`|<a href="activities/index.htm">Activities and Events</a>|`

Linking up from a file in a subdirectory to a file in the parent directory

`|<a href="../index.htm>Home</a>|`

FIGURE B-7: Linking from a first-level subdirectory

Dot slash notation directs browser to parent directory

Design Matters

Creating a Text-Based Navigation Bar

Including a text-based navigation bar is an easy method of enhancing your site's accessibility and usability. Properly formatted text-based navigation bars are easy to read, understand, and click. The following tips will help you create effective text-based navigation bars. 1) Never include spaces between the opening link tag and the start of the linked text, or between the end of the linked text and the closing link tag; doing so causes spaces on either side of the linked text to be formatted as underlined spaces. 2) Set off links by surrounding each one with characters such as pipes, |linked text|, or square brackets, [linked text] to make them easier to click. 3) To prevent your linked text item from "wrapping" between the text and the pipe or bracket, make sure that no spaces occur between the pipe or bracket and the start of the opening link tag or the end of the closing link tag. 4) Insert a single space between the linked item to make them easier to select. 5) Avoid the use of decorative fonts in your text-navigation bars. Decorative fonts are difficult to read and can negate the effectiveness of your text navigation bar.

Creating External Links

An excellent method of providing additional resources and information for your site visitors is to create links to **external Web files**—files that are hosted on another server or Web site. External links are easy to create. In an external link, use an absolute URL as the href property value. An **absolute URL** is the complete URL including the protocol (http://), server name, domain name, path, and filename of the file you want to open. To create a link to an external file, type its absolute URL between the opening and closing quote marks that follow the href attribute. 🎨 The Paradise Mountain Family Resort home page contains references to several area events of interest to Paradise Mountain's visitors. You want to create links from your home page to existing online information about those events.

STEPS

1. If necessary, open your paradise\index.htm file in your text editor, from the paradise folder in the directory where you save your site files

2. Click in front of the word annual in the phrase annual PRCA Rooftop Rodeo in the fourth paragraph, then type `<a href="http://www.estesnet.com/events/rooftoprodeo.htm">`

QUICK TIP

To save a file using the keyboard, press [Ctrl][S].

3. Click just after Rodeo, type `</a>`, click File on the menu bar, then save your work
   Your text should look similar to Figure B-8.

4. Open paradise\index.htm in your browser, move the mouse pointer over the linked text
   The text that you typed between the link anchor tags appears underlined. When you point to the link, the pointer changes to the hand icon and the target URL appears in the status bar.

QUICK TIP

If the target page does not appear, check your code to make sure that you typed the URL correctly, that you have included (http://), and that you have enclosed the entire href attribute value in quotation marks. If the page still does not appear, use your favorite search engine to search for the appropriate URL or check the Student Online Companion.

5. Click the link to display the PRCA Rooftop Rodeo page, scroll down the page to view its content, shown in Figure B-9, then click your browser's Back button to return to the index.htm page
   While the target page is displayed, the external URL is shown in the browser address location box.

6. Click the text editor program button on the taskbar, click in front of Boulder in the first sentence of the last paragraph, type
   `<a href="http://www.bouldercolorado.gov/index.php?option=com_content&task=view&id=8845&Itemid=3026"`, click after "Week" in "Boulder Walk and Bike Week", then type `</a>`

7. Click before Scottish in the last paragraph, type `<a href="http://www.scottishgames.org/">`, click after Festival, then type `</a>`

8. Save the document, click the browser program button on the taskbar, then click your browser's Reload or Refresh button
   The updated version of your page appears in the browser window.

QUICK TIP

If the appropriate target URLs do not display, refer to QuickTip next to step 5.

9. Click each link to verify that it works properly, then click the text editor program button on the taskbar

FIGURE B-8: External link code

External link

```
<p>In addition to hiking activities, during the summer months guests can enjoy
horseback riding, white-water rafting, or fly fishing for trout in one of our many
private streams. Rodeo fans arriving in mid-July will be sure to catch some of the
events at the <a href="http://www.estesnet.com/events/rooftoprodeo.htm">annual
PRCA Rooftop Rodeo</a> at the nearby Stanley Park Fairgrounds.</p>
```

FIGURE B-9: External link displayed in browser

External URL

Content may
have changed

HTML

Creating E-Mail Links

E-mail links are simple code instructions that give your site visitors an additional way to contact you for information. E-mail links use the mailto protocol with an e-mail address as the href attribute value, as shown in Figure B-10. When a site visitor clicks the e-mail link, an e-mail message window appears, similar to the one shown in Figure B-11. The new message is addressed using the mailto value you entered. You decide to update your "Contact Us" page to include clickable e-mail links with each person's contact information.

STEPS

1. In your text editor, open the paradise/contact.htm page from the location where you store your paradise site files

2. Locate the Paradise Mountain Family Resort paragraph at the bottom of the page, click before `</p>`, type `<br />`, press [Enter], then type `E-mail: <a href="mailto: info@paradisemtn.com">info@paradisemtn.com</a>`

3. Locate the Reservations paragraph near the top of the page, click before `</p>`, type `<br />`, press [Enter], then type `E-mail: <a href="mailto:reservations@paradisemtn.com"> reservations@paradisemtn.com</a>` as shown in Figure B-10

4. Locate the Activities and Events paragraph near the top of the page, click before `</p>`, type `<br />`, press [Enter], then type `E-mail: <a href="mailto: activities@paradisemtn.com">activities@paradisemtn.com</a>`

5. Locate the Business Office paragraph, click before `</p>`, type `<br />`, press [Enter], then type `E-mail: <a href="mailto:business@paradisemtn.com"> business@paradisemtn.com</a>`

6. Click after `</p>` in the "modified by" paragraph at the bottom of the page, type `<p>For questions or comments about this site, contact: <br /> <a href="mailto:web-master@paradisemtn.com">webmaster@paradisemtn.com</a> </p>`, then press [Enter]

7. Save the contact.htm file, then open it in your browser

8. In your browser, click the Reservations e-mail link

   Your e-mail program creates an untitled message, similar to that shown in Figure B-11.

9. Close the e-mail message window

FIGURE B-10: Mailto link source code

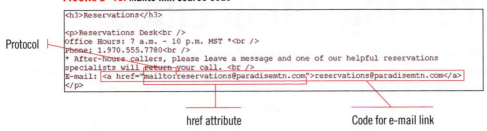

Protocol

```
<h3>Reservations</h3>

<p>Reservations Desk<br />
Office Hours: 7 a.m. - 10 p.m. MST *<br />
Phone: 1.970.555.7780<br />
* After-hours callers, please leave a message and one of our helpful reservations
specialists will return your call. <br />
E-mail: <a href="mailto:reservations@paradisemtn.com">reservations@paradisemtn.com</a>
</p>
```

href attribute   Code for e-mail link

FIGURE B-11: A mailto link and e-mail message window

Clicked mailto link
opens e-mail
message window

Clues to Use

Enhancing e-mail links

You can enhance your e-mail links to automatically include a subject line and to carbon copy another recipient. To add a subject line to your e-mail links, insert the append character, ?, at the end of the e-mail address as follows: `<a href="mailto:webmaster@paradisemtn.com?subject=Site_comments">webmaster@paradisemtn.com</a>`. To add a second enhancement, use the concatenation character (&) as follows: `mailto:webmaster@paradisemtn.com?subject=Site_comments&cc=business@paradisemtn.com`. Not all browsers support enhanced e-mail links, so be sure to test your links in a variety of browsers before making the decision to enhance them. For additional e-mail link enhancements, see the Student Online Companion for this text.

Creating Jump Links

When you must create an exceptionally long page, it is handy to create **jump links**, also known as **menu links**, that allow users to jump from a link on a page to a specific point on that page or a specific point on another page. Jump links are unlike other links in that they target HTML element IDs rather than an entire file. An **ID** is an identifier for any HTML element that can serve as an anchor point for jump links. The URL for a jump link on the same page is a pound sign (#) followed by the target element's ID. The URL for a jump link to another page is the file URL with the # and ID appended to the end of the file name. You decide to create jump links at the top of the page to specific locations on the same page. You also want to create links back to the top of the page.

STEPS

1. Click the text editor program button to return to your contact.htm source code

QUICK TIP
Make sure that no two elements on the page use the same ID.

2. Locate the level-one heading at the top of the page, click between h1 and > in the opening tag, press [Spacebar], then type id="top"
   You just set the ID value of "top" for the navigation bar paragraph, which you will use as an anchor point for creating links that allow visitors to navigate back to the top of the page.

3. Locate the level-three heading, Reservations, near the top of the page, click just after h3 in the opening tag, press [Spacebar], then type id="reservations"

4. Locate the level-three heading, General Information, click just after h3 in the opening tag, press [Spacebar], then type id="geninfo"

5. Locate the level-three heading, Paradise Garden Day Spa and Fitness Center, click just after h3 in the opening tag, press [Spacebar], then type id="spa"

6. Locate the level-three heading, Front Desk, click just after h3 in the opening tag, press [Spacebar], then type id="fdesk"

QUICK TIP
Don't forget to type square brackets ([....]) around each jump link.

7. Locate the level-two heading near the top of the page, click after </h2>, press [Enter] twice, then type the following, pressing [Spacebar][Enter] after each item:
```
<p>[<a href="#reservations">Reservations</a>]
[<a href="#geninfo">General Information</a>]
[<a href="#spa">Paradise Garden Day Spa</a>]
[<a href="#fdesk">Front Desk</a>]</p>
```
   You created jump links to each of the id points you set on the page.

8. Locate the paragraph containing the Reservations contact information near the top of the page, click before </p>, press [Enter], then type
<a href="#top">Return to top</a>

9. Drag to select the Return to top link you just created, including the opening and closing anchor tags, copy it to your clipboard, then paste it before </p> in the Human Resources Office and the Paradise Mountain Family Resort paragraphs
   Your page code appears similar to that shown in Figure B-12.

10. Save the file, then reload it in the browser to test your links
   Your completed page should resemble Figure B-13.

Jump link to anchor point

Anchor point

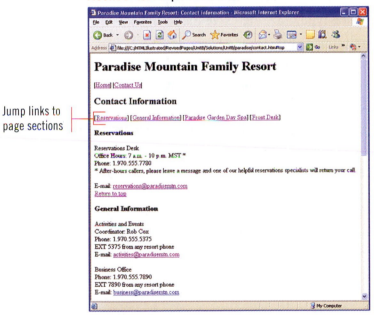

FIGURE B-13: Completed menu bar

Jump links to page sections

Clues to Use

Creating jump links with anchor name points

For years jump links were set using named anchor points rather than element IDs. Jump links created in this manner require two parts: the link and the named anchor point. Named anchor points have been deprecated by the W3C, but they are still in use today; consequently you might be called upon to modify pages with jump links to named anchor points, so it is good to know how they are created.

Links to named anchors are created in exactly the same manner as those to element IDs (<a href="URL#">Linked text</a>). To set the anchor point, click in front of the desired target element and type the anchor name code as follows: <a name="name"></a>. Set the name value as appropriate, as you would for an ID.

HTML

Opening Links in New Windows

Earlier you learned that the target URL is the page that opens when users click a link. By default, that URL opens in the same window as the page containing the link. However, there is another type of target associated with links; this target opens a page in a new window. Use the target attribute of the anchor tag with a value _blank as shown in Figure B-14. You want to create a link to one of the many Rocky Mountain National Park sites. The site is large and your site visitors might lose their way back to your site, so you want the link to open in a new window.

STEPS

1. **Open the index.htm page from your paradise site folder in your text editor**

2. **Click before Rocky Mountain National Park in the second paragraph**

3. **Type `<a href="http://www.nps.gov/romo" target="_blank">`**

   The value, _blank, is one of four **magic targets**, each of which begins with an underscore character. Although magic targets are generally reserved for use in sites that use **frames** (sites that display parts of the page in several windows simultaneously), the _blank target is useful for opening linked files in a new window from any page. Using the _blank target ensures that a new window will open every time and no content will be hidden behind already opened windows.

4. **Click after Park, type `</a>`, then save the document**

5. **Open paradise/index.htm in your browser**

   The page opens in your browser and the words "Rocky Mountain National Park" appear blue and underlined.

6. **Click the Rocky Mountain National Park link**

   The target URL opens in a new window as shown in Figure B-15.

7. **Close the target window to return to your home page**

   When the new window closes, the original page appears.

8. **Click the text editor program button to return to your source code**

Clues to Use

Targeting windows

When coding a link to open in a new window, some designers like to use "new" or "new_window". Declaring a value other than "_blank" causes the browser to assign an internal name to the generated window. Whenever a target attribute value is declared in a link tag, the linked file will open in another window provided that no other window of the same name is already open. However, one cannot always count on users closing the pop-up window after viewing its contents. This can cause content to open in hidden windows. Your option, then, is to give each target a unique name or to use the _blank name, which opens a file in a new window every time.

FIGURE B-14: Code for opening a file in a new window

```
<a href="http://www.nps.gov/romo/" target="_blank">Rocky Mountain National Park</a>
```

Target value

FIGURE B-15: Linked URL opened in new window

Targeted link

Targeted page opened in new window

Adding Link Titles

Link titles produce ScreenTips (pop-up text balloons) that appear when site visitors rest the mouse pointer over a link in which a link title has been specified. Link titles are useful **accessibility tools**—objects that make a site more usable to disabled users. They also give visitors extra information about the link. Visitors using a standard browser see a ScreenTip as shown in Figure B-16 when they rest the mouse pointer over the link. When visitors using a text reader come to a titled link, they hear the contents of the link title. This description can be much more valuable to site visitors than hearing only the link's URL. Link titles can be used to describe the content at the other end of the link, display file size, or supply download time information. Link titles can also be used to add additional, searchable information to a page. You want to warn site visitors that your external Rocky Mountain Park link opens a page in a new window. You also want to make your site more accessible to all visitors, so you decide to add link titles to your page links.

STEPS

1. Locate the opening Rocky Mountain National Park anchor tag, click after the the href attribute value "_blank", press [Spacebar], then type `title="Rocky Mountain National Park home page - opens in new window."`
   Your code should resemble Figure B-16.

2. Locate the "PRCA Rooftoop Rodeo" opening anchor tag, click just after "...rooftoprodeo.htm", press [Spacebar], then type `title="PRCA Rooftop Rodeo Web site. Click here for event schedules and dates."`

QUICK TIP
Because link titles are descriptions, you can use punctuation (except quotation marks) and spacing within a link title.

3. Locate the Boulder Walk and Bike Week opening anchor tag, click after the closing quotation mark after the href attribute value, press [Spacebar], then type `title="Experience the fun and excitement of Boulder Walk and Bike Week. Visit Boulder Walk and Bike Week's Web site."`

4. Locate the Scottish Highlands Festival opening anchor tag, click after the closing quotation mark after the href attribute value, press [Spacebar], then type `title="Visit the official Estes Park/Scottish Highlands Festival Web site for more information."`, then save the document

5. Click the browser program button on the taskbar, then click your browser's Reload or Refresh Button

6. Move the mouse pointer over the Rocky Mountain National Park link; observe that a ScreenTip displays the sentence, Rocky Mountain National Park home page - opens in new window., as shown in Figure B-17

7. Move the mouse pointer over the other three links; observe that the ScreenTip displays the title text for each link

8. Click the text editor program button on the taskbar to return to your code, print and close all files, then transfer your updated files to your remote server directory

FIGURE B-16: Code for link title

```
<p>Located just outside of
<a href="http://www.nps.gov/romo/" target="_blank" title="Rocky Mountain National
Park home page - opens in new window.">Rocky Mountain National Park</a> in Colorado,
Paradise Mountain Family Resort is the perfect getaway place for the whole family.
Adults can enjoy discounted golf and complimentary use of our health club and tennis
facilities while the little ones participate in our popular children's program.</p>
```

Link title code

FIGURE B-17: Linked text with title in ScreenTip

Link title screen tip

Paradise Mountain Family Resort

|Home| |Contact Us| |Activities and Events|

Located just outside of Rocky Mountain National Park in Colorado, Paradise Mountain Family Resort is the perfect getaway place for the whole family. Adults can enjoy discounted golf and complimentary use of our health club and tennis facilities while the little ones participate in our popular children's program.

Friday night dances are always a hit with the teens, and our new skate park offers one of the finest courses designed to entertain and challenge skaters, whether they are beginners or more experienced.

Hiking is a must-do activity in the beautiful Rocky Mountains. Guests can participate in one of our wilderness treks (designed for both experienced and beginning hikers), or strike out on their own for a more intimate wilderness experience.

In addition to hiking activities, during the summer months guests can enjoy horseback riding, white-water rafting, or fly fishing for trout in one of our many private streams. Rodeo fans arriving in mid-July will be sure to catch some of the events at the annual PRCA Rooftop Rodeo at the nearby Stanley Park Fairgrounds.

Wintertime guests are sure to enjoy a snowshoe trek along our well-manicured trails, a brisk downhill ski run, or the comfort of a cozy fire in our rustic ski lodge.

Other on-site or nearby seasonal events and activities include Boulder Walk and Bike Week (June), 4th of July Fireworks, The Paradise Mountain Cycling Road Rally (July), and the Scottish Highlands Festival (the week following Labor Day).

Send inquiries regarding rates and reservations to:
Paradise Mountain Family Resort
PO Box 17602
Estes Park, CO 80517
Phone: 1.970.555.7777

Page modified by Your Name, May 18, 2008

Design Matters

Creating effective link titles

Link titles help users predict where they are going and what they can expect from the linked page or site when they arrive. However, titles are not a substitute for good visual clues—descriptive icons and detailed text in and around the link that give site visitors navigation information. Visitors should be able to navigate your site even without link titles. If the link leads the visitor out of the current site, the link title can include the name of the linked site; the predicted page download time—especially if the linked page is graphic heavy; whether the link will open a page in a new window; whether any specific scripting has been applied to the linked page that might require users to change their browser settings; and if the site requires user registration. Although you can write link titles in sentence format, try to limit them to between 60 and 80 characters.

HTML

Practice

▼ CONCEPTS REVIEW

Identify the function of each numbered item in Figure B-18.

FIGURE B-18

Match each directory path with its correct browser interpretation.

8. http://
9. href
10. Link
11. id
12. ../

a. The object a user clicks to navigate to another file or location
b. An attribute that can be set in almost any HTML element and can be used as an anchor point for jump links
c. Hypertext transfer protocol designation—must be part of the link path when the file is on another server
d. Directs the browser to move up one level to the parent directory
e. Most often-used anchor tag attribute—when paired with a file URL, creates a hyperlink

Select the best answer from the list of choices.

13. **Which of the following statements about brochure sites are true? (Choose all that apply.)**
   a. Brochure sites contain information similar to what one would find in a printed brochure.
   b. Brochure sites often serve as start-up sites for businesses that later develop more comprehensive sites.
   c. Brochure sites offer the greatest degree of flexibility in design.
   d. Brochure sites utilize shopping carts and order-tracking pages.

14. Which Web structure is best for organizing sites with a potential for fast growth?

a. Cluster

b. Net

c. Linear

d. Hierarchical

15. In the URL, `http://www.paradisemountain.com/spa/wraps.htm`, **"spa" is a** _____.

a. Root directory

b. Top-level page

c. Subdirectory

d. File name

▼ SKILLS REVIEW

1. Plan a site

a. Although a part of Paradise Mountain Family Resort, the Garden of Eden Day Spa offers its services to community members and resort visitors. The spa and salon do offer a few items for sale, but the key focus is spa services. Which type of site is best?

b. List three main objectives you think the site should satisfy.

c. Identify and describe your site's target audience.

d. What are some potential content sources for the new site?

e. What type of structure do you think it best suited for the site?

2. Create internal links

a. Locate and open the **UnitB** folder in the location where you store your Data Files, then copy the hands.htm, packages.htm, salon.htm, services.htm, and thermacore.htm files.

b. Paste the files you just copied into the paradise/spa directory in the location where you save your site files.

c. Open the **salon.htm** page in your text editor and link the text in the top-level navigation bar as follows: Spa Services/services.htm; Spa Packages/packages.htm; Aphrodite's Salon/salon.htm; and Hand and Foot Care/hands.htm. (*Hint*: Place an href tag inside the opening square bracket of each navigation bar item, remembering to include closing tags after the linked items.)

d. Save your work.

3. Create links to other directories.

a. Click before "Paradise Mountain Resort" in the top-level navigation bar, then type `<a href="../index.htm">` to start a link to the resort home page.

b. Click after the Paradise Mountain Resort text and type `</a>` to close the link.

c. Click in front of Day Spa in the same navigation bar, then type the code to create a link to the index.htm file in the spa directory, then save your work.

d. Open the **paradise/index.htm** page in the parent directory. (*Hint*: A parent directory is one that contains the current directory.)

e. Click after Events</a>|, insert a space, then type the code to create a link to the spa index.htm page that is one level down in the directory structure using Day Spa as the linked text.

f. Save your work, then open your **spa/salon.htm** page in your browser and click the links to move between pages to test your links, clicking the Back button as necessary to return to your salon.htm page.

4. Create external links.

a. Open your **salon.htm** file in your text editor.

b. Locate the line of text that begins "Aphrodite's Salon uses only …," then create external links to the Web sites for the hair-care products listed in that line using the information shown in Table B-1.

c. Save your work, then open your **salon.htm** file in your browser to test your links.

d. Return to your text editor.

TABLE B-1: External links for salon.htm page

Product	Link URL
Redken	http://www.redken.com
Nioxin	http://www.nioxin.com
Tigi	http://www.tigihaircare.com
Paul Mitchell	http://www.paulmitchell.com

5. **Create e-mail links.**

   a. In your salon.htm file, locate the questions and comments paragraph at the bottom of the page, click before spainfo@paradisemtn.com.

   b. Using the e-mail address listed in the line, type the code to create an e-mail link. (*Hint*: E-mail links use the mailto protocol. Be sure to display the e-mail address on the page.)

   c. Replace Your name with your own name, then save your work.

   d. Open your **salon.htm** page in your browser to test the link, then return to your text editor program.

6. **Create jump links.**

   a. On the salon.htm page, click inside the opening level-one heading tag between the h1 and the >, press [Spacebar], then type `id="top"` to set the heading id.

   b. Locate the level-three heading in front of Hair Care, click between the h3 and the >, press [Spacebar], then type `id="haircare"`.

   c. Set the remaining IDs as indicated in Table B-2.

   d. In the second menu bar at the top of the page, click in front of the text "Hair Care" and type `<a href="#haircare">`.

   e. Click between "Care" and "|" in the menu bar and type `</a>`.

   f. Create the rest of the menu bar links as indicated in Table B-3, then save the document

   g. Click in front of `</p>` in the hair care list, type `<br /> <a href="#top">Return to menu</a>`

   h. Copy the line break and link you just typed and paste it before the `</p>` tag in the Facials, Depilatory Services, Makeup, and Limited-time specials lists. (*Hint*: The facials list is long. Be sure to set your "Return to menu" link before the closing paragraph tag of the "Super-Lifting" item.)

   i. Save the salon.htm file then test the links in your browser.

TABLE B-2: Name anchor points

ID location	ID value
Inside of <h3> next to Facials	facials
Inside of <h3> next to Depilatory	depil
Inside of <h3> next to Makeup	makeup
Inside of <h3>, next to Limited-time specials	specials

TABLE B-3: Menu bar links

Linked text	URL
Facials	#facials
Depilatory	#depil
Makeup	#makeup
Specials	#specials

7. **Open a link in a new window.**

   a. Click the text editor program button to return to your salon.htm page code.

   b. Click in front of Thermacore in the list of hair care services.

   c. Type the code to create a link to the thermacore page. (*Hint*: You copied the thermacore.htm file into your spa directory at the beginning of this Skills Review.)

   d. Click inside the link you just created and type the code `target="_blank"` to cause the link to open in a new window.

   e. Click after Thermacore and type the code to close the link.

   f. Cause the Paul Mitchell link that you created earlier to open in a new window, then save your work.

8. **Add link titles.**

   a. Verify that your **salon.htm** file is still open.

   b. Click after the closing quotation mark of the Redken URL inside the opening anchor tag for the redken link, then press [Spacebar].

   c. Type `title="Redken introduces Color Extend for color-treated hair"`, then save the page.

   d. Create the rest of the link titles on the salon page as shown in Table B-4.

   e. If necessary, replace Your Name at the bottom of any open code files with your own name and today's date.

   e. Save all source code files, test them in your browser, then print and close the files.

   f. Transfer your spa folder and it contents to your remote site.

TABLE B-4: Link titles for salon external

Product	Link Title
Nioxin	Skincare for the scalp - keep healthy-looking hair longer
Tigi	The fastest-growing professional hair care company in the industry
Paul Mitchell	Site opens in new window. Site is graphic-heavy and uses Flash animation - visitors may experience download delays

▼ INDEPENDENT CHALLENGE 1

You are developing a Web site for your new resort rental business, Star Vacations. You know that supplying listing and rental information as well as Frequently Asked Questions (FAQs) and featured resorts pages on your site will make your business more successful. You want to use the skills you have learned to link the pages you are developing. You also want to create links to some of your featured resorts. Your featured resorts page should contain at least three links to off-site resorts.

a. Determine your organizational structure and sketch a site storyboard.

b. Copy the files faq.htm, features.htm, and rentals.htm, and the listings folder from the location where you store your Data Files and paste them into your vacations directory in the location where you store your site files.

c. In your text editor, open the features.htm page from the place where you save your site files.

d. Click after `<p>|` in the navigation bar that is positioned below the comment that reads, `<!-- Add links to the navigation bar below -->`

e. Type the code `<a href="index.htm">` to link the text "Home" to the site home page, then click after Home and type the closing anchor tag to complete the link.

FIGURE B-19: Tomahawk resort link target opens in new window

f. Link the rest of the navigation bar text as follows: Featured Resorts (features.htm), Find a Rental (rentals.htm) and Frequently Asked Questions (faq.htm).

g. Click after the pipe following the Frequently Asked Questions link, insert a space, add a link to the listings/index.htm page, using the text "List a Rental," then save your work.

h. Create external links to the featured resorts using the link information indicated in Table B-5, then type the code to cause each link to open in a new window as shown in Figure B-19. (*Hint*: If a target page fails to appear, go to the Student Online Companion for this book and click the appropriate link.)

l. Use the contact text at the bottom of the page to create an e-mail link, then replace "Your Name" with your own name.

m. Save your work, then preview your vacations/features page in the browser, click each link to check it, then return to your source code.

n. Make any necessary corrections to your page code, then save your work, print the page code, and transfer your updated files to your remote vacations directory on the server.

Advanced Challenge Exercises

■ Copy the navigation bar from your features.htm page, then paste it after the closing level-one heading tag on your vacations/index.htm page.

TABLE B-5: Features page links

Resort	Link
Paradise Mountain Family Resort	Use the absolute URL to your paradise site on your remote server. If you are not transferring the paradise site to a server, create a relative path to the site.
Dolphin's Cove Resort	`http://www.resortime.com/resorts/profile.asp?resortid=18`
Tomahawk Resort	`http://www.tomahawkresort.com/`
Skytop Lodge	`http://www.skytop.com/`

■ Surf the Web to find and read the privacy statements of several Web sites.

■ Create a new page with your own privacy statement, then save it as privacy.htm in your vacations directory.

■ At the bottom of your privacy.htm page, create a paragraph that contains the text, "Close the window to return to the previous page," then save your work.

■ Return to the source code for your vacations/index.htm page, place the insertion point below the "Page modified by" paragraph at the bottom of the page and create a new paragraph containing a link to your privacy statement.

■ Supply an appropriate link title, then add the code to cause the target URL to open in a new window.

■ Replace Your Name with your own name, save and preview the file, then print and close all files.

▼ INDEPENDENT CHALLENGE 2

You have been researching water-conservation issues for your employer, Metro Water, and are ready to begin creating and linking your pages in order to present your findings to the people of Denver, Colorado and surrounding areas. Your site will contain a home page, a resources page, tips on water conservation and a landscaping and irrigation section. (*Hint*: You created the index.htm page for this site in Unit A. If you did not complete Independent Challenge 2 in Unit A, follow the instructions in Unit A to create this file or obtain a copy from your instructor.)

a. Copy the outside.htm, inside.htm, and saver.htm files, as well as the irrigation folder with all its files, from the place where you store your Data Files, and paste them into the water directory you created in Unit A.

b. Open the **inside.htm** page in your text editor and scroll through the code to observe that three level-three page headings have been given IDs and that the phrase "Return to menu" which appears in several locations on the page, has been linked to #menu.

c. Locate the level-three subheading tag for the "What about water?" subheading near the bottom of the page, insert a space, then set the heading id as "wells."

d. Locate the paragraph near the top of the page that begins, <p>[General Tips, and assign an id of "menu" to the opening paragraph tag.

e. Click just before General Tips in the same line and type the code `<a href="#tips">` to start a link to the tips heading on the page, click after General Tips and type the code, </a>, to finish the link.

f. Link the rest of the text in the menu bar as follows: "Conserving in the Kitchen," #kitchen, "Conserving in the Bathroom," #bathroom, and "What about Wells," #wells.

g. Locate the line of text at the bottom of the page that reads, "For more information about saving water, contact:
 Your Name at: yourname@metrowater.net" and create an e-mail link substituting your own name for the text "yourname", edit the "Page modified by" paragraph at the bottom of the page using your own name and today's date, then save your work.

h. Locate the site navigation bar at the top of the page and link the navigation bar text to the files as indicated: "Home," index.htm; "Conserving Inside," inside.htm; "Conserving Outside,"outside.htm; "Resources," resources.htm, "Super Saver," saver.htm; "Landscaping and Irrigation," irrigation/index.htm," then save the page and test it in your browser. (*Hint*: Click the browser Back button to return to the inside.htm page. If you did not complete the ACE steps in the Unit A Independent Challenge 2, open htm_b-1.txt then save it as resources.htm in your water site folder.)

i. Copy the site navigation bar from inside.htm, open water/irrigation/index.htm in your text editor and paste the navigation bar above the level-two page heading. Then modify the link paths by using dot-slash notation (../) to direct the browser to the parent directory before searching for the pages.

j. Save your work, then preview the page in your browser to test the links. (*Hint*: Click the Back button when you access pages without a link bar.)

k. Preview your page in your browser and click to test each link, then print the page and close the browser.

l. Close all files, then transfer your new and updated pages to your remote directory.

Advanced Challenge Exercises

- Use your favorite search engine to find sites about agricultural irrigation and water conservation.
- Using the information you found, write some content describing best agricultural irrigation practices.
- Create a Web page with appropriate page headings and title information, to display your information and add links to the cited sources, then create appropriate link titles.
- Add a "Page modified by" paragraph using your own name and today's date, then save the page as **agri_irrigation.htm** in your irrigation subdirectory, then print your page source code.
- Open your **irrigation/index.htm** page, then create a link from the text "agricultural irrigation" to your new page, then save the irrigation/index.htm page
- Edit the "Page modified by" paragraph to the bottom of the page using your own name and today's date, then save your work and transfer your updated pages to your remote directory.

▼ INDEPENDENT CHALLENGE 3

You have been using link titles because you know that they are part of the accessibility initiative. You are interested in learning more about the use of link titles and their part in making Web sites more accessible. You also want to find out what else you can do to make your site more user-friendly.

a. Go to the W3C Web Accessibility page and review the information regarding HTML links in section 6.1. Go to the Student Online Companion for this text, then locate the Unit B links. Write one or two paragraphs answering the following questions:

  1. How can the use of link titles make your site more user-friendly?
  2. What other steps can you take to enhance the effectiveness of your site's navigation interface to make it more accessible?
  3. Add your name and today's date to the top of your paper, then print it.

▼ INDEPENDENT CHALLENGE 4

Now that you've studied site structure and linking principles, you are ready to add and link additional pages to your Web site.

a. Determine what additional pages your proposed site requires and whether it would benefit from the use of sub-directories, then make a sketch of your proposed site structure, labeling each of your intended pages.

b. In addition to your home page, create at least four placeholder pages with appropriate page titles, headings and placeholder text. (You may add actual content if you wish.)

  - Make sure to name your home page file, and the main file in each directory, index.htm or use the default file name given to you by your instructor or server administrator.
  - Make sure each page contains page headings and titles. (*Hint*: Page titles belong in the head section of your document.)
  - Name one file about_me.htm and add some information about yourself. (*Hint*: If you are creating a business, name the file about_us.htm and add information about the business.)
  - Create at least one page in a subdirectory of your site.
  - Create at least one page with a list of links to sites related to your site content. (*Hint*: If you are creating a personal site, off-site links could be a list of your favorite Web sites, vacation places, work-related sites, or sites belonging to your family and friends.)

c. Add appropriate content to your home page. (*Hint*: Content can be changed as necessary as your site develops.)

d. Add a navigation bar to the top of each page to link all the pages.

e. On your site home page or your about_me.htm page, create at least one e-mail link.

f. On at least one page, create a jump-link menu to take the site visitor to specific points on that page.

g. Make sure to create a link that will take the site visitor back to the jump-link menu.

h. Add appropriate link titles to all your external links.

i. Cause at least one external link to open in a new window.

j. Save all your pages and transfer them to your remote server.

▼ VISUAL WORKSHOP

You are excited as you continue to build your Bits and PCs Web site and you decide to organize the entire site into logical folders and files. Create a directory structure and some placeholder pages with page heads and titles based on the site design shown in Figure B-20, then create navigation bars for each file based upon its relative placement in the file structure.

FIGURE B-20

UNIT
C
HTML

Formatting Page Elements with HTML

OBJECTIVES

Understand HTML formatting methods
Align text
Format characters
Define an address block
Control font selection
Customize fonts
Create ordered lists
Create unordered lists

Just as HTML allows you to include different kinds of text elements on your Web pages, it also enables you to determine the way text appears in the browser window. You can use HTML formatting and style tags to alter text appearance. You can apply attributes to block-level tags—tags that define an entire section of content—to modify the alignment of page content in the browser window. You can also use tag attributes to add color to your page or to change text appearance by altering fonts. Formatting text in your Web pages can improve the organization of information and make it easier for users to find what interests them. You are excited to start enhancing the pages you are developing for the Paradise Mountain Family Resort Web site using text formatting.

Understanding HTML Formatting Methods

HTML provides some effective methods of organizing page content by allowing you to format text at the tag level, making it easier for users to identify valuable content and navigate your site. Because HTML was not designed to format text in complex ways, you cannot use traditional HTML formatting alone to format a Web page in the same manner you would if you created the page in a word processor. However, HTML does include several tags that allow you to add basic formatting to your Web pages, and there are literally millions of pages on the World Wide Web to which formatting of this type has been applied. Figure C-1 shows a sample page that uses several of these formats. The HTML code that produced it is shown in Figure C-2. You begin to review the formatting methods that you want to use for the Paradise Mountain Web site.

DETAILS

HTML pages can be formatted using the following methods:

- **Alignment**

  By default, Web page text is aligned along the left edge of the browser window. HTML's alignment options allow you to quickly and easily customize your Web page's appearance. **Alignment attribute options**—left, right, center, and, justify—can be applied to paragraphs, headings, and text blocks.

- **Character Formatting**

  HTML character formatting can affect text **weight** (such as boldfaced), **posture** (such as italicized), and **decoration** (such as underlined). Character formatting is useful for emphasizing words or short sections of text.

- **Font Formatting**

  HTML includes a tag set for changing the font formatting in small sections of text as well as a tag for specifying font formatting at the page level. When used appropriately, both of these tags let you customize your Web page appearance by changing the typeface, color, and size of text. Font formatting is useful for creating pages that appeal to specific target audiences and for adding personality to your pages.

- **Block-Level Formatting**

  Block-level tags—tags in which other elements, such as paragraphs and headings can be nested—allow you to control entire sections of content. Some block-level tags require the use of attributes and values. Others are predefined to produce changes and are often used without additional attributes. Block-level tags include **division** (`<div>...</div>`), which uses attributes to effect changes in text, **blockquote** (`<blockquote>...</blockquote>`), which alters the amount of white space on either side of the effected text, and **address** (`<address>...</address>`), which both alters the physical appearance and marks content to make it recognizable to text readers as well as to indexing and cataloging software.

- **Lists**

  The most commonly used lists are **ordered lists**, in which list items appear with sequential numbers or letters, and **unordered lists**, which have bullets instead of numbers or letters. To format an ordered list, you designate a series of text lines as list items and then enclose them in the appropriate **parent element**—a tag set in which another tag set is nested. You use the same method to create an unordered list. The parent list element for an ordered list is `<ol>...</ol>`, and the parent list element for an unordered list is `<ul>...</ul>`. Both ordered and unordered lists use the **child element** (an element within a parent tag) list item, `<li>...</li>`, to define each item in the list.

FIGURE C-1: Web page with applied formatting

Centered text

Colored text

Unordered list

Ordered list

FIGURE C-2: Code for formatted text

Centers navigation bar

Sets font color

Creates unordered list

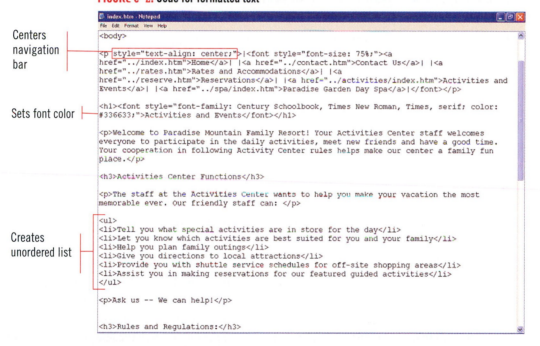

Guidelines for Web page formatting

Using element formatting in moderation can make your Web pages easier to use. However, the overuse of formatting can make pages more difficult to understand and navigate. Web users tend to scan text rather than read it, so presentation is critical in the Web environment. Properly formatted items such as page headings and navigation elements help users to quickly determine the most important content on a page; however, applying the same formatting technique to all page elements makes none of them stand out. Adhering to the "rules of three" can help make your pages more inviting to users: Increase the amount of white space on your page by limiting text blocks (paragraphs) to three average sentences. When possible, constrain your page length to scroll no more than three screens. Select no more than two or three font faces, usually one for the body type, one for headings, and a third, if necessary, for captions and/or non-text navigation elements. Use no more than three main colors consistently throughout your site.

HTML

Aligning Text

One of the most effective methods of setting off page elements is text alignment. HTML provides some basic control over where text appears on the page. Attribute values such as "text-align: center;" can be applied to block elements such as the paragraph (`<p>...</p>`) and heading (`<h1>...</h1>` through `<h6>...</h6>`) tag sets. The default text-align style value is left, meaning that if no style alignment value is applied, each line of text is flush with the left edge of the browser window. Other text-align style settings are right, which sets each line of text even with the right edge of the window, center, which centers each line between the two edges of the window, and justify, which stretches each line of text so it is flush with both the left and right edges of the browser window. Using justified text can cause text spacing problems. This is especially problematic when text wraps around an image or when a window is resized. Therefore, it is best to leave justified text in the hands of textbook publishers and keep it off your Web pages. Table C-1 summarizes the text-align attribute. You think your page navigation bars would look better centered on the page. You also want to experiment with other alignment options.

STEPS

1. **Open the rates.htm file in your text editor from the location where you store your data files, then save it as rates.htm in your paradise site folder**

2. **Locate the opening paragraph tag of your site navigation bar at the top of the page, then click between p and >**

3. **Press [Spacebar], then type** `style="text-align: center;"`
   You may have seen earlier versions of HTML documents in which alignment was specified using the `align="value"` method as follows: `<p align="center">`. Although this is easier to type, formatting text in this manner has been deprecated by the W3C. Therefore, it is best to learn to format to newer standards so that you are prepared to apply newer formatting techniques at a later date.

4. **Locate the paragraph that begins with "Call the resort office," click just before > in the opening paragraph tag, press [Spacebar], then type** `style="text-align: justify;"`

5. **Locate the next paragraph, which begins "For questions or comments," click in the opening paragraph tag just before >, press [Spacebar], then type** `style="text-align: center;"`

6. **Locate the "Page modified by" paragraph, click in the opening paragraph tag just before >, press [Spacebar], then type** `style="text-align: right;"`
   Your code should appear similar to that shown in Figure C-3.

7. **Save your work, start your browser program, then view the rates.htm file in your browser**
   As shown in Figure C-4, the site navigation bar and contact paragraph are aligned in the center of the page. However, the "Page modified by" paragraph is right aligned and the "Call the resort office" paragraph displays some odd spacing due to justified alignment. You are not pleased with the results produced by the right and justify align styles.

8. **Click the text editor program button on the taskbar, locate the "Call the resort office" paragraph, click and drag to select the style attribute and value in the opening paragraph tag, press [Delete], then press [Backspace], if necessary, to remove the extra space**
   The justified formatting has been removed from the paragraph.

9. **In the opening paragraph tag of the "Page modified by" paragraph, drag to select "right" after "text-align:", press [Delete], type center, then save the page and reload it in your browser**
   The right alignment formatting has been removed from the paragraph and center alignment has been applied.

FIGURE C-3: Style text-align attribute values

```
<body>

<p style="text-align: center;">|<a href="index.htm">Home</a>|
|<a href="contact.htm">Contact Us</a>| |<a href="rates.htm">Rates and
Accommodations</a>|  |<a href="activities/index.htm">Activities and
Events</a>| |<a href="spa/index.htm">Paradise Garden Day Spa</a>|</p>

<h1>Rates and Accommodations</h1>

<p>Watch this space! Information on Paradise Mountain Family Resort
rates and accommodations will be here soon. </p>

<p style="text-align: justify;">Call the resort office at:
1.970.555.7890, or the reservations desk at: 1.970.555.7780 to get
details regarding our deluxe accommodations, find out about our summer
specials, request a brochure or to make reservations.</p>

<p style="text-align: center;">For questions or comments about this
site, contact: <br /> <a
href="mailto:webmaster@paradisemtn.com">webmaster@paradisemtn.com</a>
</p>

<p style="text-align right;">Page Modified by: Your Name, May 25,
2008</p>

</body>

</html>
```

Center alignment

Justified alignment

Right alignment

FIGURE C-4: Web page with applied text-align style attribute values

Center-aligned text

Justified text with irregular spacing

Right-aligned text

TABLE C-1: HTML text-align attribute values

value	examples	results
text-align: left	`<p style="text-align: left;"> This text has been aligned to the left. </p>`	This text has been aligned to the left.
text-align: right	`<p style="text-align: right;"> This text has been aligned to the right. </p>`	This text has been aligned to the right.
text-align: center	`<p style="text-align: center;"> This text is centered. </p>`	This text is centered.
text-align: justify	`<p style="text-align: justify;"> This text is justified. Justified text can cause display problems like this. </p>`	This text is justified. Justified text can cause display problems like this.

HTML

Formatting Characters

Sometimes words or phrases on your Web pages need to stand out. In documents created in a word processor, this is most often accomplished using three standard formats: **bold**, *italic*, and underline. While you can easily add any of these formats to your Web page text, their use in HTML comes with some restrictions. Additionally, both bold and italic formatting can each be created by using two different tag sets. The most obvious choices—`<b>...</b>` for bold and `<i>...</i>` for italic—are available only to devices that can visually display text. Because of this restriction, these formats are known as **physical formats**. However, some Web users require different interfaces—for example, audio devices that read Web content to visually impaired people. To render character formatting in such a manner that it can be heard as well as seen, one must use the **logical formatting** tags `<strong>...</strong>`, for boldfaced text, and `<em>...</em>` for emphasized text. Table C-2 summarizes the tags available for character formatting. You have identified a small section on two pages where extra formatting would provide a needed contrast. You decide to apply bold and italic formatting using logical character formatting tags to ensure that Paradise Mountain Family Resort page content is accessible to the widest possible audience.

STEPS

1. **In the rates.htm file, locate the text Watch this space! in the first paragraph under the page heading**

2. **Click before the word Watch, then type `<strong><em>`**
   The `<strong>` tag marks the beginning of the section you want to appear as boldfaced; `<em>` marks the beginning of the section of text you want to italicize.

3. **Click after space! then type `</em></strong>`**
   The `</em>` tag ends the emphasized formatting; `</strong>` ends the boldfaced formatting. Following the rules of tag order that you learned in Unit A, the first tag opened is the last tag closed in these nested tags.

4. **Save the rates.htm file**
   Compare your code to that shown in Figure C-5.

5. **Click the browser program button on the taskbar**

6. **Click the Reload or Refresh button on the browser toolbar to update your rates.htm page**
   The phrase "Watch this space!" stands out from the rest of the text as shown in Figure C-6, because it is boldfaced and italicized.

Design Matters

Using text emphasis

As you have learned, linked text is underlined by default. Therefore, to avoid confusing users, it is best not to underline unlinked text on a Web page. If you need to emphasize text, use bold, italic, a font color, or a combination of these three methods instead.

FIGURE C-5: Logical formatting tags

```
<p><strong><em>Watch this space!</em></strong> Information on Paradise
Mountain Family Resort rates and accommodations will be here soon. </p>
```

Opening and closing
emphasized tags

FIGURE C-6: Logical formatting elements displayed in browser

|Home| |Contact Us| |Rates and Accommodations| |Activities and Events| |Paradise Garden Day Spa|

Rates and Accommodations

Watch this space! Information on Paradise Mountain Family Resort rates and accommodations will be here soon.

Call the resort office at: 1.970.555.7890, or the reservations desk at: 1.970.555.7780 to get details regarding our deluxe accomodations, find out about our summer specials, request a brochure or to make reservations.

For questions or comments about this site, contact:
webmaster@paradisemtn.com

<strong> ... </strong> and <em> ... </em>
formatting displayed in browser

TABLE C-2: HTML text formatting tags

name	tag(s)	function	notes
Underlined text	<u>...</u>	Adds underline format to text	Avoid using; may be confused with linked text
Boldface text	<b>...</b>	Adds bold format to text	Applies to visual format only; use <strong>...</strong> instead to allow widest accessibility
Italicized text	<i>...</i>	Adds italic format to text	Applies to visual format only; use <em>...</em> instead to allow widest accessibility
Strong text	<strong>...</strong>	Marks text as strong; interpreted by browsers as bold	Interpretable by different Web interfaces; use instead of <b>...</b>
Emphasized text	<em>...</em>	Marks text as emphasized; interpreted by browsers as italic	Interpretable by different Web interfaces; use instead of <i>...</i>

Defining an Address Block

Just as character formatting allows you to change the appearance of text and to add logical formatting at the character level by enclosing small sections of text in character formatting tags, HTML also offers a method of applying logical formatting at the block level. One such tag set, **blockquote** (`<blockquote>...</blockquote>`), allows you to control white space on the page by indenting the affected text approximately 40 pixels on each side. Although there are other methods of controlling white space on the page, the block quote is still useful when a "quick-fix" is necessary. Another block-level tag set that appeared to be "on the way out" is making a comeback: The **address tag** (`<address>...</address>`) was originally designed to be recognized as address content by indexing and cataloging software, but it is also recognized by most accessibility devices, such as text readers and is, therefore, an accessibility tool recommended by the Web Accessibility Initiative (WAI). In most browsers, address text is rendered using an italic typeface. You decide to format your contact and "modified by" content using the address tag set.

STEPS

1. **Click the** text editor program button **on the taskbar to display the rates.htm page code**

2. **Locate the "For questions or comments" paragraph near the bottom of the page**

3. **Click inside the opening paragraph tag directly after the p, press** [Backspace]**, then type** address

   You changed the opening paragraph tag into an opening address tag, but left the formatting that you applied earlier.

4. **Click directly after the p in the closing paragraph tag, press** [Backspace]**, type** address, **then save your work**

   Your page code appears similar to that shown in Figure C-7.

5. **Click the** browser program button **on the taskbar, then reload your page in the browser window**

   The "For questions or comments" address block appears in italic type as shown in Figure C-8.

6. **Click the** text editor button **on the taskbar to display the rates.htm page code**

   You want the navigation bar on your home page to match the one on your rates page, so you decide to copy it.

7. **Locate the navigation bar code near the top of the body selection, drag to select from the opening paragraph tag through the closing paragraph tag, then copy the selected code to your clipboard**

8. **Open the** paradise/index.htm **file, drag to select the navigation bar code, press** [Delete]**, then paste the copied code and save your work**

> **TROUBLE**
>
> If you deleted the space between the tag name, "address," and the tag style attribute, click after "address" and press the space-bar once.

Design Matters

Using address blocks for inline display

Many designers like to use address blocks in the middle of a line to emphasize inline e-mail links. However, some browsers display address blocks with extra white space above and/or below them. If you use inline address blocks, be sure to test your page in several browsers.

FIGURE C-7: Address block code

Opening tag

```
the reservations desk at: 1.970.555.7780 to get details regarding our deluxe
accomodations, find out about our summer specials, request a brochure or to
make reservations.</p>

<address style="text-align: center;">For questions or comments about this
site, contact: <br />
<a href="mailto:webmaster@paradisemtn.com">webmaster@paradisemtn.com</a>
</address>

<p style="text-align: center;">Page Modified by: Your Name, May 25, 2008</p>
```

Closing tag

Address block

FIGURE C-8: Address block text displayed in browser window

|Home| |Contact Us| |Rates and Accommodations| |Activities and Events| |Paradise Garden Day Spa|

Rates and Accommodations

Watch this space! Information on Paradise Mountain Family Resort rates and accommodations will be here soon.

Call the resort office at: 1.970.555.7890, or the reservations desk at: 1.970.555.7780 to get details regarding our deluxe accomodations, find out about our summer specials, request a brochure or to make reservations.

Address block

For questions or comments about this site, contact:
webmaster@paradisemtn.com

Controlling Font Selection

You have used character- and block-formatting features to change the weight, posture, and alignment of text. You can also alter text appearance by changing its typeface. You can do this by using the `<font>...</font>` tag in the body of the document. You can also apply changes to text at the page level by adding formatting instructions in the head section of your document using the `<basefont />` tag. The style value `font-family` changes the typeface in which text appears. In recent years, basefont and font tags have been deprecated by the W3C in favor of newer formatting methods; however, there are literally millions of pages on the Web that still use font tags to format pages, so it is a good idea to learn how to use these tags. You are accustomed to working with different fonts in a word processor, and now you want to see how the Paradise Mountain Resort pages look in another font.

STEPS

1. **Open paradise/index.htm in your browser program and view the formatting**

   As shown in Figure C-9, the page heading is heavier than the rest of the text, but the heading and body text all use the same typeface.

2. **Return to the paradise/index.htm page in your text editor**

QUICK TIP

The semicolon (;) at the end of the style value signifies the end of that style element. While some browsers apply the style correctly when the semicolon is missing, not all do, so it is important to include the semicolon at the end of the value string and before the closing quotation mark.

3. **Click between `<h1>` and the page heading text, type `<font style="font-family: Century Schoolbook, Times New Roman, Times, serif;">`**

   You used an **inline style**—a style applied as an attribute—to change the page heading text to the serif typeface, Century Schoolbook, which is available on most systems. To make sure your page appears as close to your design as possible, you decide to list similar-looking font families used in three operating systems in case your chosen font is not available. You did this by creating a **font stack**—a list of acceptable fonts—in which you specified Times New Roman—the default serif font on Windows systems, Times (Macintosh), and serif (UNIX).

4. **Click after Resort and before `</h1>`, then type `</font>`**

   The opening and closing font tags surround the page heading text. You want to add basefont formatting to format the rest of the text on the page in a sans serif font. For information on modifying fonts without using style attributes, see the appendix.

5. **Click before the closing head tag in the head section, type `<basefont style="font-family: Verdana, Arial, sans serif;" />`, then press [Enter] twice**

   The basefont tag is now inserted in the head section of your code as shown in Figure C-10.

TROUBLE

Based on your monitor size and display settings, your output may appear differently.

6. **Save your file, click the browser program button on the taskbar, then reload your paradise/index.htm page in the browser window**

   The page heading is now set in the Century Schoolbook (or the default serif font on your computer), and the rest of the document is set in Verdana or a sans serif font as shown in Figure C-11. You like the new look, but notice that the navigation bar now wraps to a second line.

Design Matters

Understanding fonts and typefaces

A **font** is a complete set of characters, including letters, numbers, and special characters, in a particular size and style of type. A **typeface** contains a series of fonts such as Times Bold, Times Italic, and Times New Roman, which are different fonts in the same family. In Web design, the terms "font," "typeface," "font family," and "font face" are used interchangeably. Typefaces are divided into families. The majority of fonts fall into one of two categories: serif or sans serif. **Serif** fonts take their name from the decorative "tails," called serifs, at the ends of the lines that make up each letter. The most common serif fonts are Times New Roman, the default serif font on most Windows computers, and Times, the default serif font on most Macintosh computers. **Sans serif** literally means "without serifs"; fonts in this group do not have decorative "tails." In traditional print media, large blocks of normal-sized text usually appear in a serif font so they are easier to read. Page headings traditionally appear in sans serif. On a computer screen, however, light emissions from the monitor make serif fonts more difficult to read. Therefore, the roles of serif and sans serif fonts are often reversed on the Web.

FIGURE C-9: Paradise Mountain home page before formatting

Heading and body are all the same typeface

Paradise Mountain Family Resort

|Home| |Contact Us| |Rates and Accommodations| |Activities and Events| |Paradise Garden Day Spa|

Located just outside of Rocky Mountain National Park in Colorado, Paradise Mountain Family Resort is the perfect getaway place for the whole family. Adults can enjoy discounted golf and complimentary use of our health club and tennis facilities while the little ones participate in our popular children's program.

Friday night dances are always a hit with the teens, and our new skate park offers one of the finest courses designed to entertain and challenge skaters, whether they are beginners or more experienced.

FIGURE C-10: Home page code with applied formatting

Basefont formatting in head section

Opening font tag with style formatting

Closing font tag

```
<title>Paradise Mountain Family Resort</title>

<meta name="Keywords" content="Resort vacations, Estes Park, Estes Park lodging,
family vacation, spa, day spa" />

<basefont style="font-family: Verdana, Arial, san serif;" />

</head>

<body>

<h1><font style="font-family: Century Schoolbook, Times New Roman, Times,
serif;">Paradise Mountain Family Resort</font></h1>

<p style="text-align: center;">|<a href="index.htm">Home</a>| |<a
href="contact.htm">Contact Us</a>| |<a href="rates.htm">Rates and Accommodations</a>|
|<a href="activities/index.htm">Activities and Events</a>| |<a
href="spa/index.htm">Paradise Garden Day Spa</a>|</p>
```

FIGURE C-11: Paradise Mountain home page with text formatting

Serif font in level-one heading

Paradise Mountain Family Resort

|Home| |Contact Us| |Rates and Accommodations| |Activities and Events| |Paradise Garden Day Spa|

Sans serif font applied with <basefont /> tag

Located just outside of Rocky Mountain National Park in Colorado, Paradise Mountain Family Resort is the perfect getaway place for the whole family. Adults can enjoy discounted golf and complimentary use of our health club and tennis facilities while the little ones participate in our popular children's program.

Friday night dances are always a hit with the teens, and our new skate park offers one of the finest courses designed to entertain and challenge skaters, whether they are beginners or more experienced.

Hiking is a must-do activity in the beautiful Rocky Mountains. Guests can participate in one of our wilderness treks (designed for both experienced and beginning hikers), or strike out on their own for a more intimate wilderness experience.

In addition to hiking activities, during the summer months guests can enjoy horseback riding, white-water rafting, or fly fishing for trout in one of our many private streams. Rodeo fans arriving in mid-July will be sure to catch some of the events at the annual PRCA Rooftop Rodeo at the nearby Stanley Park Fairgrounds.

Clues to Use

Selecting and specifying page fonts

Rules governing typeface selection apply to both print and screen media: If you are going to use more than one font face, use one family (serif or sans serif) for headings and select a font from the other family for body text. Do not mix several different font faces from the same family. A sans serif font such as Verdana, which was designed for Web display, Arial, or Helvetica are all excellent choices for Web page text. Although you can specify any font family for a document or marked section of text, only the fonts that are installed on the user's system are available for display in the user's browser. If the font you specified is not installed, the user's computer displays the system's default font. Consequently, the best practice is to use fonts that are commonly available. When in doubt, you can "stack" multiple font families. When multiple font families are listed, the browser checks each family until it finds one that is available or, finding none, displays the system font.

Customizing Fonts

In addition to specifying a font family, the `<font>...</font>` and `<basefont />` tags also allow you to change the color and size of text on a page. By applying the color style and specifying a color code value such as the following, `<font style="color: #339999;">affected text</font>`, you can change text to a color other than black. (The color shown in the example is teal, but you can use any color code.) You also can customize font appearance by changing font size with the font style size value as follows `<font style="font-size: 80%;">`. Size can be specified in percentages or in point sizes. An older method of customizing fonts is to use the attributes **face**, **color**, and **size** as follows: `<font face="Century Schoolbook" size="5" color="#339999">Affected text</font>`. While this method of specifying fonts has been deprecated by the W3C, it is still widely in use today. The appendix summarizes the attributes and values for working with fonts in traditional HTML. You think adding color to the text on the Paradise Mountain Family Resort page will make the page more interesting to your site visitors. You also want to resize the navigation bar so that it does not wrap in the browser window.

STEPS

QUICK TIP
You can use descriptive words such as "green" or "navy" to specify your color choices; however, not all browsers interpret color words in the same manner.

1. **Return to the paradise\index.htm page in your text editor, locate the opening font tag in the level-one page heading, click between the semicolon (;) and the closing quotation mark, press [Spacebar], type** `color: #336633;` **(including the semicolon), then save the page**
   The number #336633 is a hexadecimal color code for a medium-green color. When setting text colors, be sure to select colors that are different from your link colors.

2. **Locate the basefont tag in the head section, click between ";" and the closing quotation mark, press [Spacebar], then type** `color: #333366;` **(including the semicolon)**
   The hexadecimal code you just typed sets the document text to a steel blue color, which you think is a good match for the company's image. By adding the color value to the style attribute, you are creating a series of attributes called an **attribute string**. Attribute strings allow you to assign more than one attribute to the same tag. This is useful when you want to display all of the marked content in the same manner. Using attribute strings rather than several individual tags of the same type enable you to keep your code neater and reduce the possibility of code errors.

3. **Locate the navigation bar at the top of the page, click after the opening paragraph tag and just before the first pipe, then type** `<font style="font-size: 75%;">`
   The font-size style you set causes the affected text to appear at 75 percent of (25 percent smaller than) the surrounding text. When no font size is specified, the page appears in the default font size. Font sizes can also be specified in traditional HTML as `<font size="4">affected text</font>`.

4. **In the site navigation bar, click between the final pipe and the** `</p>`**, type** `</font>`**, then save the page**
   Your page code should resemble the code shown in Figure C-12.

5. **Click the browser program button on the taskbar, then reload your page**
   The site navigation bar appears smaller than the rest of the page text, and the text colors change, as shown in Figure C-13.

FIGURE C-12: HTML code for typeface formatting

Basefont tag with font style and color values

```
<basefont style="font-family: Verdana, Arial, san serif; color: #333366;" />

</head>

<body>

<h1><font style="font-family: Century Schoolbook, Times New Roman, Times, serif;
color: #336633;">Paradise Mountain Family Resort</font></h1>

<p style="text-align: center;"><font style="font-size: 75%;">|<a
href="index.htm">Home</a>|  |<a href="contact.htm">Contact Us</a>|  |<a
href="rates.htm">Rates and Accommodations</a>|   |<a
href="activities/index.htm">Activities and Events</a>|  |<a
href="spa/index.htm">Paradise Garden Day Spa</a>|</font></p>
```

Font tag nested inside level-one heading tag

Font size attribute

FIGURE C-13: Page with font family, color, and size formatting

Navigation bar is 75% of surrounding text size

Body text is blue

Heading is green

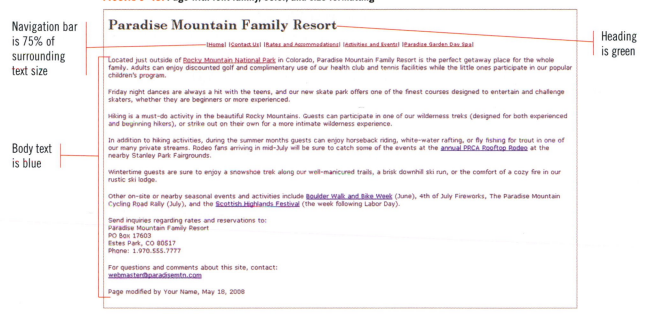

Design Matters

Working with hexadecimal colors

Hexadecimal is a base 16 numbering system that uses numerical and character values from 0 (zero) through 9 and "A" through "F." A color code is composed of three pairs of numbers. The code "#FF6666," produces a rose pink color. Although you can use descriptive words for colors, such as "green" or "navy," to specify your color choices, using the hexadecimal equivalent is a good habit to develop. Hexadecimal code tells the browser mathematically how to create the color you want and is interpretable by a wider range of browsers than are color names. There are literally millions of hexadecimal colors. However, there are only 216 colors that are considered "browser-safe." A table of browser-safe hexadecimal color codes is included in the appendix and in the Online Companion for this text.

Creating Ordered Lists

One of the keys to an effective online layout is to divide text into small pieces that users can easily comprehend. HTML list formats provide an easy avenue for keeping your pages Web friendly. An ordered list is an ideal format for steps, rankings, and other sets of information for which order is important. The Paradise Mountain Family Resort Activities Center staff prints a list of rules and regulations for guests using the Activities Center facilities and equipment. They have asked you to publish this list in the activities directory of the Paradise Mountain Family Resort Web site.

STEPS

QUICK TIP

If you are using a Microsoft browser, you can open your page source code from the browser menu bar. Simply click View on the menu bar and then click Source.

1. In your text editor, open the file htm_C-2.txt from the location where you store your Data Files, click File on the menu bar, then click Save As

2. Navigate to the location where you store your paradise site files, double-click activities, click the Save as type list arrow, click All Files, type the filename index.htm, click Save, then click Yes to replace the existing index file

3. Click the browser program button on the taskbar, then open the activities/index.htm file from the location where you store your site files

    The file includes a list of Activity Center rules. You think this content would look better formatted as a numbered list.

QUICK TIP

Most HTML tags are abbreviations; "ol" is short for "ordered list."

4. Click the text editor program button on the taskbar, drag to select <p> below the level-three heading, press [Delete], type <ol>, then press [Enter]

    The <ol> tag marks the start of an ordered list. By pressing [Enter] after the ordered list tag, you move the list text down one row and make it easier to identify.

5. Locate the end of the the rules list after "...the following day", drag to select the </p>, press [Delete], type </ol>, then press [Enter] twice

    You have just specified the beginning and end of the ordered list. You still need to format the list items.

6. Click before "Guests" in the line below the opening ordered list tag, then type <li>

    The <li> tag marks the text that follows it and identifies it to the browser as a list item.

7. Select the "<br />" tag at the end of the line, press [Delete], then type </li>

    The </li> marks the end of a list item. Some designers choose not to include the closing list tag. However, according to newer coding standards, list item tags, like all other tags, must be closed. On the other hand, <br /> tags aren't necessary in lists because each list item automatically starts on a new line.

TROUBLE

Be sure that you do not replace the line break in the contact paragraph with a closing list item tag.

8. Type <li> tags before the remaining list items, as shown in Figure C-14

9. Replace the remaining line break tags with closing list item tags, click just before the </ol>, type </li> to mark the end of the last list item as shown in Figure C-14, save the file, then view it in your browser

    Your completed file should resemble Figure C-15.

FIGURE C-14: Marked ordered list

```
<ol>

<li>Guests under the age of 16, must be accompanied by an adult</li>

<li>Please sign in before using any computer equipment</li>

<li>Guests are asked to refrain from using pool cues in any manner not
intended by the manufacturer</li>

<li>Please, no throwing of billiard balls</li>

<li>Darts must be checked out through the Activities Center desk</li>

<li>Children using darts and dartboards must be accompanied by an adult</li>

<li>Anyone using the Activities Center equipment in a manner for which is was
not intended will be asked to leave the Activities Center</li>

<li>Guests displaying unsportsmanlike behavior will be asked to leave the
Activities Center</li>

<li>Internet access is reserved for adult guests; however, a selection of
video games are available for youngsters</li>

<li>Video games may be checked out for up to three days at a time</li>

<li>Guests checking out videos and DVDs are reminded that all movies are due
for return by noon the following day.</li>

</ol>
```

FIGURE C-15: Completed page with ordered list

|Home| |Contact Us| |Rates and Accommodations| |Activities and Events| |Paradise Garden Day Spa|

Activities Center

Welcome to Paradise Mountain Family Resort! Your Activities Center staff welcomes everyone to participate in the daily activities, meet new friends and have a good time. Your cooperation in following Activity Center rules helps make our center a family fun place.

Rules and Regulations:

1. Guests under the age of 16, must be accompanied by an adult
2. Please sign in before using any computer equipment
3. Guests are asked to refrain from using pool cues in any manner not intended by the manufacturer
4. Please, no throwing of billiard balls
5. Darts must be checked out through the Activities Center desk
6. Children using darts and dartboards must be accompanied by an adult
7. Anyone using the Activities Center equipment in a manner for which is was not intended will be asked to leave the Activities Center
8. Guests displaying unsportsmanlike behavior will be asked to leave the Activities Center
9. Internet access is reserved for adult guests; however, a selection of video games are available for youngsters
10. Video games may be checked out for up to three days at a time
11. Guests checking out videos and DVDs are reminded that all movies are due for return by noon the following day.

For questions or comments about this site, contact:
webmaster@paradisemtn.com

Page Modified by: Your Name, May 25, 2008

Clues to Use

Nesting lists

Sometimes information is more easily organized when you break your lists down even further. For example, it might be necessary to include a list of subitems within a parent list. This process is known as **nesting** a list. You can nest lists of any type. You can nest an ordered list inside an unordered list, an unordered list inside of an ordered list, or you can nest lists of the same type. When nesting lists, make sure that you nest the sublist completely. In other words, make sure that you include an opening as well as a closing list tag and the opening and closing tags for all list items. Also remember to close the parent list. Figure C-16 shows the code used to produce a nested list as well as the browser output the code produces.

FIGURE C-16: Nested list code and browser output

```
<p>You can nest lists of any sort. Following are examples of nested lists:
</p>

<ol>
<li>This is the first list item in an ordered list</li>
<li>This is the second list item. What are some reasons that you might want
to nest a list?
   <ol type="a">
   <li>To organize your content (we set the list type attribute for this
nested list to "a".)</li>
   <li>To demonstrate your superb cod
   <li>Because it's so cool </li>
   </ol>
<li>This is list item three in the p
unordered list.</li>
   <ul>
   <li>This is unordered list item 1<
   <li>This is unordered list item 2.
      <ul>
      <li>This is unordered list ite
      <li>This is unordered list ite
      <li>This is unordered list ite
      </ul>
   <li>This is unordered list item 3
   </ul>
<li>This is the last list item in th
</ol>

<p>Indentions in your code help you
ends.</p>
```

You can nest lists of any sort. Following are examples of nested lists:

1. This is the first list item in an ordered list
2. This is the second list item. What are some reasons that you might want to nest a list?
   a. To organize your content (we set the list type attribute for this nested list to "a".)
   b. To demonstrate your superb coding abilities
   c. Because it's so cool
3. This is list item three in the parent list. It precedes a nested unordered list.
   o This is unordered list item 1
   o This is unordered list item 2. We'll add another nested list here:
      ▪ This is unordered list item 1 in the nested list.
      ▪ This is unordered list item 2 in the nested list.
      ▪ This is unordered list item 3 in the nested list.
   o This is unordered list item 3 in the first unordered list
4. This is the last list item in the master list

Indentions in your code help you to keep track of when and where each list ends.

UNIT
C
HTML

Creating Unordered Lists

Like an ordered list, an unordered list is a simple way to divide Web page text into smaller, easier-to-read portions. While the items in an ordered list are numbered in order, unordered list items appear with bullets before each item. This format works well for organizing a list of links or listing sets of ideas when each item is equally important and order doesn't matter. Table C-3 explains the HTML tags used to create an unordered list. The Activities Center director has asked you to post some additional information on the Center's main page.

STEPS

1. **In your text editor, open the file htm_C-3.txt from the location where you store your Data Files, drag to select all the text on the page, click Edit on the menu bar, click Copy, then close the file**

2. **If necessary, open your activities/index.htm page in your text editor, locate the paragraph that ends with "… our center a family fun place," click after </p>, press [Enter] twice, click Edit on the menu bar, then click Paste**

   The text and markup from htm_C-3.txt has been pasted into the activities/index.htm file between the welcome paragraph and the list of rules. This information would look better as bulleted text.

3. **Drag to select <p> in the line that begins "Tell you what," press [Delete], type <ul>, then press [Enter]**

   The <ul> marks the start of an unordered list. As with the ordered list, the paragraph tag is not necessary. Pressing [Enter] causes the first sentence of the pasted text to move to the next line.

4. **Verify that the insertion point is before the word "Tell" in the first sentence of the list, then type <li>**

5. **Drag to select <br /> at the end of the line, press [Delete], then type </li>**

   Just as in an ordered list, <li> marks the text that follows as a list item, and </li> closes that item. Line breaks are not required because each list item starts a new line.

QUICK TIP

You can use the Copy and Paste commands on the Edit menu to speed your work.

6. **Repeat Steps 4 and 5 to set an opening and closing list item tag before and after each line, replacing the <br /> tags with </li> tags, then save the file**

7. **Drag to select the </p> after the list item that ends with "guided activities," press [Delete], type </ul>, then compare your screen to Figure C-17**

8. **Save your work, click the browser program button in the taskbar, reload the activities/index.htm page, then print the page**

   The Activity Center functions appear next to bullet characters, while the Rules and Regulations list items are numbered, as shown in Figure C-18.

9. **Close all files, then transfer your updated files to your remote directory on the server**

Clues to Use

Customizing lists

Be default, ordered lists are displayed in the browser with items numbered sequentially beginning with 1. However, you can use attributes to customize the <ol> tag to display lists with letters or Roman numerals. Set the "type" attribute to "a" for lowercase letters, "A" for uppercase letters, "i" for lowercase Roman numerals, or "I" for uppercase Roman numerals. You can also change the starting point of a list by setting a start value. For example, to format a numbered list to begin with the number 4, add start="4", to the <ol> tag. You can also customize bulleted lists using type="value" to specify the appearance of the bullet as follows: <ul type="circle"> <li>Item 1</li></ul>. The bullet produced by the preceding code is an open circle rather than the usual filled disc. Possible values for unordered list types are: circle, square, and disc.

FIGURE C-17: Code for unordered list

```
<p>The staff at the Activities Center wants to help you make your vacation the most
memorable ever. Our friendly staff can: </p>

<ul>
<li>Tell you what special activities are in store for the day</li>
<li>Let you know which activities are best suited for you and your family</li>
<li>Help you plan family outings</li>
<li>Give you directions to local attractions</li>
<li>Provide you with shuttle service schedules for off-site shopping areas</li>
<li>Assist you in making reservations for our featured guided activities</li>
</ul>

<p>Ask us -- We can help!</p>
```

FIGURE C-18: Unordered and ordered lists displayed in Web page

|Home| |Contact Us| |Rates and Accommodations| |Activities and Events| |Paradise Garden Day Spa|

Activities Center

Welcome to Paradise Mountain Family Resort! Your Activities Center staff welcomes everyone to participate in the daily activities, meet new friends and have a good time. Your cooperation in following Activity Center rules helps make our center a family fun place.

Activities Center Functions

The staff at the Activities Center wants to help you make your vacation the most memorable ever. Our friendly staff can:

- Tell you what special activities are in store for the day
- Let you know which activities are best suited for you and your family
- Help you plan family outings
- Give you directions to local attractions
- Provide you with shuttle service schedules for off-site shopping areas
- Assist you in making reservations for our featured guided activities

Ask us -- We can help!

Rules and Regulations:

1. Guests under the age of 16, must be accompanied by an adult
2. Please sign in before using any computer equipment
3. Guests are asked to refrain from using pool cues in any manner not intended by the manufacturer
4. Please, no throwing of billiard balls
5. Darts must be checked out through the Activities Center desk
6. Children using darts and dartboards must be accompanied by an adult
7. Anyone using the Activities Center equipment in a manner for which is was not intended will be asked to leave the Activities Center

TABLE C-3: HTML tags for creating ordered and unordered lists

tag	description	example

`<ol>...</ol>`	Marks beginning and end of an ordered list	`<ol>`
		`<li>Item 1</li>`
		`<li>Item 2</li>`
		`</ol>`

`<ul>...</ul>`	Marks beginning and end of an unordered list	`<ul>`
		`<li>Item 1</li>`
		`<li>Item 2</li>`
		`</ul>`

`<li>...</li>`	Marks the beginning and end of each item in an ordered or unordered list; as with most other tags, the closing tag is required	`<li>Item 1</li>` `<li>Item 2</li>`

HTML

Practice

▼ CONCEPTS REVIEW

Identify the function of each item labeled in Figure C-19.

FIGURE C-19

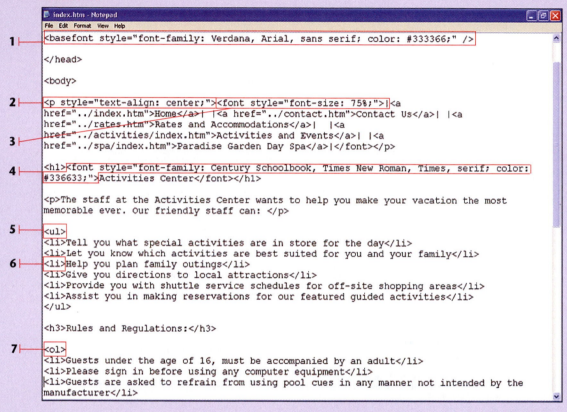

Match each tag with its function.

8. `<ol>`

9. `<ul>`

10. `<font>`

11. `<address>`

12. `<blockquote>`

a. Alters the default white space on either side of the affected text

b. Useful for creating pages that appeal to specific target audiences and for adding personality to your pages

c. Produces a series of list items where a bullet character, instead of a number or letter, designates each list item

d. Produces a series of list items in which the items appear with sequential numbers or letters

e. Alters the physical appearance of a block of content and is recognized by some indexing and cataloging software

Select the best answer from the list of choices.

13. **Which of the following HTML codes could you use to change a character style to bold? (Choose all that apply)**
    a. `<p property="bold">`
    b. `<strong>...</strong>`
    c. `<b>...</b>`
    d. `<font color="#FFCC33">...</font>`

14. **Which one of the following HTML codes does not center-align a paragraph?**
    a. `<p style="text-align: center;">`
    b. `<p align="center">`
    c. `<ol>...</ol>`
    d. `<address style="text-align: center;">`

▼ SKILLS REVIEW

1. **Align text.**
    a. Start your text editor, then open the **salon.htm** file from your paradise/spa directory in the place where you save your site files. (If you did not complete the Skills Review in Unit B, see your instructor for a copy of the files you need.)
    b. In your text editor, locate the level-one heading that begins with "<h1 id="top" >Aphrodite's..." at the top of the page content section, then click directly before the > in the <h1> tag.
    c. Insert a space, then type the code `style="text-align: center;"` to center the page heading on the page.
    d. Apply the centered style you used on the page heading to both navigation bars and the "questions or comments" paragraph near the bottom of the page.
    e. Save the page, then open it in your browser to verify that the page heading, both navigation bars, and the questions and comments paragraph are centered.

2. **Format characters.**
    a. In your text editor, locate the line near the top of the page that starts with, "<p>Aphrodite's Salon full-service hair and nail salon", click directly before the phrase "full-service", then enter an `<em>` tag.
    b. Click directly after "full-service," then enter the closing tag `</em>`.
    c. Locate the "Limited-time specials" section heading near the bottom of the page.
    d. Apply the emphasized formatting to the "Limited-time specials" text using the same method you applied in Steps a and b above.
    e. Locate the line that begins "* Summer Special:".
    f. Click just before the *, then enter `<strong>`.
    g. Click just after the colon following the word "Special," enter a closing `</strong>` tag, then save your work.
    h. Reload the **salon.htm** page in your browser to verify that your formatting appears.

3. **Define an address block.**
    a. Return to your code, locate the questions or comments paragraph that you centered earlier, then click directly after the p in the opening paragraph tag.
    b. Press **[Backspace]**, then type `address`.
    c. If necessary, modify the content so that you are listed as the contact source.
    d. Locate the closing paragraph tag after </a> and change the closing paragraph tag into a closing address tag, then save your work.
    e. Reload the **salon.htm** file in your browser to verify that the contact paragraph is now an address block with italicized text.

4. **Control font selection.**
    a. In your text editor, locate the head section of the salon.htm page, click after </title>, then press **[Enter]** twice.
    b. Enter the code `<basefont style="font-family: Franklin Gothic Book, Arial, Helvetica, sans serif;" />`.
    c. Locate the level-one page heading at the top of the body section, click directly before the word "Aphrodite's," then enter the code `<font style="font-family: Pristina, Viner Hand ITC, Script MT Bold, serif;">`.

   d. Click between the word "Salon" and the </h1>, then type `</font>`.

   e. Save your work.

   f. Reload the page in your browser to verify that all the text on the page appears in a sans serif font and that the page heading appears in a decorative or serif font.

5. **Customize fonts.**

   a. In your text editor, locate the level-one page heading at the top of the page, click after the semicolon and before the closing quotation mark inside the opening font tag, then press **[Spacebar]**.

   b. Enter the code `color: #336633;`

   c. In the "Summer special" paragraph near the bottom of the document, click before the asterisk (*), then add a font tag that includes a color style set to `#FF3333;`

   d. Click directly after the colon (:) in the same line, then insert the `</font>` tag.

   e. Click directly before the first square bracket in the top-level navigation bar, then enter an opening font tag with a code that sets the font-size at 80% of the default font.

   f. Move to the end of the navigation bar and set a closing font tag directly before </p>, then save your work.

   g. Reload the **salon.htm** page in your browser to verify that the text color is changed in the heading and in the "Summer special" paragraph, and that the navigation bar appears smaller than the rest of the text on the page.

6. **Create ordered lists.**

   a. In your text editor, locate the line beginning with "<p>Apollo's haircut" under the level-three heading "Hair Care" near the top of the file, click after the <p>, then type `Aphrodite's has a number of hair-care services to make you feel like a god or goddess. View our list below:</p>`.

   b. Press **[Enter]** twice, enter the code `<ol>`, then press **[Enter]**.

   c. Enter the opening list item tag `<li>` before "Apollo's", then replace the line-break tag at the end of the line with the closing list item tag, `</li>`.

   d. Repeat Step c on the following lines through the line that begins "Chemical straightening." Replace the </p> with a closing ordered list tag. (*Hint:* The link tag and the Thermacore text are part of the same line.)

   e. Click before the Return to Menu link at the bottom of the list and enter the code `<p>`. (*Hint:* Recall that you deleted the original opening paragraph tag at the start of the parent list.)

   f. Save your file, then reload the page in your Web browser to verify that the ordered list appears as shown in Figure C-20.

7. **Create unordered lists.**

   a. In your text editor, locate the line <p>Eyebrow shaping - $18.00
, under the level-three heading tag near the bottom of the page, replace the opening paragraph tag with an opening unordered list tag, then press **[Enter]**.

   b. If necessary, click before "Eyebrow," and type the code to start a list item, then at the end of the line, replace the line break tag with a closing list item tag.

   c. Repeat Step b in the next five lines, adding opening list item tags and replacing the line break tags with closing list item tags.

   FIGURE C-20

   Aphrodite's Salon

   |Paradise Mountain Resort| |Day Spa| |Spa Services| |Spa Packages| |Aphrodite's Salon| |Resort Activities|

   Aphrodite's Salon *full-service* hair and nail salon - services include:

   |Hair Care| |Facials| |Depilatory Services| |Makeup| |Specials|

   Hair Care

   Aphrodite's has a number of hair-care services to make you feel like a god or goddess. View our list below:

   1. Apollo's haircut - $18.00
   2. Aphrodite's haircut - $40.00
   3. Shampoo and styling - $35.00
   4. Single process color - $65.00
   5. Highlighting/foil work - Partial - $55.00
   6. Highlighting/foil work - Full - $85.00
   7. Permanent - Short hair - $65.00
   8. Permanent - Long hair - $95.00
   9. Thermacore Therapy - $45.00
   10. Chemical straightening - $65.00

   d. Press **[Enter]** after the final </li> tag, type the code to end the unordered list, press **[Enter]**, then type the code `<p>` to restore the opening paragraph tag that was removed from the beginning of the list section.

▼ SKILLS REVIEW (CONTINUED)

e. Use the steps above to format the content under the level-three heading "Makeup" as an unordered list, then save your work.

f. Reload the page in your browser to verify that the unordered lists appears correctly, then print the page.

g. Save and close **salon.htm**, then transfer your updated file to your remote directory.

▼ INDEPENDENT CHALLENGE 1

You are developing a Web site for your new resort rental business, Star Vacations. You want to use the skills you have learned to enhance your site and to highlight one of your new featured resorts. You've decided to use two primary fonts, Arial—a sans serif font—for the page content, and Lucida Calligraphy—a more modern, serif font—for the page headings. As alternate fonts, you have chosen Magneto and serif. You also want to apply special formatting and organize some of your content in lists to emphasize some of the new resort's amenities.

a. Open the **htm_C-4.txt** file from the place where you store your Data Files, then save it as **IslandSeas.htm** in your vacations folder in the place where you save your site files.

b. Use the basefont tag to set the page font family to Arial and specify an alternate font choice of sans serif, then set the page text color as `#000066`.

c. Apply a style to center the level-two heading at the top of the page as well as the level-three heading that follows it.

d. Add `<font>...</font>` tags to all the page headings and specify a style that changes the font to Lucida Calligraphy with alternate fonts Magneto, and serif, then include a style that changes the color of the affected text to the aqua color, `#009999`. (*Hint*: If your system does not have Magneto or Lucida Calligraphy, use another readable calligraphic font or choose a serif font that you think most users will have on their systems.)

e. Format the contact paragraph at the bottom of the page as an address block.

f. Locate the paragraph that begins with "<p>Nestled serenely," then format the words "you've DISCOVERED PARADISE" at the end of the paragraph by applying strong and em formatting to the text.

g. Locate the section of text that begins with "Rollaway Bed," and use the `<ol>...</ol>` and `<li>...</li>` tags to format the text starting with "Rollaway Bed" through "Hot Tub/Whirlpool," as a numbered list.

h. Use the `<ul>...</ul>` and `<li>...</li>` tags to format the paragraphs under Snorkeling Excursions and Tours into bulleted lists.

i. Update the "Page Modified by" paragraph, using your name and today's date. Save the file and preview it in your browser, then print the page.

j. Close the file, then transfer it to your remote vacations directory.

Advanced Challenge Exercises

- Open **htm_C-5.txt** from your Data Files folder, then save it as **faq.htm**, replacing the existing file.
- Locate the comment tag, `<!-- Format the paragraphs below this comment as a bulleted list. -->`, then format the paragraphs below it as a bulleted list.
- Locate the comment that reads `<!-- Format the items below this comment as a nested list using lowercase letters. -->`, then format the next three lines as directed in the comment tag. (*Hint*: Do not format any Return to top links.)
- Add your name and the date to the "Page Modified by" paragraph at the bottom of the page, save and print your work, close all programs, then transfer your updated page to your remote directory on the server.

▼ INDEPENDENT CHALLENGE 2

The water-conservation Web site you have been developing for your employer, Metro Water, is coming along nicely. Now that you have created several informational pages and linked them to your home page, you are ready to start enhancing those pages by formatting text, adding lists, and aligning page elements. You also want to use colors that will make your site visitors think about water and nature.

a. In your text editor, open **inside.htm** from your Data File location, then save it as **inside.htm** in the water folder in the place where you save your site files, replacing the file if prompted.

b. Format the top-level navigation bar to align in the center of the page, then use a font tag to make the navigation bar display at 85 percent of the size of the rest of the text on the page.

c. Copy the alignment and font formatting from the navigation bar paragraph to the jump menu in the middle of the page and to the "For more information" paragraph at the bottom of the page.

d. Use a basefont tag to change the default page font to Verdana and specify Arial, Helvetica, and sans serif as alternate fonts, then specify the default page text color as #333333.

e. Change the color of the level-two page heading to #000066 and change the page heading font to Georgia, specifying alternate fonts Times New Roman, Times, and serif.

f. Locate the sentence that ends with "substantially reduce your water usage." At the end of the line, type `Every drop helps . . . You CAN make a difference!`

g. Use logical formatting styles to italicize "You CAN make a difference!" and to cause the word "CAN" to be displayed in boldfaced type, then emphasize the word "CAN" even more by making it red. (*Hint*: Refer to the browser-safe color chart in the appendix of this text for a list of color codes.)

h. Format the questions in the second paragraph on the page as an ordered list.

i. Add your name and update the date at the bottom of the page, then save your file and preview it in your browser.

j. Transfer your updated page to your remote directory.

Advanced Challenge Exercises

- Format the paragraphs under the page headings, "General Tips," "In the Kitchen," "Conserving Water in the Bathroom," and "What About Well Water" as bulleted items, creating a new list for each section. (Hint: Do not make the page headings part of the lists.)
- Use the type attribute on each of your bulleted lists to make the bullets in each list appear as square.
- Save your page, then view it in your browser.
- Transfer your updated page to your remote directory.

▼ INDEPENDENT CHALLENGE 3

You are concerned about text colors and lists because you know that they are part of the accessibility initiative. You are interested in learning more about the use of text colors and their part in making Web sites more accessible. You want to use the latest and most elegant methods of creating lists, but you are concerned about accessibility. You also want to find out what else you can do to make your site more pleasing to customers.

a. Go to the Online Companion for this book and locate the links for this unit. Click the W3C Web Accessibility page link and review the information regarding HTML color contrast in section 9.1, then write one or two paragraphs answering the following questions:

1. How can the use of text color make your site more user friendly?

2. How would you test your site to see whether color contrast is sufficient to be read by people with color deficiencies?

b. From the color section on the W3C Web Accessibility pages, click to follow the Lighthouse links until you arrive at the Lighthouse site.

▼ INDEPENDENT CHALLENGE 3 (CONTINUED)

c. Type "Color" in the search box to find information about effective color contrast, then find what three things a designer can do to make effective color choices.

d. Write your name at the top of your report and print the page.

▼ INDEPENDENT CHALLENGE 4

Now that you've studied formatting and creating lists, you are ready to add these features to the pages on your Web site.

a. Based on your site content and purpose, determine what formatting your site requires, then make a list describing your choice of colors and font families.

- Tell why you have chosen each of your font and color style elements.
- Plan what your page background color will eventually be and make sure it contrasts with your font color. (*Hint*: If you are going to use a dark background and light text, you may have to choose a temporary font color until you learn how to set page backgrounds.)

b. Format your home page using at least two font families in appropriate sizes, with at least one color change from the default font color.

c. Add at least one list to one of your pages.

d. Add appropriate content to your home page. (*Hint*: Content can be changed as necessary as your site develops.)

e. Apply formatting to your site navigation bar, then apply it to all pages.

f. Add a centered address block to your home page or your about_me.htm page, then apply other alignment formatting to the rest of your site elements to achieve the look you want.

g. Preview the modified pages in your browser, then print them and mark on the printouts the areas you modified.

▼ VISUAL WORKSHOP

As you develop the PC history Web site for Bits and PCs, you have obtained quite a bit of information on the history of Apple Computers. Because Apple played such a large role in making personal computing accessible to a wider audience, you want to present this chronology right away. Open the file **htm_C-6.txt** from the place where you store your Data Files, then save it as **apple_hist.htm** in the History folder in your bitspcs site file location. Add a page heading and apply color, alignment, font, and list formatting to resemble the Web page shown in Figure C-22. When you finish, link the file to your apple page in your BitsPCs history folder and cause the page to open in a new window. Save and print the apple.htm page code, then preview it in your browser. Click the new link and print the page from the browser window. (*Hint:* The basefont is Arial.)

FIGURE C-22

Adding Graphics and Multimedia

OBJECTIVES

Plan graphics use
Insert images
Optimize images
Specify image size
Add a background image
Link images
Insert an image map
Explore multimedia options
Use multimedia

While text is often the most significant element of a Web page, graphics are also an important part of Web design. In addition to sometimes conveying information better than text, graphics can make a page easier to read and can give a page a unique style and mood. When resized and optimized for quick download, images can effectively serve as graphic content, page backgrounds, and navigation elements. Pages usually contain static graphics, but many also supplement content with multimedia, including animated graphics, sound, and video. You are leading the team of designers who are working to create the new Web site for Paradise Mountain Family Resort. Because so many of the resort's special features are better described in pictures, you want to use images to enhance the Web site and to better convey the information you are presenting. You also want to look into the possibility of using multimedia to further enhance the site.

Planning Graphics Use

The use of graphics is a popular and practical way to enrich Web pages. However, as with other design tools, moderation is the key to effective graphics use. A Web page filled with text but devoid of graphics can be uninviting and difficult for users to read. On the other hand, devoting too much space to graphics can overwhelm and distract users from the focus of the page. To use graphics most effectively, first clarify the goal of your Web page or Web site. Then plan and incorporate a graphics style that supports your layout without overwhelming it. Figure D-1 shows a Web page that balances text and graphics. ▰▰▰ You plan to incorporate the Paradise Mountain Family Resort logo into the Web site you are creating. You also want to add some graphics that depict some of the resort's many activities.

DETAILS

While planning the use of graphics, it's important to keep these few guidelines in mind:

- ### Use supported file formats

  Unlike Web page text, which is actually a part of the HTML document that creates a Web page, Web page graphics are separate files that are referenced in a page's HTML code. Images that are displayed as content on the page are called **inline images** because the code used to **call** (pull in) the images is written "inline" with the other code on the page. Many graphic file formats exist, but only three are widely supported by Web browsers: GIF, JPG, and PNG. You can tell the format of a file by checking the filename's extension. For example, the name of a JPG file ends with .jpg or .jpeg. As you create or acquire graphics for your Web site, make sure they are GIF, JPG, or PNG files. When you request graphic files from others, you must either specify that they be in one of the three Web-compatible formats or you must have the ability to convert them into a Web-compatible format. Table D-1 gives more information about each of these three formats.

- ### Add alternate text

  Although images are widely supported by most of today's browsers, not all users are able to benefit from image-based content. Some users still surf the Web on computers without access to high-speed connections and choose not to view images in order to speed up Web page download time. What is more important to consider, however, is the fact that there are many individuals who are unable to view Web page images because of a visual impairment. To accommodate these users, it's important that Web pages convey the same information with or without the images. The HTML tag for adding an image to a Web page also supports an attribute that allows you to specify a text alternative that appears when your image does not. As you plan how you will incorporate graphics into your layout, you must also determine a text alternative that is appropriate for each graphic.

- ### Keep file size small

  Web page download time is an important usability factor in which the size of graphics plays a large role. Download time is the amount of time it takes for the page and its associated files to transfer from their location on a Web server to a user's computer. HTML files alone are relatively small, and, without their graphics, most download within a few seconds—even over the slowest Internet connection. Graphic files, however, can be much larger and can take much longer to download. High-speed technologies such as **DSL** (digital subscriber line), **ISDN** (Integrated Services Digital Network), **cable modem**, **T-1**, and **T-3** connections that allow faster downloads are becoming more widespread. Universities and many large corporations also have Web connections that enable near-instantaneous downloads. However, many parts of the world still use slower dial-up connections; this means that your design should ensure that your pages are easily viewable over all types of Internet connections.

- ### Use graphics wisely

  Some novice designers believe that if a few images are good, a lot of images are better. This is usually not the case. Placing too many images on a page can make the page difficult to understand and can distract the user from your intended message. The most reliable way to effectively use images on your Web pages is to restrict their use to those that support your page's structure and function. It is important that there be a purpose for every element, including images, on your page.

FIGURE D-1: Web page with text and graphics

Logo image

Top-border background image

Inline image

FIGURE D-2: Displaying file extensions in Windows Explorer

Hide extensions for known file types unchecked

TABLE D-1: Web-compatible graphic formats

format	best for	notes
GIF	Line art and animations; also supports 1-bit transparency, which sets a single color as the transparent color	A proprietary format by CompuServ/Unisys: No licensing or fees required for using, viewing, or selling GIF images; companies producing software programs that *create* GIF images must pay licensing fees to CompuServ/Unisys
JPG (or JPEG)	Photographs and other images with gradient color	Variable compression allows a trade-off between better image quality and smaller file size
PNG	Line art and photographs, also supports 32-bit (gradient) transparency	Recently developed format; browser support not as widespread; in many browsers 32-bit transparency does not appear as expected; file size might be significantly larger or smaller depending upon image content—test image in more than one format

Clues to Use

Changing image file formats

While you can use your system's file management utility, such as Windows Explorer or Desktop Manager, to edit the name of an image file, you cannot use it to *convert* an image file from one type to another. In other words, you can use the utility to rename the file to use a lowercase extension, to remove spaces from folders or file names, to give the file a new name, or to change a JPG file extension from .jpeg to .jpg because .jpeg and .jpg, like .txt and .htm, are the same file type. But you cannot change a file type by renaming a file, such as changing logo.bmp to logo.gif, because BMP (bit mapped) files and GIF (Graphic Interchange Format) files are different file types. To convert a file from one type to another, you must open that file in an image-editing program and *convert* it to another file type.

HTML

Inserting Images

HTML uses the `<img />` tag to display images on a Web page. Because the `<img />` tag is not part of a tag set, you must close it by typing a closing slash at the end of the tag, just as you do for line break tags. Like the opening tag for a link, the `<img />` tag always requires an attribute. This required attribute for all image tags is the source attribute, src, which indicates the name and location of the graphic file. Another important image attribute is the alt attribute. Also known as alt statements, **alt attributes** are part of the Web Accessibility Initiative (WAI) because they supply alternative text that appears in the browser if for any reason the image does not appear. Alternative text is also used by screen readers to describe your graphics or your graphic links when you use graphics to create navigation bars. It is, therefore, critically important that you use good alt statements—simply stating the image's file name or size is not a good use of alt statements. The `<img />` tag supports many other attributes—several of which are explained in Table D-2. You want to add a logo graphic to the Paradise Mountain Family Resort's home page.

STEPS

TROUBLE

If you have already created an images folder in your paradise site, open the paradise\images folder from your Data Files directory and copy all of the images, then paste them into your existing images folder.

1. **Copy the paradise\images folder from the place where you store your Data Files and paste it into the paradise folder in the place where you store your site files; open htm_D-1.txt from your Data Files folder and save it as index.htm in your paradise folder, replacing the existing file**

   You want to try out the look of your page with a sans serif font, so you have removed the font reference from the basefont formatting.

2. **Locate the level-one heading at the top of the body section, click directly after `<h1>`, then type `<img src="images/pm_logo1.jpg" alt="Paradise Mountain Family Resort" />`**

   The code you typed adds the new company logo inline with the level-one page heading. The src attribute value maps a relative path from the index.htm file to the pm_logo1.jpg file in the images directory. By storing all of your image files in your images folder, you are able to better organize your site. Now you want to add a second image to the page.

QUICK TIP

Be sure to insert a single space between the closing quotation mark and the closing slash (/) in the image code.

3. **Locate the line that starts with `<p>` Located just outside of, click directly before `<p>`, type `<img src="images/trail_ride1.jpg" alt="The end of the trail -- A Paradise Mountain guide and guests return from a long day's ride exploring the resort wilderness areas." />`, press [Enter] twice, then save your work**

4. **Start your Web browser, then open index.htm from your paradise site folder**

   The resort logo and the photograph both appear on the left side of the page, and the page text has been pushed below the photo, leaving large amounts of white space, as shown in Figure D-3. Setting image alignment properties can help correct these problems.

QUICK TIP

The `<img />` align values set image alignment in relation to page text, not the page margins

5. **Click the text editor program button on the taskbar, click directly before `/>` inside the trail_ride1.jpg image tag, type `align="right"`, press [Spacebar], then save your file and reload it in your browser**

   Setting the `align="right"` property instructs the photograph to align on the right side of the text.

6. **Click the text editor program button on the taskbar, click directly before `/>` in the logo image tag, type `align="middle"`, press [Spacebar], then save your work**

   Your code should resemble Figure D-4.

7. **Reload the index.htm page in your browser, then rest the pointer over the photo**

   The heading text fills the white space to the right of the logo, and the alternate text appears, as shown in Figure D-5.

FIGURE D-3: Images with large amounts of white space

Logo and image
left-aligned on page

White space

FIGURE D-4: `<img />` tag code with attributes

Logo image inside
heading block

Image alt attribute

Image tag for
photo image

Image align
attribute

```
<body>

<h1><img src="images/pm_logo1.jpg" alt="Paradise Mountain Family Resort" align="middle" />
<font style="font-family: Century Schoolbook, Times New Roman, Times, Serif; color:
#336633;">Paradise Mountain Family Resort</font></h1>

<p style="text-align: center;"><font style="font-size: 75%;">|<a
href="index.htm">Home</a>|  |<a href="contact.htm">Contact Us</a>|  |<a
href="rates.htm">Rates and Accommodations</a>|  |<a href="activities/index.htm">Activities
and Events</a>|  |<a href="spa/index.htm">Paradise Garden Day Spa</a>|</font></p>

<img src="images/trail_ride1.jpg" alt="The end of the trail -- A Paradise Mountain guide
and guests return from a long day's ride exploring the resort wilderness areas."
align="right" />

<p>Located just outside of <a href="http://www.nps.gov/romo" target="_blank"
title="Rocky Mountain National Park home page - opens in new window.">Rocky Mountain
National Park</a> in Colorado, Paradise Mountain Family Resort is the perfect getaway
place for the whole family. Adults can enjoy discounted golf and complimentary use of our
health club and tennis facilities while the little ones participate in our popular
children's program.</p>
```

FIGURE D-5: Paradise Mountain home page with aligned images and alt statement

Logo image with
middle alignment

Right-aligned image

Hovering mouse pointer
displays alt text

TABLE D-2: Commonly used `</img>` tag attributes

attribute	specifies	possible values	examples
src	Name and location of image file	Name, including extension and path of image file	`src="filename.jpg"` or `src="filepath/filename.jpg"`
alt	Alternate text for users who don't use graphics	Almost any text, including spacing and punctuation—but not double quotation marks	`alt="Guests enjoy resort activities"`
align	Image's alignment in relation to page text, not in relation to page margins	Left, right, top, texttop, middle, absmiddle, baseline, bottom, absbottom, and center	`align="right"`
height	Image's display height in pixels	Whole number representing image height—do not use to resize image	`height="200"`
width	Image's display width in pixels	Whole number representing image width—not for use in resizing image	`width="275"`
border	Image border size	Whole number representing border width in pixels	`border="2"`

HTML

Optimizing Images

A picture may be worth a thousand words, but on the Web, that picture could also take up a thousand times more disk space. Images that are excessively large in file size cause problems for end users because large file sizes translate into long download times. Even one large image file can cause your page to download slowly. If you want your pages to download quickly, you must learn to optimize your images for display on the Web. To **optimize** an image is to make sure that it is properly sized and formatted for Web display. The four main factors affecting image file size are resolution, dimension, file type, and color depth. **Resolution** is specified in pixels per inch (ppi). **Pixels** (short for "picture elements"—abbreviated "px") are the points of light that make up the display on a computer screen. **Dimension** is the physical size of your image in terms of width and height. You can control dimension by changing file resolution, cropping out unnecessary elements, or by resizing the file in a graphics-editing program. **File type** is the format in which your file is saved, and **color depth** is the number of colors an image uses. You want your pages to download quickly, so you investigate methods of optimizing Web images for faster download time.

DETAILS

You can optimize your Web images by doing the following:

- **Use the proper Web image resolution**

  Print media uses dpi (dots per inch) to specify image resolution. A higher resolution for print media is advantageous because high-resolution images produce a better printed output. On the Web, however, high-resolution images take up too much file space and browser "real estate." The optimum resolution for Web images is 72 ppi. This might not seem like much, but as shown in Figure D-6, it is perfect for screen display. Sometimes, setting the resolution to 72 ppi is all that is required to optimize your Web image.

- **Crop out unnecessary elements**

  The next step in optimizing your images is to crop out any unnecessary image elements. Web designers often use photos or other images that contain unnecessary information. By cropping the image, you can trim unnecessary elements and cut the file size dramatically. Cropping an image can also make it more interesting by focusing on on the image subject.

- **Resize the image**

  After you have changed your file's resolution and cropped out unnecessary information, your image may still be too large for effective display. When selecting an output size for your Web images, it is important to consider browser dimensions and size your page elements accordingly. Most users have monitor resolution settings of 800 × 600 or 1024 × 768. Therefore graphic banners and headings should not exceed 700 pixels in width, and page content images should not exceed more than 300 pixels in width or height.

- **Use the proper file format**

  The format you choose for saving your Web images can greatly affect the image's file size. Save flat-color, clipart-type graphics as GIF or PNG files and save full-color images, such as photographs and images with gradient fills, in JPG format. Improperly saved images could be more than 10 times larger in file size than one that is saved in the proper format.

- **Control the color depth**

  Color depth is defined by the number of bits per pixel that can be displayed on a computer screen. In a computer system, data is stored in bits. Each color bit represents two colors because it has a value of 0 or 1 (on or off). The more bits per pixel an image has, the more colors can be displayed. Since each bit represents two colors, it is easy to work out the number of colors for the various color depths. The number of possible colors is two to the power of the number of bits per pixel. Table D-3 demonstrates the relationship between color bits and the number of available colors. Some flat-color images use only four or five colors, but are saved with an 8-bit color depth (256 available colors—the maximum color depth for GIF or PNG-8 images). When this is the case, reducing the number of available colors can substantially reduce the file size of your image.

  Figure D-6 shows examples of a Web page before and after image optimization.

FIGURE D-6: A Web page before and after image optimization

Optimized image fits in one screen (file size: less than 28KB)

Page after optimization

Oversized image scrolls off page (file size: nearly 569 KB)

Page before optimization

TABLE D-3: Color depth (bits) and available colors

color bit number	mathematic formula	number of available colors
1-bit	2^1 (2)	2
2-bit	2^2 (2 × 2)	4
3-bit	2^3 (2 × 2 × 2)	8
4-bit	2^4 (2 × 2 × 2 × 2)	16
5-bit	2^5 (2 × 2 × 2 × 2 × 2)	32
6-bit	2^6 (2 × 2 × 2 × 2 × 2 × 2)	64
7-bit	2^7 (2 × 2 × 2 × 2 × 2 × 2 × 2)	128
8-bit (the greatest number of colors available for a GIF or PNG-8 image)	2^8 (2 × 2 × 2 × 2 × 2 × 2 × 2 × 2)	256
24-bit (the greatest number of colors available for a JPG or PNG-24 image)	2^{24} (2 × 2 × 2 × 2 × 2 × 2 × 2 × 2 × 2 × 2 × 2 × 2 × 2 × 2 × 2 × 2 × 2 × 2 × 2 × 2 × 2 × 2 × 2 × 2)	16,777,216 (also called "millions of colors" in some monitor settings)
32-bit (generally refers to monitor color quality—not used for Web images)	2^{32} (2 × 2 × 2 × 2 × 2 × 2 × 2 × 2 × 2 × 2 × 2 × 2 × 2 × 2 × 2 × 2 × 2 × 2 × 2 × 2 × 2 × 2 × 2 × 2 × 2 × 2 × 2 × 2 × 2 × 2 × 2 × 2)	4,294,267,296 (also called "billions of colors" in some monitor settings)

Specifying Image Size

As you learned earlier, the `<img />` tag supports many attributes, which are applied collectively as an attribute string. Among the attributes that should be added to your image attribute string are **width** and **height**, which specify a graphic's display dimensions in terms of pixels. An important use of width and height attributes is to reserve space on the page for the graphic as the page loads. This practice eliminates an event known as **text jumping**, an annoying condition in which text on a page begins to load and then must "jump" out of the way to make room for an image that appears later in the page-load process. Eliminating text jumping allows your pages to load more smoothly and gives the illusion that they load more quickly. Two other attributes that are usually part of an image attribute string are hspace and vspace. The **hspace** attribute controls the amount of horizontal white space and **vspace** controls the amount of vertical white space around an image. You want to add the height and width attributes to your page images to make the page load more smoothly. You also want to use an optimized image in the body of your document and add some additional white space around it.

STEPS

TROUBLE

If you are using Internet Explorer and the Internet Explorer information bar appears telling you that Internet Explorer has "restricted the file from showing active content," right-click the information bar, choose Allow Blocked Content from the shortcut menu, then click Yes.

1. **In your browser, right-click the Paradise Mountain Family Resort logo in the upper-left corner of the page, then click Properties on the shortcut menu**
   As shown in Figure D-7, the Properties dialog box appears. You can see that the image is 159 pixels wide by 156 pixels high and that the image file size is 5342 bytes or slightly more than 5 KB — there are 1024 bytes in a kilobyte.

2. **Click OK to close the dialog box**

3. **Click the text editor program button on the taskbar, locate the image tag that references pm_logo1.jpg, click just before the closing /, type `width="159" height="156"`, then press [Spacebar]**

4. **Locate the `<img />` tag that references the graphic trail_ride1.jpg, click just after the "1" in the file name, press [Backspace], then type 2**
   You changed the source file to trail_ride2.jpg, a file that has been optimized for display on the Web. To prevent text jumping, you decide to reserve space for the graphic as the page loads.

5. **Click directly before the closing / in the same tag, then type `hspace="15" vspace="5"`**
   The hspace attribute adds horizontal space between the image and the page elements to the left and right of the image. The vspace attribute adds vertical space above and below the image. Although these attributes have been deprecated by the W3C in favor of CSS formatting, you see them in older pages and find that they still effectively control the amount of space around an image and are valuable tools for use until you are able to learn and apply style sheet formatting.

6. **Press [Spacebar], type `width="261" height="400"`, press [Spacebar], then save your work**
   See Figure D-8.

7. **Click the browser program button in the taskbar, then reload index.htm**
   Your completed page resembles the page shown in Figure D-9, with extra white space around the smaller, optimized image.

Clues to Use

Resizing Images

Although it is possible to use image width and height properties to cause an image to display on a Web page smaller than the image's actual dimensions, it is important that you not use these attributes for such a purpose. A large image with a large file size is still a big image—even if you have managed to make it appear smaller. If you need to use an image that is too large for your page design, use an image-editing program to reduce the file dimensions as well as the file size.

FIGURE D-7: Properties dialog box in browser window

Properties dialog box

Image file size

Image dimensions

Internet Explorer security information bar

FIGURE D-8: Web page code for sized image

Image tag appears in code before other main page content

Align="right" attribute causes image to align to right of content

```
href="index.htm">Home</a>|  |<a href="contact.htm">Contact Us</a>|  |<a
href="rates.htm">Rates and Accommodations</a>|  |<a
href="reserve.htm">Reservations</a>|  |<a href="activities/index.htm">Activities
and Events</a>|  |<a href="spa/index.htm">Paradise Garden Day Spa</a>|</font></p>

<img src="images/trail_ride2.jpg" alt="The end of the trail -- A Paradise Mountain
guide and guests return from a long day's ride exploring the resort wilderness areas."
align="right" hspace="15" vspace="5" width="261" height="400"  />

<p>Located just outside of
<a href="http://www.rmnp.com" target="_blank" title="Rocky Mountain National Park
home page - opens in new window.">Rocky Mountain National Park </a> in Colorado,
Paradise Mountain Family Resort is the perfect getaway place for the whole family.
```

FIGURE D-9: Paradise Mountain Family Resort home page with optimized image

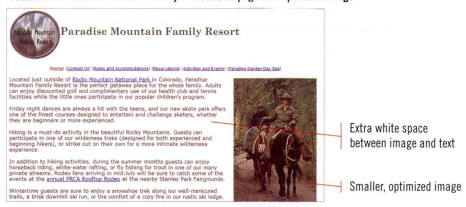

Extra white space between image and text

Smaller, optimized image

HTML

Adding a Background Image

Just as Web page images are separate files that the browser calls up for display when the page is loaded, Web page **background images**—graphics that appear behind other page elements—are stored as separate image files in the site's images directory. Traditionally, background images are specified in the opening body tag <body> as background="value". Although body tag attributes have been deprecated by the W3C in favor of more advanced formatting techniques such as CSS, you will most likely have to edit or update pages with body tag attributes, so it is good to know about them. Most background images are very small in both dimension and file size so they display quickly when the page is loaded. Although small, a background image can fill a page because it is **tiled**, meaning that it repeats itself across and down the page until the entire page is filled. A well-designed background tile is **seamless**, making it almost impossible for the viewer to tell where one repetition of the image ends and the next begins. See the appendix for more information on applying body attributes and values. One of your design team members has created a background sampler page. You want to view the samples, then enhance the Paradise Mountain home page by adding a background graphic.

STEPS

1. **In a separate instance of your browser, open the file** bkg_samples.htm **from the samples folder in your paradise\images folder**

2. **Click each of the background samples to view the actual file, clicking the Back to samples link after viewing each file, then close the** bkg_samples.htm **browser window**

   You notice that each background image is quite small. You decide that the file pm_bkgnd.gif is the best choice for the Paradise Mountain home page.

3. **Click the text editor program button on the taskbar to return to your page code, click inside the** <body> **tag, directly before the closing >, press [Spacebar], then type** background="images/pm_bkgnd.gif"

   The body's background attribute is similar to the src attribute of the image tag in that it directs the browser to find and display an image.

4. **Save your work, click the browser program button on the taskbar, then reload** index.htm

   As Figure D-10 shows, the small background image repeats, creating a border across the top of the page. However, a white square appears around the logo image. Because JPG images do not support transparency, the white matte—solid-colored, non-image area of a graphic that "frames" the graphic content—is displayed against the blue background image.

5. **Click the text editor program button on the taskbar, locate the logo image code, click directly before the closing quotation mark in the image file name, press [Backspace] five times, then type** 2.png

   You removed the .jpg file extension, the dot, and the number "1" from the file name. Then you replaced the image with one that supports transparency. You want to move the page content so it is somewhat higher on the page.

6. **Click directly before the > in the opening body tag, press [Spacebar], type** topmargin="5", **then save your work**

   Your code should be similar to that shown in Figure D-11. By default, most browsers have a top-border margin of approximately 10 pixels. By setting the topmargin attribute value in the opening body tag to "5," you reduced the size of the top margin and allowed the page content to move up five pixels on the page.

7. **Click the browser program button on the taskbar, then reload** index.htm

   As shown in Figure D-12, the logo and heading text have moved up slightly on the page, and the logo graphic no longer appears with a white background.

FIGURE D-10: Home page with background image and logo in JPG format

Logo image appears in white box

Paradise Mountain Family Resort

Page background image

|Home| |Contact Us| |Rates and Accommodations| |Activities and Events| |Paradise Garden Day Spa|

Located just outside of Rocky Mountain National Park in Colorado, Paradise Mountain Family Resort is the perfect getaway place for the whole family. Adults can enjoy discounted golf and complimentary use of our health club and tennis facilities while the little ones participate in our popular children's program.

Friday night dances are always a hit with the teens, and our new skate park offers one of the finest courses designed to entertain and challenge skaters, whether they are beginners or more experienced.

Hiking is a must-do activity in the beautiful Rocky Mountains. Guests can participate in one of our wilderness treks (designed for both experienced and beginning hikers), or strike out on their own for a more intimate wilderness experience.

In addition to hiking activities, during the summer months guests can enjoy horseback riding, white-water rafting, or fly fishing for trout in one of our many private streams. Rodeo fans arriving in mid-July will be sure to catch some of the events at the annual PRCA Rooftop Rodeo at the nearby Stanley Park Fairgrounds.

Wintertime guests are sure to enjoy a snowshoe trek along our well-manicured trails, a brisk downhill ski run, or the comfort of a cozy fire in our rustic ski lodge.

Other on-site or nearby seasonal events and activities include Boulder Walk and Bike Week (June), 4th of July Fireworks, The Paradise Mountain Cycling Road Rally (July), and the Scottish Highlands Festival (the week following Labor Day).

FIGURE D-11: Web page code to adjust graphic elements

Background image inserted in opening body tag

Call to image file changed

```
<body background="images/pm_bkgnd.gif" topmargin="5">

<h1><img src="images/pm_logo2.png" alt="Paradise Mountain Family Resort"
align="middle" width="159" height="156" /><font style="font-family: Century
Schoolbook, Times New Roman, Times, Serif; color: #336633;">Paradise Mountain Family
Resort</font></h1>
```

FIGURE D-12: Web page with transparent PNG-formatted logo and alignment adjustments

Transparent PNG image replaces opaque JPG image

Top margin reduced and image and text moved

Paradise Mountain Family Resort

|Home| |Contact Us| |Rates and Accommodations| |Activities and Events| |Paradise Garden Day Spa|

Located just outside of Rocky Mountain National Park in Colorado, Paradise Mountain Family Resort is the perfect getaway place for the whole family. Adults can enjoy discounted golf and complimentary use of our health club and tennis facilities while the little ones participate in our popular children's program.

Friday night dances are always a hit with the teens, and our new skate park offers one of the finest courses designed to entertain and challenge skaters, whether they are beginners or more experienced.

Hiking is a must-do activity in the beautiful Rocky Mountains. Guests can participate in one of our wilderness treks (designed for both experienced and beginning hikers), or strike out on their own for a more intimate wilderness experience.

In addition to hiking activities, during the summer months guests can enjoy horseback riding, white-water rafting, or fly fishing for trout in one of our many private streams. Rodeo fans arriving in mid-July will be sure to catch some of the events at the annual PRCA Rooftop Rodeo at the nearby Stanley Park Fairgrounds.

Wintertime guests are sure to enjoy a snowshoe trek along our well-manicured trails, a brisk downhill ski run, or the comfort of a cozy fire in our rustic ski lodge.

Other on-site or nearby seasonal events and activities include Boulder Walk and Bike Week (June), 4th of July Fireworks, The Paradise Mountain Cycling Road Rally (July), and the Scottish Highlands Festival (the week following Labor Day).

Body content moved up slightly on page

Design Matters

Creating effective backgrounds

When you use backgrounds, make sure that there is enough contrast between the text and the background by using body attributes that determine text colors: **text**, for page text; **link**, for unclicked links; **vlink**, for visited links; and **alink**, for active links. In addition to using an image, you also can specify a background color for your Web page. A **background color** is the color that appears behind page text when no background image is supplied, if the background image is specified incorrectly, or when part of the page background image is transparent. You indicate a color in the <body> tag by setting the **bgcolor attribute** equal to the color's hexadecimal equivalent. As with a background image, it is important to select a background color that contrasts well with a page's text.

Linking Images

Just as you can link text, you can also add link formatting to Web page images. To do so, surround the `<img/>` tag with the `<a>...</a>` tag set, and add the appropriate href attribute. When using linked images as site navigation elements, it is good practice to place the images in the same location on every page for a consistent look. Most pages with linked images are more attractive when image borders are set to zero (0) using the `border="0"` attribute and value. Table D-4 lists additional image attributes. You have placed the Paradise Mountain logo in the upper-left corner of the home page and want to add it to your other pages as well. You think the logo would make an excellent link point to help keep users oriented as they view the site.

STEPS

1. Click the **text editor program button** on the taskbar, drag to select all of the code from the basefont tag through the navigation bar, as shown in Figure D-13, then copy the code

2. Open the **contact.htm** page in your text editor from the paradise folder in your site file location, click directly before `</head>`, drag to select all of the page code through `</p>` at the end of the site navigation bar, then paste the copied code

    The contact page is updated. You want to add an image link back to your home page.

QUICK TIP
Link titles may not appear on linked images with alt statements, but they still provide information for users with disabilities.

3. Click between the `<h1>` and the `<img` in the heading and logo section at the top of the page content code area, then type `<a href="index.htm" title="Return to Paradise Mountain Family Resort Home page">`

TROUBLE
If your image border is blue, you either have never displayed your home page in the browser, or your file path is incorrect.

4. Click directly after the `/>` at the end of the image tag, type `</a>`, save your work, click the **browser program button** on the taskbar, open **contact.htm** in your browser, then move the mouse pointer over the **Paradise Mountain** graphic logo

    The mouse pointer changes to a pointing hand, letting the site visitors know that the image is linked. Browsers handle alt statements and link titles differently. As shown in Figure D-14, the image alt statement rather than the link title appears in Internet Explorer. (Other browsers may display the link title rather than the alt statement.) In Internet Explorer, the image is bounded by a purple box, which spoils your page design.

5. Click the **Paradise Mountain** logo

    The Paradise Mountain home page opens.

6. Click the **text editor program button** on the taskbar to return to your contact.htm page code, click directly after the closing quotation mark following the align attribute "middle," press **[Spacebar]**, type `border="0"`, then save your work

7. Click the **browser program button** on the taskbar, then click the **Contact Us link** to reload the contact page

    The linked logo now appears without the border, as shown in Figure D-15.

8. Return to your contact.htm source code, drag to select all the code from the basefont tag through the `</p>` of the top navigation bar, then copy the code

    You want to work with your rates.htm page next, so you begin by updating the logo and navigation bar with your most recent changes.

9. Open the **rates.htm** page in your text editor, drag to select from `</head>` through the closing `</p>` of the navigation bar paragraph, paste the copied code, then save your work

FIGURE D-13: Selected code for copying

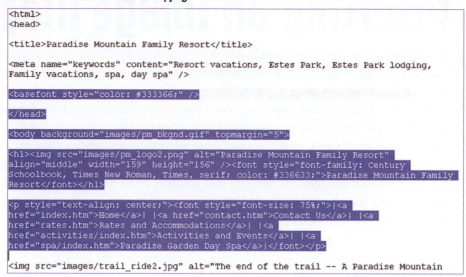

```
<html>
<head>

<title>Paradise Mountain Family Resort</title>

<meta name="keywords" content="Resort vacations, Estes Park, Estes Park lodging,
Family vacations, spa, day spa" />

<basefont style="color: #333366;" />

</head>

<body background="images/pm_bkgnd.gif" topmargin="5">

<h1><img src="images/pm_logo2.png" alt="Paradise Mountain Family Resort"
align="middle" width="159" height="156" /><font style="font-family: Century
Schoolbook, Times New Roman, Times, serif; color: #336633;">Paradise Mountain Family
Resort</font></h1>

<p style="text-align: center;"><font style="font-size: 75%;">|<a
href="index.htm">Home</a>| |<a href="contact.htm">Contact Us</a>| |<a
href="rates.htm">Rates and Accommodations</a>| |<a
href="activities/index.htm">Activities and Events</a>| |<a
href="spa/index.htm">Paradise Garden Day Spa</a>|</font></p>

<img src="images/trail_ride2.jpg" alt="The end of the trail -- A Paradise Mountain
```

FIGURE D-14: Web page containing linked graphic in Internet Explorer

Linked logo image displays border

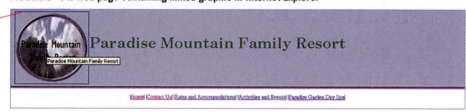

FIGURE D-15: Logo without border

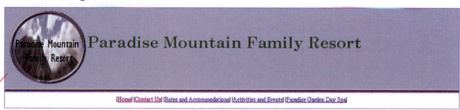

Border="0" attribute removes border from linked image

TABLE D-4: Additional `<img />` attributes

attribute	specifies	possible values	example
border	The width of an optional border placed around the image; by default, a blue border appears around a linked graphic	A number representing this width, in pixels; to remove default border from linked images, set value to 0	border="0"
vspace	The size of the space between the top and bottom of the graphic and the surrounding page elements; short for "vertical space"	A number representing this space, in pixels	vspace="5"
hspace	The size of the space between the left and right edges of the graphic, and the surrounding page elements; short for "horizontal space"	A number representing this space, in pixels	hspace="5"

Inserting an Image Map

Although the ability to link an image to a Web file is useful in Web page design, sometimes a single graphic conveys information that's appropriate for more than one link. You can take advantage of such an image by making it into an **image map**, a graphic that has different areas that are linked to different Web files. Each of these areas, known as **hot spots**, is defined with a coordinate system that uses the `<map>` and `<area>` tags. The image map information associated with a graphic can be located anywhere in a Web document; you specify a name for each map, and use the usemap attribute to reference the map name in the `<img />` tag that uses it. Because it is a challenging task to specify the exact pixel coordinates of areas within a graphic, most Web designers use software that simplifies image map creation by allowing you to draw the hot spots over the graphic. Table D-5 shows the available attributes for an image map. You designed a graphic that shows a floor plan of a two-bedroom suite at Paradise Mountain Family Resort. You also created an image map for the graphic; the image map splits the image into seven hot spots. You want to insert the image map code into the Rates and Accommodations page you are designing for the resort.

STEPS

1. **Start another instance of your text editor program, then open the file imagemapParadise.txt from the paradise folder in the location where you store your Data Files**

   This file contains your image map information. Along with inserting the correct values in the `<map>` and `<area>` tags, the graphics software you used to create it also generated the `<img />` tag for the associated graphic.

2. **Drag to select all the text in the file, copy it to the clipboard, then close the file**

3. **In your rates.htm file, locate the line that begins with** `<p><strong><em>Watch this space!`**, drag to select the entire paragraph including** `<p>` **and** `</p>`**, then press [Delete] twice**

   You deleted the placeholder information and the blank line after it.

4. **Find the paragraph that ends with** `or to make reservations.</p>`**, click after** `</p>`**, press [Enter] twice, type** `<p>Click a spot in the map below to view the rooms in one of our 2-bedroom units.</p>`**, press [Enter] twice, paste the image map code from the clipboard, then press [Enter]**

   Figure D-16 shows the image map code in the Web page.

5. **Save your work, click the browser program button on the taskbar, then open the rates.htm page**

   The image map showing the floor plan of one of the units appears, as shown in Figure D-17.

6. **Move the mouse pointer over the graphic showing the two-bedroom floor plan**

   The text specified for each `<area>` tag's alt attribute appears in a box when the mouse pointer is over the matching hot spot. In addition to the pointing hand icon, the appearance of this text is another cue for the user that this image contains links.

7. **Click the master bath hot spot on the image map**

   An image of the master bath opens in a new window.

8. **Close the new window and return to the image map**

9. **Repeat Steps 7 and 8 for each of the other hot spots in the image map**

   All the hot spots work as you intended.

FIGURE D-16: Code for image map in Web page

Pasted image map code

```
<p>Click a spot in the map below to view the rooms in one of our 2-bedroom
units.</p>

<p><map name="resortMap">
<area target="_blank" href="images/masterbedroom.jpg" shape="rect" coords="12,
6, 123, 108" alt="view the master bedroom" />
<area target="_blank" href="images/masterbath.jpg" shape="rect" coords="5, 118,
101, 193" alt="The master bathroom features a Whirlpool hot tub"/>
<area target="_blank" href="images/bed2.jpg" shape="rect" coords="30, 252, 149,
342" alt="Two queen-sized beds and a sitting area provide ample comfort for
your family in the second bedroom." />
<area target="_blank" href="images/frontroom.jpg" shape="rect" coords="160, 48,
259, 183" alt="The DVD, 32-inch TV, and stereo system make this room ideal for
entertaining. The pull out queen-sized sleeper sofa is a delightful extra."  />
<area target="_blank" href="images/dine2.jpg" shape="rect" coords="112, 112,
156, 182" alt="U-shaped booth seating with additional chairs, gives plenty of
room for seating your entire family." />
<area target="_blank" href="images/bath2.jpg" shape="rect" coords="5, 203, 148,
242" />
<area target="_blank" href="images/kitchen.jpg" shape="polygon" coords="161,
302, 162, 187, 257, 188, 259, 253, 198, 303" alt="In the kitchen, built-in
Whirlpool appliances make cooking and cleanup a breeze." />
</map>
<img border="0" src="images/floorplan2bedroom.gif" width="266" height="351"
usemap="#resortMap"align="left" ></p>

<br clear="all" /><br /><br />

<address style="text-align: center;">For questions or comments about this site,
contact: <br /> <a
```

FIGURE D-17: Floor plan image map displayed in rates.htm page

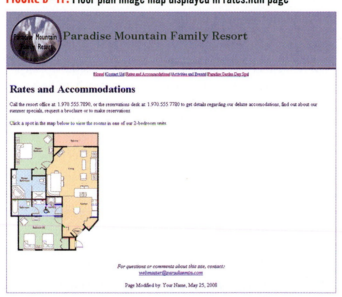

TABLE D-5: Image map tags

tag or tag set	function	attribute	specifies	example
`<map>...</map>`	Marks a section of HTML code as a named image map	name	Name of image map (for reference by `<img />` tag)	`<map name="2bedroom">`
`<area />`	Describes the shape and function of a hot spot	href	Target link address	`<area href="images/masterbedroom.jpg"`
		shape	Geometric shape of area; can be "circle," "rect" (rectangle), "poly" (polygon) or "default"	`shape="rect"`
		coords	pixel coordinates that describe the boundaries of the hot spot	`coords="12, 6, 123, 108"`
		alt	alternate text to display or speak	`alt="Click to view the master bedroom" />`

Exploring Multimedia Options

Advances in Web page design bring dynamic interactive pages to users instead of the static pages of yesterday. In addition to adding features to HTML, today's cutting-edge technology moves toward integrating sound and video with a page's basic text and graphics. The product of this integration is known as **multimedia**. In the past, **bandwidth**—the data transfer capacity of a Web user's Internet connection—was an obstacle to designers who wanted to incorporate multimedia in their sites. Because video and audio files are much larger than HTML and image files, the download time for a Web page that included video or audio blocked its smooth integration into Web pages. Recent trends in multimedia technology have enabled designers to provide a multitude of multimedia options knowing that most users will be able to experience all that the sites have to offer. These trends include **high-bandwidth Internet connections** (DSL and cable modems), **improved compression** that shrinks the size of video and audio files, and **streaming multimedia technology** (the ability to configure multimedia files to begin playing before they are fully downloaded). Table D-6 summarizes the requirements for creating and playing back the main multimedia technologies. You think multimedia would enhance your site and so you decide to explore your multimedia options to learn more about them.

DETAILS

Multimedia implementations on the Web include:

QUICK TIP

Animated gifs are inserted using the image tag, like any other image.

- ### Animated GIF
  The oldest of all multimedia options, and the easiest to use, the GIF file format allows you to combine two or more images into a single file and to include instructions on how the images are presented. Creating such a file, known as an **animated GIF**, was for years the only widely viewable multimedia effect on the Web. It costs very little and is often free, and online software is readily available for creating such effects. Animated GIFs are most often used in Web page banner advertisements, as they allow advertisers to display one or more images to attract a reader's interest before displaying the company logo or other target information. However, this type of advertising has been known to drive users away from a site, so be careful how often you use such a feature.

- ### Macromedia Flash animation
  A Macromedia innovation, Flash animation is rapidly becoming the most widely used Web animation. Flash animation requires a proprietary player. However, the **object tag set** <object>...</object> used to implement Flash multimedia embeds a call to the Flash player download site, making it easy for users to obtain and install the program. Therefore a great majority of Web users have the Flash player installed on their machines. As early as March 2005, nearly 98 percent of Web users worldwide had the ability to view and listen to Flash video and sound, as shown in Figure D-18. Moreover, the Macromedia Flash program is no longer necessary to create Flash animation; other licensed software allows designers to create complex and highly compressed multimedia animations.

- ### Streaming media
  Recent higher-bandwidth connections and more compressed formats have facilitated the wider incorporation of traditional audio and video media into Web sites as streaming media. Many news organizations, such as printed newspapers and television stations, include relevant video clips alongside articles on their Web sites; musicians and record companies also use the Web to promote music and videos. Although clips are often embedded as links for downloading, today's faster Internet connections allow Web users to experience the audio or video without leaving the site. In addition, many radio and television stations have added **Webcasting** to their Web sites, meaning that they make their stations' normal programming available live on their Web sites. This technology also has allowed people and organizations to disseminate video and audio media programming without the financial costs of using traditional media channels.

- ### Embedded audio and video
  One of the easiest methods of making sound and video files available to site visitors is by delivering **embedded media**—simple sound and video files that are inserted through the use of the embed (<embed />) tag. Embedded media options are supported by most of the traditional audio and video types such as WAV, AVI, MPG, and MP3. When properly formatted, embedded media options allow site visitors to control the player and to stop or start a file as they see fit. Embedded media options are available for both sound and video files.

FIGURE D-18: Macromedia Flash statistics page

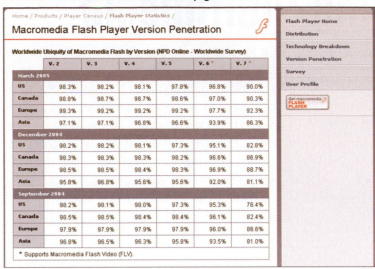

TABLE D-6: Comparison of multimedia options

technology	creation tool(s)	how used	playback tool
Animated GIF	Software commonly available for free or at low cost, or professional graphic editing tools such as Adobe ImageReady	`<img />` tag; implemented exactly like standard images; requires src attribute	Web browser
Flash animation	Macromedia Flash software and other tools such as Adobe ImageReady, Techsmith Camtasia, or free Web-based tools	`<object >...</object>` tag with specified param elements, required object attributes: classid with Flash class value, codebase, width, height, and name or id; required param names, movie with value	Web browser with Flash Player plug-in
Traditional audio and video	Audio and/or video computer translation hardware with associated software	`<embed />` tag, requires src attribute	Web browser with player plug-ins, such as Windows Media Player, Apple QuickTime Player, or one of the Real media players
RealOne Streaming audio and video	Audio and/or video computer translation hardware with associated software and streaming server	`<object >...</object>` with specified param elements, requires object attributes—classid with RealOne class value, width, height, and id; required param names, src with .rpm value; additional files—rpm file, which tells browser how to stream video or audio file	Web browser and add-on such as RealOne Player, QuickTime, or Windows Media player

Using Multimedia

If your page's only purpose is to serve as a download site for media files, you can make them available to your site visitors by creating links. However, in most cases, you want media files to enhance, not supplant, page content. One method of delivering media within the context of the Web page is to use the **embed tag** <embed />. Embed tags use most of the same attributes used by image tags including src, width, height, hspace, vspace, align, and title. Embed tags also use the additional attributes **hidden**—which allows the designer to choose to display the player, and **autostart**—which controls whether the file plays on page load or not. Sound or video files embedded in a Web file require few attributes. The only one that is absolutely required is the source attribute (src), which specifies the path to the media file. However, adding other attributes makes your sound or video file easier to use. You decide to provide a simple video file that site visitors can access from your Rates and Accommodations page to show site visitors some of the activities available at Paradise Mountain Family Resort.

STEPS

1. **Copy the media folder from the paradise folder in the place where you store your Data Files to the paradise folder in the place where you save your site files**

2. **Click the text editor program button on the taskbar to return to your rates.htm source code, click directly before `<br clear="all" /><br /><br />` near the bottom of the page, type `<p><embed src="media/paradise.wmv" width="300" height="400" /></p>`, press [Enter] twice, then save the file**

    The paradise.wmv file is a video clip. Most video clips display well at 300 × 400 pixels.

> **TROUBLE**
> If you open your file in Internet Explorer and the Information bar displays, right-click it and choose "Allow blocked content." Then click Yes to the prompt, "Are you sure you want to let this file run active content."

3. **Click the browser program button on the taskbar, then reload your rates.htm file**

    Depending upon your browser version, the file could start to play almost immediately. You realize that this is not necessarily in the best interests of the user, so you decide to add some attributes to allow the user to control the playback. You also notice that the object is too close to the floor plan image.

4. **Click the text editor program button on the taskbar to return to your rates.htm source code, locate the height attribute for the media file, click directly after the closing quotation mark following it, press [Spacebar], type `autostart="false" align="right" vspace="10" hspace="10"`, then save your work**

    The autostart="false" attribute prevents the player from starting automatically, thus enabling the users to decide whether they want to play the video. The align attribute moves the file to the right side of the page, and the vspace and hspace attributes add extra white space so the video is not crowded by other content on the page. The embedded file needs a title.

5. **Click after the closing quotation mark following the "hspace" attribute value, press [Spacebar], type `title="Click to play resort features video, or visit the site home page to learn more about the resort."`, make sure that your name and today's date appear in the "Page modified by" paragraph at the bottom of the page, then save your work**

    See Figure D-19. Although alt is not a supported attribute for the embed tag, you can use the title attribute to supply additional information for people whose disabilities prevent them from seeing the video display.

> **QUICK TIP**
> The multimedia file format can play a significant role in its initial appearance. Some files, like the WMV file you are using, are smaller in file size, but display no image until activated. Others are larger in file size but initially more attractive.

6. **Click the browser program button on the taskbar, reload the page, then print it**

    The page appears with a media player for the embedded media file, but the video does not start automatically.

7. **Click the Play button ⊙ on the media player to activate the video clip**

    The video plays in the media player, as shown in Figure D-20.

8. **Close any open files, then transfer your updated files to your remote directory on the server**

```
<p><map name="resortMap">
<area target="_blank" href="images/masterbedroom.jpg" shape="rect" coords="12,
6, 123, 108" alt="View the master bedroom" />
<area target="_blank" href="images/masterbath.jpg" shape="rect" coords="5, 118,
101, 193" alt="The master bathroom features a Whirlpool hot tub"/>
<area target="_blank" href="images/bed2.jpg" shape="rect" coords="30, 252, 149,
342" alt="Two queen-sized beds and a sitting area provide ample comfort for your
family in the second bedroom." />
<area target="_blank" href="images/frontroom.jpg" shape="rect" coords="160, 48,
259, 183" alt="The DVD, 32-inch TV, and stereo system make this room ideal for
entertaining. The pull out queen-sized sleeper sofa is a delightful extra."  />
<area target="_blank" href="images/dine2.jpg" shape="rect" coords="112, 112,
156, 182" alt="U-shaped booth seating with additional chairs, gives plenty of
room for seating your entire family." />
<area target="_blank" href="images/bath2.jpg" shape="rect" coords="5, 203, 148,
242" />
<area target="_blank" href="images/kitchen.jpg" shape="polygon" coords="161,
302, 162, 187, 257, 188, 259, 253, 198, 303" alt="In the kitchen, built-in
Whirlpool appliances make cooking and cleanup a breeze." />
</map>
<img border="0" src="images/floorplan2bedroom.gif" width="266" height="351"
usemap="#resortMap"align="left" ></p>

<p><embed src="media/paradise.wmv" width="300" height="400" autostart="false"
align="right" vspace="10" hspace="10" title="Click to play resort features
video, or visit the site home page to learn more about the resort." /></p>

<br clear="all" /><br /><br />
```

Embed code ┤ (label pointing to the `<p><embed` line)

Practice

▼ CONCEPTS REVIEW

Name the function of each section of code indicated in Figure D-21.

FIGURE D-21

Match each statement with the term that best describes it.

8. A graphic that links different areas to Web pages

9. A linked area of a graphic

10. A graphic that allows any user to see text in a font selected by the designer

11. A group of technologies that allows faster downloads

12. One of the points of light that makes up the display on a computer screen

a. Broadband

b. Hot spot

c. Pixel

d. Image map

e. Text image

Select the best answer from the list of choices.

13. Which of the following is a graphics file format commonly used on the Internet? (Choose all that apply.)
    a. GIF
    b. JPG
    c. TIFF
    d. BMP

14. Which one of the following attributes for the `<img />` tag adds space to the left and right of the image?
    a. align
    b. vspace
    c. src
    d. hspace

▼ SKILLS REVIEW

1. Insert images.

a. In your text editor, open the file **htm_D-2.txt** from the place where you store your Data Files, then save it as **index.htm** in your paradise/spa folder in the place where you save your site files, replacing the existing file.

b. Locate the level-two heading tag with the id "slogan", drag to select Paradise Garden Day Spa, press [Delete], then type the code `<img src="../images/spa_logo.gif" />`. (*Hint*: Because the spa site is in a subdirectory of the paradise site, the images folder is in the parent directory. Make sure that your src attribute correctly identifies the file path.)

c. Add an alt statement to the image that indicates to the user that the image represents Paradise Gardens Day Spa, then save the file. (*Hint*: Use the code `alt="Paradise Garden Day Spa"`)

d. In your text editor, open the **htm_D-3.txt** file from your Data Files location and save it as **hands.htm** in the spa folder in your site files location, replacing the existing file. Repeat Steps b and c to set the logo graphic at the top of the page, replacing Paradise Garden Day Spa, then add an appropriate alt statement.

e. Click directly before the level-three heading tag for Hand Care, and insert the code to display the image pedi.jpg from your paradise images folder. (*Hint*: Use the code `<img src="../images/pedi.jpg" />`)

f. Click inside the pedi.jpg image tag and insert the code to cause the image to align to the right, then type the code to insert an alt statement using the text, **Indulge yourself with a professional pedicure**, then save your work.

2. Specify image size.

a. Open your **spa/hands.htm** file in your browser, locate and right-click the logo image and open the Image Properties dialog box, then record the width and height of the image. (*Hint*: In the Image Properties window, the width is always listed first.)

b. Repeat Step a with the photograph, then click the text editor program button to return to your page code.

c. Add the correct width and height attributes and set the hspace value for each image to 10 pixels, update the "Page modified by" paragraph with your name and the current date, then save your work.

d. Open your **spa/index.htm** file in your text editor and use the information you recorded in Step a above to specify the proper image width and height for the page logo.

e. Save your work, reload your **spa/hands.htm** file to view your changes, then click the Paradise Garden Day Spa link in the navigation bar to view changes to the spa/index.htm file.

3. Add a background image.

a. Make sure that your **spa/index.htm** page is open in your text editor.

b. Click directly after "body" in the opening body tag, insert a space, then type the code that causes the image bkg_spa.gif from the paradise/images folder to appear as the background image for your page. (*Hint*: Use the code `background="../images/bkg_spa.gif"`)

c. Add a leftmargin attribute and value to the body tag that moves the page content 150 pixels from the left page margin and 50 pixels from the right margin. (*Hint*: Use the code `leftmargin="150" rightmargin="50"`)

d. Save your work.

e. Repeat Steps b through d to add the same background image and margins to your hands.htm page.

f. Save and load each page in your browser to test your images.

4. Link images.

a. Click the text editor program button to return to your hands.htm page code.

b. Locate the `<img />` tag that references the spa logo graphic, click directly before `<img` and enter an opening anchor tag with the code to create a link to the spa/index.htm page, then click at the end of the image tag and type the closing anchor tag. (*Hint*: For the opening anchor tag, type `<a href="../spa/index.htm">`.)

c. Click inside the opening link tag and directly after the href value, then insert the link title, **Link to Paradise Garden Day Spa home page**.

d. Click inside the image tag and insert the code `border="0"` to prevent a border from being displayed on your linked image.

e. Save your work, view the file spa/hands.htm in your browser, then click the logo graphic to make sure it links to the spa/index.htm page.

5. Insert an image map.

a. In your text editor, open the file **imagemap.txt** from the UnitD spa folder in the location where you store your Data Files, select and copy all the text in the file, then return to your spa/index.htm file.

b. In the spa/index.htm file, locate, then delete the second-level navigation bar that starts with `<p id="spaNav" style="text-align: center;">`, and paste the image map code from the Clipboard.

c. Save your work, then reload the file **spa/index.htm** in your browser.

d. Copy the wraps.htm file from your Data Files spa folder and paste it into your paradise/spa folder.

e. Return to **index.htm** in your browser, then click the image map hot spots to test the image map.

6. Use multimedia.

a. Copy the media folder and its contents from the UnitD spa folder in the place where you store your Data Files to your paradise/spa folder in the place where you save your site files.

b. Make sure that your **spa/index.htm** file is open in your text editor, click directly after the second line break following the image map, then press [Enter] twice.

FIGURE D-22

c. Insert an embed tag with the source attribute and value `src="media/spa.wmv"` and the title `Tour our facilities`.

d. Right-align the embedded file, insert additional attributes to set the width and height to 300, then add an additional 10 pixels of horizontal white space around the player.

e. Type the code `hidden="false"` to make sure the player is visible in all browsers, then insert the code that prevents the file from playing when the page is loaded. (*Hint*: Set the autostart attribute to "false.")

f. Ensure that the "Page modified by" paragraph contains your name and the date is today's date, then print the code.

g. Save your work, then reload the file **spa/index.htm** in your browser.

h. Test your embedded multimedia file by clicking the Play button on the media player. Your page should resemble Figure D-22.

i. Close all files and transfer your updated files to your remote directory.

▼ INDEPENDENT CHALLENGE 1

As you continue developing the Web site for your resort rental business, Star Vacations, you want to use the skills you have learned to add graphics and multimedia to enhance the site.

a. Locate and copy the **images** directory with all of its contents, as well as the files, **eu.htm**, **ak.htm**, and **hi.htm**, from the UnitD vacations folder in the place where you store your Data Files.

b. Paste the copied folder and files inside your vacations site folder in the place where you store your site files.

c. In your text editor, open your **IslandSeas.htm** file from your vacations folder in the place where you save your site files (or obtain a copy of the file from your instructor).

d. Click just after "body" in the <body> tag and type the code to display the graphic **bkg_vaca.gif** as a background image. (*Hint:* The image is saved in your images folder.)

e. Click after the </h3> tag following the resort address at the top of the page, then enter two line breaks to move the rest of the content down on the page.

f. Locate the paragraph that begins with "<p>Nestled serenely", click before <p>, and enter the code `<img src="images/resort.jpg" hspace="10" vspace="10" align="right" />`, then insert an alt statement **Find fun in the sun at Island Seas**, update the "Page modified by" section with your name and today's date, then save your work.

g. Open **htm_D-4.txt** from the UnitD Data Files, save it as **index.htm** in your vacations folder, then repeat Step d to place the background graphic, bkg_vaca.gif, on the page and save your work.

h. Open a separate text editor window, open the **map.txt** file from the UnitD vacations Data Files folder, replacing the existing file, then copy all of the text to the Clipboard and close the map.txt file.

▼ INDEPENDENT CHALLENGE 1 (CONTINUED)

i. In the index.htm file, locate and select the comment tag, `<!-- Insert image map here -->`, then paste the copied code.

j. Update the "Page Modified by" section with your name and today's date, save your work and display the index.htm file in the browser, check your image map links, close all files, then transfer your completed pages to your remote directory.

Advanced Challenge Exercises

- Copy the media folder from your vacations_ace Data Files into your vacations folder, then edit the index.htm file to embed the audio file islandseas.wav in a separate centered paragraph just above the address block.
- Set the width and height attributes of the embed tag to 150 wide by 40 pixels high to cause only the media player control buttons to appear, then add code to prevent the file from playing automatically.
- Locate the text "Come to the Land of the Midnight Sun," currently linked to features.htm, and change its link to the Alaska Resort page, ak.htm.
- Locate the text "A tropical paradise awaits!", then change its link to the Hawaii Resorts page, hi.htm; if necessary, add your name and today's date to the "Page Modified by" section.
- Edit the Island Seas image map area to cause the page to open in a new window.
- Save your work, then reload the **vacations/index** file in your browser, and check all links; close all files, then transfer them to the remote site.

▼ INDEPENDENT CHALLENGE 2

The water conservation Web site you have been developing for your employer, Metro Water, is coming along nicely. You are ready to start enhancing your pages with graphics and sound.

a. Copy the images and media folders, as well as the saver.htm file from the water folder in the place where you store your Data Files and paste them into your water folder in the place where you save your site files. (*Hint:* If prompted to replace files, click Yes.)

b. In your text editor, **open htm_D-5.txt** from your Data File location, then save it as **index.htm** in your water folder, replacing the existing file.

c. Click after the closing paragraph tag in the "Page modified by" paragraph at the bottom of the page, then insert a return and enter the code to place and center the mw.gif file (located in the images folder) below the "Page modified by" text. (*Hint:* To center an image, place it in a paragraph or division and set alignment attributes in the parent element.)

d. Set the width and height of the graphic to 50 × 50, and add the alt attribute, "Metro Water reminds you that every drop counts" and link the graphic to saver.htm. (*Hint:* Be sure to remove the border from the linked graphic.)

e. Click just after `</a>` following the linked image at the bottom of the page, insert a line break, and embed the conserve.wav file. Set the media player to appear at 200 pixels by 20 pixels, update the "Page modified by" paragraph as necessary, then save, preview, and close your page and transfer your file to your remote directory.

Advanced Challenge Exercises

- Open **water/index.htm** and add the background image water_bg1.jpg or water_bg2.jpg.
- Replace the level-one heading text with the graphic waterHead2.gif, then add an alt statement for the graphic, then save your work.
- If necessary, open the page in your browser and view it to determine the best text and link color choices for the background, then use the color chart in the appendix of this text to help determine an appropriate text, link, and background color palette for this page.
- Use the text attribute of the body tag to set your page text color.
- Use the link, vlink, and alink body tag attributes to set the link, visited link, and active link colors.
- Use the bgcolor attribute to set a page background color that closely matches the background graphic.
- Save, preview, print, and close your file and transfer it to the remote site.

▼ INDEPENDENT CHALLENGE 3

Graphics and multimedia are a necessary part of presenting content on the Web today. You want to use the latest and most elegant methods of displaying graphics, but you are concerned about accessibility.

a. Go to the Student Online Companion, then click the link to open the W3C Web Accessibility page and review the information regarding graphics and multimedia, then answer the following:

1. How can the use of graphics make your site more user friendly?
2. How would you test your site to see whether the graphics you included can be read by people with sight deficiencies?
3. What steps should you take when using graphics and multimedia to ensure accessibility?
4. What are the issues of accessibility when using sound on your pages?
5. Add your name and today's date to the top of your paper, then print it.

▼ INDEPENDENT CHALLENGE 4

Now that you've studied graphics and multimedia, you are ready to add these features to the pages on your Web site.

a. Locate or create graphics, multimedia, and background images that are appropriate for your site.
b. Make sure each page contains a background image and at least one inline graphic; include at least one multimedia file in your site. Then add appropriate content to your pages. You may include image maps, but they are optional.

VISUAL WORKSHOP

Work progresses on your Bits and PCs Web site and you decide to add images to the apple_hist.htm file. You received permission from photographer A. Luckow to use pictures he took of Steve Jobs and Steve Wozniak. Using the files provided, revise your apple_hist.htm page to resemble the page shown in Figure D-23. Copy the images and media folders from the UnitD bitspcs folder in the place where you store your Data Files into the bitspcs folder in the place where you save your site files. The images folder contains the files apple.gif, applebg.gif, and woz-jobsbyLuckow.jpg and the media folder contains the apple.wav file. (*Hint:* The base font in Figure D-23 is Arial.)

FIGURE D-23

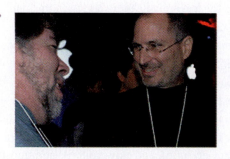

[Home] [History Information] [Advertised Specials] [Products] [Services]

Chronology of the Apple Computer until 1987

Click to hear some Apple history

- **1971** Stephen Wozniak and Bill Fernandez build their "Cream Soda computer."
- **1972** Stephen Wozniak and Steven Jobs begin selling blue boxes.
- **1973** Stephen Wozniak joins Hewlett-Packard.
- **1974** Steve Jobs joins Atari
- **1975** Apple I
- **1976** Apple becomes a company
  1. Wozniak and Jobs form the Apple Computer Company on April Fool's Day.
  2. Apple Computer opens its first offices in Cupertino and introduces the Apple II. It is the first personal computer with color graphics. It has a 6502 CPU, 4KB RAM, 16KB ROM, keyboard, 8-slot motherboard, game paddles, and built-in BASIC.
- **1978** Apple introduces and begins shipping disk drives for the Apple II and initiates the LISA research and development project.
- **1980** Apple III
- **1983** Three new products from Apple
  1. Apple Computer announces Lisa, the first business computer with a graphical user interface launched by Apple Computer Inc., Cupertino, California. The computer has 5MHz 68000 CPU, 860KB 5.25 *floppy*, B&W screen, detached keyboard, and mouse.
  2. Apple IIe
  3. Apple III+

Formatting with Cascading Style Sheets

OBJECTIVES

Explore CSS formatting
Control text formatting
Set background colors and images
Set link properties
Apply margins
Apply text alignment and format lists
Use CSS class rules
Use linked style sheets

Cascading Style Sheets (CSS) are a powerful method of formatting Web pages according to a series of rules you create and apply to your Web pages. A fundamental feature of CSS formatting is its ability to **cascade**—apply multiple styles to the same document. CSS rules allow you to control page elements in ways that traditional HTML formatting cannot. You can use CSS to control the appearance of text, set background colors, apply page margins, set link properties, and align text. Moreover, you can create style sheets that can be linked to multiple pages to instantly control formatting throughout an entire site. As the Paradise Mountain Family Resort Web site grows and matures, you begin to realize how difficult it is to implement formatting changes across all pages, so you decide to investigate the possibility of using CSS.

Exploring CSS Formatting

In the first four units of this book, you used inline styles, which you entered within formatting tags. Although useful for formatting pages, inline styles require that you format each element individually. **Cascading Style Sheets (CSS)** allow you to format your Web files efficiently without adding HTML formatting tags and attributes to the document body. You apply CSS styles by creating and using **CSS style rules**—special instructions that describe the formatting you want to apply to each element. When HTML was introduced, it was not intended as a formatting language, but rather as a method of making documents available to users on a variety of operating systems. Over the years, formatting elements, such as `<font>...</font>` were introduced to make HTML documents more appealing to the general public. With new elements being introduced yearly, the need to standardize HTML led to **Extensible Hypertext Markup Language (XHTML)**. Well-formed XHTML documents use CSS to format page output. In addition to making pages more attractive, CSS formatting also enables designers to create pages that are accessible to a wider range of display devices, such as computer screens, personal digital assistants (PDAs), and digital phone displays. You want to learn how you can use CSS to enhance your pages, so you begin to study CSS formatting options.

DETAILS

You can accomplish the following tasks using CSS:

- **Control text formatting**

  As with HTML formatting, CSS enables you to control font color and size. However, CSS moves beyond the limitations of **standard HTML** (HTML prior to version 4.0) because it allows you to control font size in fixed values, such as points and pixels, as well as in relative values such as **em** (the height of the lowercase letter "m" of your chosen font family) and in percentages. Figure E-1 shows a Web page formatted with CSS.

- **Set background properties**

  Using CSS formatting you can apply background color and images to the entire page, to page block elements such as block quotes, divisions, and address tags and to specific page elements such as paragraphs and headings. In addition, CSS allows you to control the way page backgrounds appear by controlling the background's position and its repetition behavior.

- **Control page margins and spacing**

  With CSS formatting, you have more margin control than ever before. You can specify page margins in terms of pixels, points, or percentages. You can also control white space around specific page elements by applying **padding**—added space within an element—and **margins**—added space around an element. In addition, CSS lets you also control white space by adding CSS rules to control **line spacing**—the space between lines, **character kerning**—the space between letters within a word, and **word spacing**—the amount of space between words.

- **Control element alignment and decoration**

  You can use CSS to align block-level page elements such as `<div>...</div>`, `<blockquote>...</blockquote>`, and `<address>...</address>`. Using CSS you can also add decorative borders above, below, or around page block elements, paragraphs, and headings.

- **Format multiple pages within the same site**

  Once you have created your document styles, you can save them in a separate style sheet file with a .css extension and then apply that document to multiple pages throughout your site. Formatting your documents in this manner allows you to make global changes to your site by making those changes to a single file.

Formatted navigation text

Graphic bullets

Double-spacing between lines

Design Matters

Creating a "well-formed" document

According to W3C, a "well-formed" document follows certain syntax rules. This syntax is: All attributes must be enclosed in quotation marks and assigned values; the elements must be properly nested; all elements, even empty elements, must to be closed; element names must be in lowercase; and everything must be contained within the opening and closing html tags, which are together known as the **root element**. "Well-formed" usually describes XML documents. XHTML is HTML that is written to follow the XML syntax rules for a well-formed document.

Clues to Use

Understanding XHTML variations

XHTML language rules and structure, or **syntax**, is based on the stricter XML (Extensible Markup Language) standards. These standards declare that all tag elements must be closed and recommends that all documents contain a **document type definition (DTD)** tag written as the first line of code to tell the browser what type of XHTML you are using so it knows how to interpret the page code. According to the W3C, there are three "flavors" of XHTML: Strict, Transitional, and Frameset, each with its own DTD. Use **XHTML Strict** in documents that contain no layout or formatting markup and that use CSS to apply any formatting effects. Use **XHTML Transitional** for formatting pages that take advantage of CSS but that might contain small markup adjustments, such as bgcolor or text and link attributes in the body tag, to make page formatting visible in older browers. Use **XHTML Frameset** when you want to use frames to divide the browser window into two or more windows. (You will learn more about frames in Unit H.) The W3C also recommends that XHTML documents include a meta tag to describe the document's character set. A **character set** is a defined list of characters recognized by the computer hardware and software. Most Web documents use the ISO-8859-1 character set as defined by the International Organization for Standardization (ISO); the set includes standard ASCII characters plus additional characters for European languages. Figure E-2 shows a DTD that declares the document type to be transitional XHTML. It also shows a meta tag that defines the character set as ISO-8859-1.

FIGURE E-2: Transitional DTD and meta character type tag

Transitional DTD

Meta character type tag

Controlling Text Formatting

Cascading Style Sheets provide document-formatting techniques that were previously available only for word-processed documents. You can apply styles to text as inline style attributes, as you did in Unit C. But it is much more effective to use style sheets because they can control the formatting for an entire page or for multiple pages. **Style sheets** are composed of one or more CSS rules that dictate the way page content appears. Using the `<style>...</style>` tags, you can embed style sheets within the head section of a document to control formatting on one page. You can also save style sheets as separate files to control formatting for multiple pages. **CSS rules** are made up of a selector and a declaration that together describe the characteristics of XHTML elements. As shown in Figure E-3, the **selector** specifies the element to which the style is applied. The **declaration** contains one or more properties and values that describe the style. A colon follows each declaration property and a semicolon (;) follows each declaration property value. The entire style declaration is enclosed in curly brackets ({ }). The activities center has asked you to post some information about their many activities, and you decide to use CSS to format the document.

QUICK TIP

If you did not complete Unit D, copy the images folder from your Unit D Data Files to your paradise site folder.

1. **Locate and open the UnitE folder in the drive and folder where you store your Data Files, copy the pm_bkgnd2.gif, pm_bul1.png, and pm_bul2.png files, then paste them into the paradise\images folder in the place where you save your site files**

2. **In your text editor, open htm_E-1.txt from the location where you store your Data Files, then inspect the code**

   The first tag in the file includes the XHTML doctype description (also called a **doctype declaration**), which tells the browser that this is a Transitional XHTML document. Above the `</head>` tag, the meta character set tag tells the browser to interpret the document using the ISO-8859-1 character set.

3. **Save the file as activities.htm in the paradise\activities folder in the location where you save your site files, replacing the existing activities.htm file if prompted**

4. **Click before </head>, then type the following code, pressing [Enter] after each line:**

   ```
   <style>
   <!--
   -->
   </style>
   ```

   You entered the opening and closing style tags as well as opening and closing comment tags. You place your style rules inside the comment tags to hide the style code from browsers that do not support CSS.

QUICK TIP

The curly brackets around the style declaration do not have to be on separate lines, but Web designers usually place them there because it makes them easier to see.

5. **Click after <!--, press [Enter], then type the following code, pressing [Enter] after each line:**

   ```
   body    {
           font-family: Verdana, Arial, Helvetica, sans-serif;
           font-size: 14px;
           color: #333366;
           line-height: 2em;
   }
   ```

   As shown in Figure E-4, an opening curly bracket starts the style rule declaration, which defines your font family, font size and color, and line spacing selections for the document.

6. **Save the activities.htm file, start your browser, then open activities.htm**

   Most of the formatting applied to your other pages, as well as your background graphic, are missing, as shown in Figure E-5. However, you like the readability of the double-spaced text.

FIGURE E-3: Parts of a CSS style rule

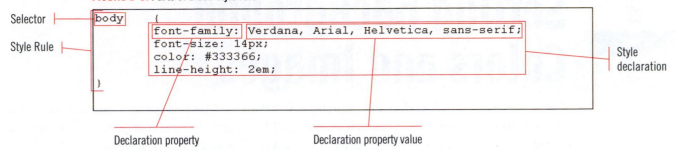

Selector — `body`

Style Rule

`{`
`font-family: Verdana, Arial, Helvetica, sans-serif;`
`font-size: 14px;`
`color: #333366;`
`line-height: 2em;`
`}`

Style declaration

Declaration property

Declaration property value

FIGURE E-4: Embedded style sheet with body style rule

```
<head>

<title>Paradise Mountain Family Resort Weekly Activities List</title>

<meta name="description" content="Paradise Mountain Family Resort weekly
activities schedule for more information contact the activities center at:
1.970.555.7890">

<meta http-equiv="Content-Type" content="text/html; charset=iso-8859-1">

<style>
<!--
body    {
        font-family: Verdana, Arial, Helvetica, sans-serif;
        font-size: 14px;
        color: #333366;
        line-height: 2em;

}

-->
</style>
</head>
```

Opening style tag

Embedded style sheet in head section

Style rule

Closing style tag

FIGURE E-5: Activities page with CSS formatting

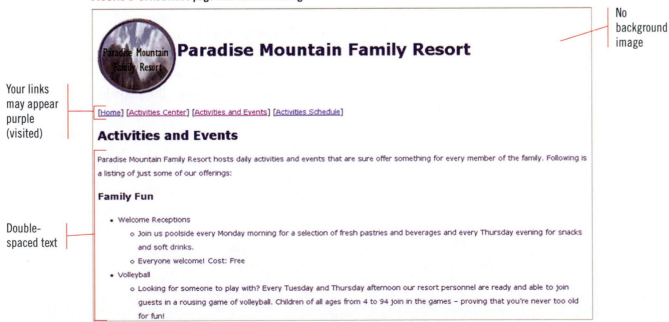

No background image

Paradise Mountain Family Resort

Your links may appear purple (visited)

[Home] [Activities Center] [Activities and Events] [Activities Schedule]

Activities and Events

Paradise Mountain Family Resort hosts daily activities and events that are sure offer something for every member of the family. Following is a listing of just some of our offerings:

Family Fun

- Welcome Receptions
  - Join us poolside every Monday morning for a selection of fresh pastries and beverages and every Thursday evening for snacks and soft drinks.
  - Everyone welcome! Cost: Free
- Volleyball
  - Looking for someone to play with? Every Tuesday and Thursday afternoon our resort personnel are ready and able to join guests in a rousing game of volleyball. Children of all ages from 4 to 94 join in the games – proving that you're never too old for fun!

Double-spaced text

HTML

Setting Background Colors and Images

Defining page background colors and images in CSS has some distinct advantages over specifying those characteristics in standard HTML. Not only can you use CSS to apply the same changes to all your Web documents; you can also use CSS to control the placement of inline and background images and the tiling of background images. (The appendix lists CSS background properties.) When you defined the style for your page in the first lesson of this unit, you used a type selector that specified the body element. **Type selectors**, also called **tag selectors**, specify elements by their names and apply the rule to all tags of the same name. The CSS rule to specify a page background also uses the body type selector. The declaration used to set the page background image is `background-image: url(imagepath);`. You decide to use CSS to apply background image and color properties. You also want to experiment with new color choices.

STEPS

1. **Click the text editor program button to return to your source code, click just before } in the body rule of your embedded style sheet, then press [Tab]**

   The insertion point is properly positioned for adding additional formatting commands to your CSS body style rule.

2. **Type the following code, pressing [Enter] after each line, save your work, then preview it in your browser:**

   ```
   background-image: url(../images/pm_bkgnd2.gif);
   margin-left: 0px;
   margin-top: 5px;
   margin-right: 0px;
   ```

   As shown in Figure E-6, you extended the CSS body rule to set a background image and margin properties for the page. Now you would like to experiment with background color.

3. **Select the color code in the color declaration, type `#FFFFFF;`, press [Enter], press [Tab], type `background-color: #336699;`, then save your file**

4. **Click the browser program button on the taskbar, then click the Reload/Refresh button to preview your updated file**

   As shown in Figure E-7, the white text is displayed against the blue background, but the link colors are almost invisible. The page is much easier to read with a white background and blue text.

5. **Click the text editor program button, change the color value to `#333366;`, change the background color to `#FFFFFF;`, then save your work and view the page in your browser**

   As shown in Figure E-7, the links are easier to read.

FIGURE E-6: Extended body rule sets background image and margin properties

Background image

Page margin zero px (pixels)

Background image and margin declarations

```
<style>
<!--
body        {
        font-family: Verdana, Arial, Helvetica, sans-serif;
        font-size: 14px;
        color: #333366;
        line-height: 2em;
        background-image: url(../images/pm_bkgnd2.gif);
        margin-left: 0px;
        margin-top: 5px;
        margin-right: 0px;

}
-->
</style>
</head>

<body>
```

FIGURE E-7: Web page output with good and bad color choices

Difficult to read

Easier to read

HTML

Setting Link Properties

As you learned in Unit D, you can change link colors using alink, vlink, and link attributes in standard HTML, but CSS allows you to do much more. With CSS formatting, you can not only change link colors from their default colors, but also cause links to be displayed in different colors on different sections of a page, and make linked text respond to **click events**—when the site visitor clicks a link—and **hover events**—when the site visitor rests the mouse pointer over the link. You format links separately for its three **states**: visited, hover, and active (those that are in the process of being clicked or that have just been clicked). You want the links on your page to stand out a little more, so you apply text decoration and other formatting to the links in their various states.

STEPS

1. Click the text editor program button on the taskbar, click just after the closing } at the end of the body CSS rule, then press [Enter] twice

2. Type the code shown below, pressing [Enter] after each line:

```
a:link      {
    font-weight: bold;
    color: #006699;
    text-decoration: underline overline;
}
a:visited{
    color: #666699;
    text-decoration: underline overline;
}
a:hover     {
    font-style: italic;
    font-weight: bold;
    color: #CC0000;
    text-decoration: underline overline;
}
a:active    {
    font-style: italic;
    font-weight: bold;
    color: #FF0000;
    text-decoration: underline overline;
}
```

> **TROUBLE**
>
> The Activities Schedule Link will not work because you haven't created that page yet.

3. Save your work, click the browser program button on the taskbar, then reload your activities.htm page

> **TROUBLE**
>
> If you have already clicked all your links, your unclicked formatting is not visible.

4. Move the mouse pointer over each link, then click to test each one

    As shown in Figure E-8, the unclicked link appears in a steel blue as boldfaced type with over- and underlining. Hovered links—those over which you rest the mouse pointer—change to boldfaced, italicized, dark red. As you click each link to make it active, the red color intensifies. Clicking the back button to return to the page allows the link to remain active until another link or another part of the page is clicked. Visited links appear gray and lose their boldfaced qualities.

Hovered link

Active link

Visited link

Unclicked link

Design Matters

Specifying alternate link colors

Many Web sites are built with a dark-colored navigation area and a light-colored page content area. Prior to CSS formatting, this meant that either all links in the navigation area had to be graphic links to ensure they would appear against the dark background, or links in the content area were difficult to read because they were too light.

CSS formatting allows you to solve this problem by defining an alternate class of link color values that can work with your dark background. You then apply the class to the dark section of the page. You will learn more about style class selectors in a later lesson.

HTML

Applying Margins

White space is any empty area on a page and may not necessarily be white. Too much white space on a page gives the reader an unbalanced, uncomfortable feeling. Too little white space, a more common occurrence, makes page elements appear overcrowded and causes eye strain for the site visitor. Applied properly, white space can be a great enhancement to Web design. CSS formatting allows you to format page elements to include not only margins around the edges of a page, but also around elements within a page. You have identified some elements of your page that need adjusting. As shown in Figure E-9, the page heading is too close to the logo and there is not enough white space on the edges of the page. You will also add some additional formatting to your headings.

STEPS

1. **Return to your page code, click just after the } that closes the active link rule, press [Enter] twice, then type the following code, pressing [Enter] after each line:**

```
h1      {
        font-family: Century Schoolbook, Times New Roman, Times, serif;
        color: #336633;
        font-size: 36px;
        margin: 0px;
}
```

Your new style rule makes the Paradise Mountain heading appear in 36-pixel green text, and sets the margins to zero. Because the logo is part of the heading, the zero-pixel margin setting ensures that the logo stays flush left with the page border. The rest of the page still needs adjusting.

> **QUICK TIP**
> In Unit D you learned that the hspace attribute applies horizontal space to both sides of an image; using CSS you can control the spacing on just one side of an image.

2. **Press [Enter] twice, then type the following code, pressing [Enter] after each line:**

```
img     {
        margin-right: 25px;
}
```

The image rule causes any image to be displayed on the page with a 25-pixel space to its right.

3. **Press [Enter] twice, then type the following code, pressing [Enter] after each line:**

```
div     {
        margin-left: 40px;
        margin-right: 40px;
}
```

Your new rule formats any page areas enclosed by <div>...</div> (division) tags with 40-pixel left and right margins. Usually used with an ID attribute, **divisions** are block-level elements often used to control several elements at once. On this page, you set a default div value to control the page-content borders. You still need to specify what block of text the div tag affects.

4. **Locate the line at the beginning of the navigation bar code that begins <p>[<a href="../index.htm">, click just before <p>, then type <div>**

5. **Move to the end of the source code, click just before the closing body tag, type </div>, press [Enter], then save the file**

6. **Preview the page in your browser**
   As shown in Figure E-10, the page content moves in 40 pixels on the left and right, leaving ample white space on the page margins.

FIGURE E-9: Activities and Events page with identified problems

Logo and heading too close

Insufficient white space

Insufficient white space

FIGURE E-10: Page with enhanced white space

No space to left of logo

40-pixel margin

25-pixel space

Applying Text Alignment and Formatting Lists

As with other tasks, you can use CSS formatting to align text and other page elements. Setting alignment properties that override the default left alignment on specified elements can give your pages interest and balance. When using text alignment properties, however, remember that a little goes a long way. Use the default left alignment for most page content and apply special alignment formatting in moderation. The most accepted uses for other alignment options include right-aligning columns containing numeric data and center-aligning main page headings, some navigation bars, photo galleries, contact blocks, and copyright information. You want to add CSS formatting to some of your page elements in order to change their default alignment. You also want to add some specialized formatting.

STEPS

1. **Return to your text editor**

2. **Locate the h1 style rule you created earlier, click just after the } that closes the rule, press [Enter] twice, then type the following code, pressing [Enter] after each line:**

```
h2      {
        font-family: Century Schoolbook, Times New Roman, Times, serif;
        color: #000066;
        font-size: 28px;
        text-align: center;

}
```

   You defined a style and set the alignment properties for level-two page headings.

3. **Click after } of the level-two heading rule, press [Enter] twice, then type the following code, pressing [Enter] after each line**

```
address     {
        text-align: center;

}
```

   You center-aligned the address block.

TROUBLE

Be sure you type the number 1 after "pm_bul" instead of the letter L.

4. **Click after } of the division rule, press [Enter] twice, then type the following code, pressing [Enter] after each line:**

```
ul      {
        list-style-image: url(../images/pm_bul1.png);

}
```

   You specified pm_bul1.png as the bullet image. Your code should resemble Figure E-11.

5. **Save your page, then view it in your browser**

   Verify that the level-two page heading and the address block are centered on the page, and that the lists now use a graphic bullet, as shown in Figure E-12.

FIGURE E-11: Text formatting code

```
h1        {
          font-family: Century Schoolbook, Times New Roman,
          Times, serif;
          color: #336633;
          font-size: 36px;
          margin: 0px;
}

h2        {
          font-family: Century Schoolbook, Times New Roman, Times, serif;
          color: #000066;
          font-size: 28px;
          text-align: center;
}

address {
          text-align: center;
}


img       {
          margin-right: 25px;
}

div       {
          margin-left: 40px;
          margin-right: 40px;
}

ul        {
          list-style-image: url(../images/pm_bul1.png);
}
```

FIGURE E-12: Activities page with centered heading, address block, and graphic bullets

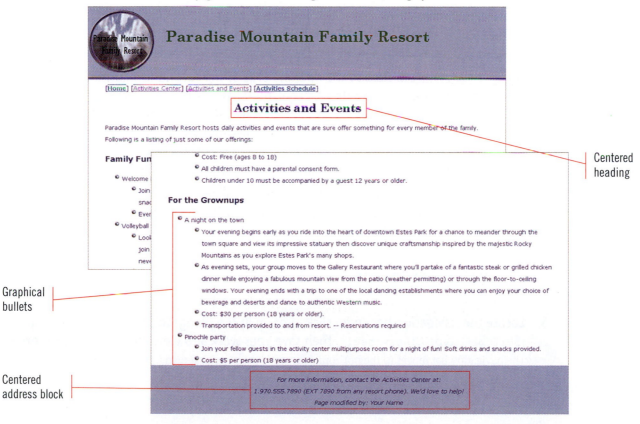

Centered heading

Graphical bullets

Centered address block

Using CSS Class Rules

Up until now, you have used type selector rules to apply CSS formatting to specific HTML elements. You have changed formatting while keeping your code relatively free of nonessential markup. However, there are times when you must go to the tag level to apply or to override a style set in your style sheet. **CSS class selector rules**—named sets of formatting instructions—allow you to define a specific-purpose style in the style sheet that can be triggered in the document code. Class selectors are preceded by a period (.), known as a **flag**, that identifies the rule as a class rule. Following the flag is the selector name. Class rules can be applied inline to any element using class="classname". When the browser sees class="classname" in an opening tag, it uses the formatting instructions specified in the style sheet for that class. When you specify a class, you do not type the flag. Once you have defined a class in the style sheet, you can change the formatting instructions for the class in the style sheet, and the instructions cascade down to any element using that class. You have identified a few areas of your Web page that still need formatting but that cannot be formatted using type selector rules. You will apply class selector rules to these elements.

STEPS

1. **Return to your code, click just after } that ends the unordered list rule, press [Enter] twice, then type the following code, pressing [Enter] after each line:**

```
.second_bul     {
     list-style-image: url(../images/pm_bul2.png);
}
```

You created a class selector rule that defines a class called second_bul. You can apply the rule to your second-level unordered lists to change the graphic bullet to pm_bul2.png, which is a square bullet.

2. **Locate the opening <ul> tag above the line of code that begins <li>join us poolside, click inside the <ul> tag just after ul, press [Spacebar], then type class="second_bul"**

As shown in Figure E-13, you have applied the second_bul class to the second-level list under "Family Fun."

3. **Apply the second_bul class to the opening tags of the second-level unordered lists that start above the following list items: "Looking for someone," "Resort counselors are on hand," "Every afternoon from 1 - 3 p.m.," "Skilled skateboarders," "Your evening begins," and "Join your fellow guests," then save your work and view it in your browser**

Each of the second-level unordered list items starts with a square bullet, as shown in Figure E-14. You notice that the navigation bar near the top of the page remains uncentered.

4. **Return to your code, click in the embedded style sheet just after the closing } following the .second_bul class selector rule, press [Enter] twice, then type the following code, pressing [Enter] after each line:**

```
.nav1     {
     text-align: center;
}
```

5. **Locate the navigation bar code, click after <p in the paragraph tag just after the <p, press [Spacebar], type class="nav1", then save your work and view your page in your browser**

The navigation bar moves to the horizontal center of the page, as shown in Figure E-15.

FIGURE E-13: Unordered list tag with applied second_bul class

Flag

```
ul          {
            list-style-image: url(../images/pm_bul1.png);
}

.second_bul      {
            list-style-image: url(../images/pm_bul2.png);
}



-->
</style>

</head>

<body>
<h1><a><img src="../images/pm_logo2.png" alt="Paradise Mountain Family Resort: Your family fun
place!" width="159" height="156" border="0" align="middle" /></a>Paradise Mountain Family
Resort</h1>

<div><p>[<a href="../index.htm">Home</a>] [<a href="../activities/index.htm">Activities Center</a>]
[<a href="activities.htm">Activities and Events</a>] [<a href="schedule.htm">Activities
Schedule</a>]</p></div>

<h2>Activities and Events</h2>
<p>Paradise Mountain Family Resort hosts daily activities and events that are
sure offer something for every member of the family. Following is a listing
of just some of our offerings: </p>

<h3>Family Fun</h3>

<ul>
<li>Welcome Receptions</li>
<ul class="second_bul">
<li>Join us poolside every Monday morning for a selection of fresh pastries
and beverages and every Thursday evening for snacks and soft drinks.</li>
```

Defined
second_bul class

Applied class

FIGURE E-14: Activities page with square second-level bullets

Square bullets

FIGURE E-15: Activities page with centered navigation bar

Centered
navigation bar

HTML

Using Linked Style Sheets

External style sheets are separate files that are saved with a .css extension and linked to documents to which their defined styles are applied. Just like embedded style sheets, external style sheets use type and class selectors. To link an external style sheet to a Web page, click inside the head section and type `<link href="folder/stylesheetname.css" rel="stylesheet" type="text/css" />` substituting the name of your style sheet file for `stylesheetname`. 🎨 You are developing some new pages to which you want to apply style sheet formatting. You also want to update some of your current pages with style sheet formatting. You decide to save your embedded style as a separate file and then use it to format the other pages in your site.

STEPS

QUICK TIP

To open a second instance of Notepad, choose All Programs/ Accessories/Notepad from the Windows Start Menu.

1. **Return to your code, locate the opening style tag in the head section of your document**

2. **Click and drag through the embedded style sheet from "body" through the } following the .nav1 style class, then copy it to the Clipboard**

3. **Open a new instance of your text editor, click anywhere in the empty document, then paste the code you copied from the Clipboard into the new document**

QUICK TIP

Use the All Files format to ensure that your file is not saved as paradise_style.css.txt. Also, if you did not complete Unit D, copy the media folder to your paradise site folder.

4. **Save your file as paradise_style.css, using the All Files format, in a new root-level folder that you create called css**
   The folder should be at the same level as the spa, activities, images, and media folders, as shown in Figure E-16.

5. **Open the file htm_E-2.txt from the place where you store your Data Files, save it as schedule.htm in the Paradise\activities folder, then preview it in your browser**
   The file contains some placeholder text, the resort logo, some bullet items, and little else. It has not been formatted. You need to insert a link to the external style sheet.

6. **Return to your schedule.htm page code, click in the head section before </head>, type `<link href="../css/paradise_style.css" rel="stylesheet" type="text/css" />`, then press [Enter] twice to insert a link to the external style sheet**
   Your code should resemble Figure E-17.

7. **Locate the navigation bar near the top of the page, click inside the paragraph tag just after <p>, press [Spacebar], then type `class="nav1"`**

8. **Replace Your Name after "Page modified by" at the bottom of the code with your own name, save the file, print the code, then view the page in your browser**
   The file appears formatted with your site styles, as shown in Figure E-18. Because there were no second-level lists, you did not need to apply that class.

9. **Close your browser and text editor**

FIGURE E-16: Paradise site structure with css folder

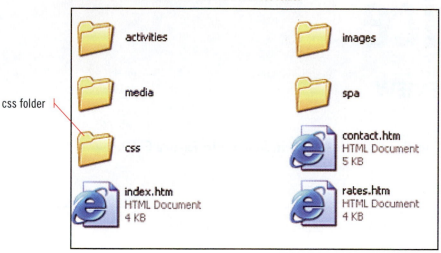

FIGURE E-17: Linked style applied to head section of document

Linked stylesheet reference typed in head section

```
<!DOCTYPE html PUBLIC "-//W3C//DTD XHTML 1.0 Transitional//EN"
"http://www.w3.org/TR/xhtml1/DTD/xhtml1-transitional.dtd">
<html>
<head>

<title>Paradise Mountain Family Resort Weekly Activities List</title>

<meta name="description" content="Paradise Mountain Family Resort weekly activities
schedule for more information contact the activities center at: 1.970.555.7890" />

<meta http-equiv="Content-Type" content="text/html; charset=iso-8859-1" />

<link href="../css/paradise_style.css" rel="stylesheet" type="text/css" />

</head>

<body>
<h1><a href="../index.htm"><img src="../images/pm_logo2.png" alt="Paradise Mountain
```

FIGURE E-18: Document formatted by linked style sheet

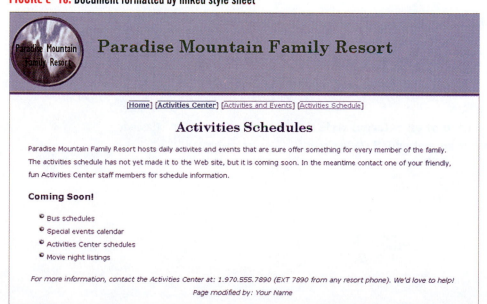

HTML

Practice

▼ CONCEPTS REVIEW

Name the function of each section of code indicated in Figure E-19.

FIGURE E-19

```
1  <!DOCTYPE html PUBLIC "-//W3C//DTD XHTML 1.0 Transitional//EN"
   "http://www.w3.org/TR/xhtml1/DTD/xhtml1-transitional.dtd">
   <html>
   <head>

   <title>Paradise Mountain Family Resort Weekly Activities List</title>

   <meta name="description" content="Paradise Mountain Family Resort weekly activities
    schedule for more information contact the activities center at: 1.970.555.7890" />

2  <meta http-equiv="Content-Type" content="text/html; charset=iso-8859-1" />

3  <style>

4  <!--

5  body  {
           font-family: Verdana, Arial, Helvetica, sans-serif;

   }

6  div      {
             margin-left: 40px;                                              9
             margin-right: 40px;

   }

7  .second {
            list-style-image: url(../images/pm_bul2.png);
   }

   -->
   </style>
8  <link href="activities_style.css" rel="stylesheet" type="text/css" />
   </head>
```

Match each statement with the term it describes.

10. A feature of CSS
11. A style that formats an individual HTML tag
12. A style sheet that can control the style of many Web pages
13. The file extension of an external style sheet
14. The location of an embedded style sheet

a. Inline
b. CSS
c. External
d. Header
e. Cascade

Select the best answer from the list of choices.

15. **Which of the following should be the first line of code in an XHTML document?**
    a. Document type definition
    b. Embedded style sheet
    c. Link to the external style sheet
    d. Inline style definition

16. **Which type of DTD should be used in an HTML document that is free of formatting attributes?**
    a. XHTML Transitional
    b. XHTML Strict
    c. XHTML Frameset
    d. XHTML Styles

17. **Which one of the following is used before a class selector?**
    a. {
    b. :
    c. ;
    d. .

18. **Where should a link to an external style sheet be placed?**
    a. Inside a comment
    b. Inside the DTD
    c. Inside the body
    d. Inside the head

19. **Where should embedded styles be placed?**
    a. Inside the head
    b. Inside the DTD
    c. Inside the body
    d. Inside `<div>...</div>` tags

20. **Which of the following is used to hide embedded styles from browsers that do not support CSS ?**
    a. `<!--...-->`
    b. `/*...*/`
    c. `<style>...</style>`
    d. `<head>...</head>`

▼ SKILLS REVIEW

1. **Explore CSS formatting.**
   a. Consider how CSS styles can be used to format the pages of the spa site. What styles are appropriate for the spa site?
   b. Which styles should be included in embedded style sheets?
   c. Which styles should be added to an external style sheet?
   d. How can classes be used to format the spa pages?
   e. How can styles be used to format the site's links?

2. **Control text formatting.**
   a. In your text editor, open the file **htm_E-3.txt** from the drive and folder where your Data Files are stored, then save it as **salon.htm** to the paradise/spa directory where you save your site files. If you are asked whether you want to replace the file, click Yes.
   b. Open the **salon.htm** file in your browser to view the unformatted page.
   c. Using your text editor, add the XHTML transitional doctype description at the top of the page above the opening `<html>` tag.
   d. Add a meta tag after the `</title>` tag with a description of the content as "Aphrodite's Salon full-service hair and nail salon."

e. Add a meta character-set tag under the previous meta tag to let the browser know the page is written in HTML. (*Hint*: Use the code `<meta http-equiv="Content-Type" content="text/html; charset=iso-8859-1" />`.)

f. Add opening and closing style tags above the basefont tag in the page head.

g. Add opening and closing comment tags inside the styles tags to hide style code from browsers that do not support CSS.

h. Add an embedded style rule after the opening comment tag that defines the body page font as Franklin Gothic Book, Arial, Helvetica, sans-serif. (*Hint*: Use the body selector with the declaration `{font-family: Franklin Gothic Book, Arial, Helvetica, sans-serif;}`.)

i. Delete the basefont style tag in the head. (Because the basefont tag has been deprecated by the W3C in favor of CSS, you replaced this style with the embedded style sheet of your page in the previous step.)

3. **Set background colors and images.**

a. Add an embedded style rule for the page body that inserts a background image using the path `../images/bkg_pillar_green1.gif`. (*Hint*: Use the body selector with the declaration `{background-image: url(../images/bkg_pillar_green1.gif);}`.) If you did not complete Unit D, copy the two files in the images folder from the folder where your Data Files are stored and paste them in the paradise/images directory. If necessary, create an images folder in the paradise folder.

b. Add an embedded style rule for the body that sets the left margin of the page to 150 pixels. (*Hint*: Use the margin-left declaration followed by a colon, with a semicolon after the rule.)

c. Add an embedded style rule for the body that sets the top margin of the page to 5 pixels.

d. Add an embedded style rule for the body that sets the right margin of the page to 0 pixels.

e. Delete the image and left margin information in the `<body>` tag of the page. (*Hint*: The `<body>` tag should not have any attributes.)

f. Save your work, then open the file in your browser to view the new formatting.

4. **Set link properties.**

a. Add an embedded style that formats the unclicked links on the page to bold, a color of #000099, and no decoration. (*Hint*: Add a style of `a:link {font-weight: bold; color: #000099; text-decoration: none;}`.)

b. Add an embedded style that formats the visited links on the page with a color of #666699 and no decoration.

c. Add an embedded style that formats the active links on the page to bold, italics, a color of #9933CC, and no decoration.

d. Add an embedded style that formats the links to bold, italics, a color of #00FF99, and no decoration when the mouse hovers over the link.

e. Save your work and view the page in your browser.

5. **Apply margins.**

a. Add opening and closing `<div>` tags to enclose the main content of the page from below the top navigation bar to just above the `</body>` tag.

b. Add a style declaration for the `<div>` tag to add 40 pixels of white space above the main page content. (*Hint*: Add `div {margin-top: 40px;}` to the embedded style sheet.)

c. Save your work, then view the file in your browser.

d. Verify that additional white space has been added between the top navigation bar and the remainder of the page.

6. **Apply text alignment and format lists.**

a. Add an embedded style to format the text in address tags as bold. (*Hint*: Add the style `address{font-weight: bold;}` to your embedded style sheet.)

b. Add an embedded style to set the color of level-three headings to #336633. (*Hint*: Add the style `h3 {color: #336633;}` to your embedded style sheet.)

c. Add an embedded style to set the font-size of level-three headings to 20 pixels. (*Hint*: Add `font-size: 20px;` to the h3 style entered in the previous step.)

d. Save your work, then reload the page in your browser.

e. Verify the changes to the address text and the level-three headings.

7. **Use CSS class rules.**

a. Create a class named circle in the embedded style sheet to format bullets in an unordered list to the open circle style. (*Hint*: Add the code `.circle{list-style-type: circle;}` to your embedded style sheet.)

▼ SKILLS REVIEW (CONTINUED)

  b. Place the code `class="circle"` in the `<ul>` tags of the page to apply the circle class to both of the unordered lists in the page.

  c. Replace Your Name between the address tags with your name.

  d. Save your work, reload the file in your browser, then verify the changes to the bullets in the page's lists.

8. Use linked style sheets.

  a. Copy the entire embedded style sheet from your salon.htm page. Do not copy the opening and closing `<style>` tags or the comment tags.

  b. Create an external style sheet by pasting the embedded style sheet into a new empty file, then save it as **salon_style.css** in your paradise/css directory. You should not have the opening or closing `<style>` or comment tags in the external style sheet.

  c. Delete the entire embedded style sheet from your salon.htm file, save the **salon.htm** file, then view the unformatted page in your browser.

  d. Place the link `<link href="../css/salon_style.css" rel="stylesheet" type="text/css" />` to the external style sheet salon_style.css in the salon.htm file's head, before the `</head>` tag.

  e. Resave the **salon.htm** file, then reload the file in your browser.

  f. Verify the page is formatted with the styles in the external style sheet, then print the page in the browser.

  g. Transfer the files to your remote directory.

▼ INDEPENDENT CHALLENGE 1

As you continue developing the Web site for your resort rental business, Star Vacations, you want to use the external and embedded style sheets to format your pages.

  a. In your text editor, open the file **htm_E-4.txt** from the drive and folder where your Data Files are stored, then save it as **features.htm** in the vacations folder where you save your site files. If you are asked whether you want to replace the file, click Yes.

  b. Add a DTD and appropriate meta tags to the page.

  c. Add an embedded style sheet to replace the basefont style information in the header. Don't forget to delete the basefont tag. (*Hint*: Place the following in the embedded style sheet: `body{font-family: Arial, sans serif; color: #000066;}`.)

  d. Add a class named square to the embedded style sheet. that formats the bullets in an unordered list as a square shape (*Hint*: Place the following in the embedded style sheet:

    `.square{list-style-type: square;}`.)

  e. Add `class="square"` to the `<ul>` tag on your page to apply the style to your unordered list.

  f. In your text editor, open a new file, then save it as **star_style.css** in your Vacations folder.

  g. Using Figure E-20 as a guide, add the following styles to your star_style.css external style sheet:

    • Set the body background color to #CCFFCC.

    • Add a top margin of 5 pixels to the body.

    • Format the links as bold, underlined, and a color of #006699.

    • Format the links to a color of #009933 and underlined when the mouse hovers over it.

    • Format level-one headings to 40 pixels with a color of #000099.

  h. Add a link in the features.htm file to the external style sheet.

FIGURE E-20

```
body {
        background-color: #CCFFCC;
        margin-top: 5px;
}
a:link {
        font-weight: bold;
        color: #006699;
        text-decoration: underline;
}
a:hover {
        color: #009933;
        text-decoration: underline;
}
h1      {
        color: #000099;
        font-size: 40px;
}
```

▼ INDEPENDENT CHALLENGE 1 (CONTINUED)

i. Using the search engine of your choice, find a new international resort. Add a link to the resort in the unordered list of the features page.

j. Replace Your Name between the address tags with your name, save your work, display the **features.htm** file in the browser to check your styles, then transfer your completed pages to your remote directory.

Advanced Challenge Exercises

■ Find a color that you would like to use as a background when the mouse hovers over the link.

■ Add a style to your external sheet that changes the link background to your color when the mouse hovers over the link. (*Hint*: Add `background:#FFFFFF;` to the a:hover style, replacing #FFFFFF with the code for your chosen color.)

■ Save your external style sheet, and check the link background color.

■ Save your files and transfer them to the remote site.

▼ INDEPENDENT CHALLENGE 2

You want to use style sheets to format the water-conservation Web site you are developing for your employer, Metro Water. You decide to put many of the styles for your pages in an external style sheet to ensure uniform formatting throughout your Web site. You will check the external styles by applying them to a page in your Web site.

a. Create an external style sheet, then save it as **metro_style.css** in the water folder where you save your site files.

b. Add rules to format the body of a Web page with the following styles:

- Background color of #CCFFCC
- Top margin of 10 pixels
- Font-family of Verdana, Arial, Helvetica, sans serif
- Font color of #333333

c. Add a style rule to format the links as underlined, a color of #0066FF, and a hover effect of bold.

d. Add a class rule named "small" to change the numbers of the ordered list to lower case alpha characters (*Hint*: Set the list-style-type to `lower-alpha`.)

e. Add a style rule to the `<div>` tag that sets the left margin to 25 pixels.

f. Save the external style sheet.

g. In your text editor, open the **htm_E-5.txt** file from the drive and folder where your Data Files are stored, then save it as **inside.htm** in the water folder where you save your site files. If you are asked whether you want to replace the file, click Yes.

h. Delete the page's basefont style information in the head section.

i. Add `<div>` tags to apply the style defined in Step e to the General Tips section of the page. (*Hint*: There are comments in the page to help you place the opening and closing `<div>` tags in the correct location.)

j. Add `class="small"` to the `<ol>` tag on the page.

k. Place a link to the metro_styles.css style sheet in the page head.

l. Replace Your Name between the address tags with your name, save your work, then display the **inside.htm** file in your browser to make sure the styles have been applied to the page. Your page should match Figure E-21.

m. Save your work and transfer the files to the remote site.

FIGURE E-21

[Home] [Conserving Inside] [Conserving Outside] [Super Saved] [Resources] [Landscaping and Irrigation]

Conservation Tips

Conserving Water Indoors:

Are you using more water than ~~
he or she would imagine. Cutting ~~
surprised at how much money th~~

If you have questions about wat~~
customer surveys, the most comm~~

  a. How can I tell how much we~~
  b. What can I do to conserve ~~
  c. Is my water usage within re~~
  d. What's the average daily wa~~
  e. What if I have a well, doesn~~

If you have ever asked yourself a~~
links below to find your answers.~~

     [General Tips]

You and your water usage:

If you want to know how much w~~
month is listed there.

Water District Household Averag~~

person per day. However, if you are at the high end of the scale or if you are using more water than average, chances are that you can substantially reduce your water usage. Every drop helps . . . *You CAN* make a difference!

General Tips

- Never pour water down the drain when there may be another use for it such as watering a plant or garden, or for cleaning around your home.
- Verify that your home is leak free. Many homes have hidden water leaks. Read your water meter before and after a two-hour period when no water is being used. If the meter does not read exactly the same, there is a leak.
- Repair dripping faucets by replacing washers. If your faucet is dripping at a rate of one drop per second, you can expect to waste 2,700 gallons per year. This adds to the cost of water and sewer utilities and adds to your water bill.
- Retrofit all household faucets by installing aerators with flow restrictors to slow the flow of water.
- Evaporative coolers require a seasonal maintenance check-up. For more water efficient cooling, check your evaporative coolers annually. Insulate your water pipes. You'll get hot water faster and avoid wasting water while it heats up.
- Install water softening systems only when necessary. Save water and salt by running the minimum amount of regenerations necessary to maintain water softness. Turn softeners off while on vacation.

In the Kitchen

- Operate automatic dishwashers and clothes washers only when they are fully loaded. Set the water level for the size of load you are using.
- When washing dishes by hand, fill one sink or basin with soapy water. Quickly rinse under a slow-moving stream from the faucet.
- Store drinking water in the refrigerator. Don't let the tap run while you are waiting for cool water to flow.
- Do not use running water to thaw meat or other frozen foods. Defrost food overnight in the refrigerator or use the defrost setting on your microwave.
- Kitchen sink disposals require lots of water to operate properly. Start a compost pile as an alternate method of disposing of food waste, instead of using a garbage disposal. Garbage disposals also can add 50 percent to

▼ INDEPENDENT CHALLENGE 2 (CONTINUED)

Advanced Challenge Exercises

- Add an embedded style section to the inside.htm page under the link to the external style sheet, just above the `</head>` tag.
- Add a style to the embedded style sheet that uses the class `small` to change the numbers of the ordered list to lower roman numerals. Add the class name to the ordered list.
- Add an inline style to the `<body>` tag of the page to set the background color to #FFFF99.
- Save your changes to the inside.htm page, and display the file in the browser to check your styles.
- Write a paragraph describing your observations of the precedence of external, embedded, and inline styles.
- Transfer your completed pages to your remote directory.

▼ INDEPENDENT CHALLENGE 3

Style sheets are used to preserve a consistent look for the pages of a Web site. You want to use style sheets, but you are concerned about accessibility and browser support.

a. Go to the Student Online Companion for this text, locate the link for this unit, then go to the W3C Web Accessibility page and review the information for CSS techniques. Write one or two paragraphs answering the following questions:

- How can the use of style sheets make your site more user-friendly?
- What are the issues of accessibility when using style sheets?
- What methods are included in CSS2 that allow content to be generated from style sheets?
- Add your name and today's date to the top of your paper.
- Print the paper.

b. Use the search engine of your choice to research the two versions of CSS: CSS1 and CSS2. Investigate the browser support for CSS1 and CSS2, and then write one or two paragraphs answering the following questions:

- When were the CSS1 and CSS2 versions introduced?
- Which browsers fully support CSS1 and CSS2?
- Which browsers partially support CSS1 and CSS2?
- Add your name and today's date to the top of your paper, then print it.

▼ INDEPENDENT CHALLENGE 4

Now that you've studied style sheets to define styles for Web pages, you are ready to add style sheets to the pages on your Web site.

a. Determine how the different types of style sheets can be used in your Web site. You need to add at least one embedded and one external style sheet to your site.

b. Add at least one style that formats the entire page body.

c. Add at least one style that formats a class.

d. Add at least one style that formats the `<div>` tag.

e. Place links to your external style sheet in the appropriate pages of your site.

f. Transfer your external style sheet and your edited files to the remote location.

▼ VISUAL WORKSHOP

Work progresses on your Bits and PCs Web site and you decide to use an external style sheet to format your pages. In your text editor, open the **htm_E-6.txt** file from the drive and folder where your Data Files are stored, then save it as **index.htm** in the bitspcs folder where you save your site files. Create an external style sheet, then save it as **bit_style.css** in the bitspcs folder where you save your site files. Your external style sheet should format your index page as shown in Figure E-22. Use classes to center the navigation bar and to format the contact information at the bottom of the page. Replace info in the e-mail link label at the bottom of the page with your name. (*Hint*: Both the level-one and level-three headings are formatted with the color #3333FF and the links, including the visited ones, are formatted with the color #006699. Level-one headings are 30 pixels in size.)

FIGURE E-22

Bits and PCs

Filling all your computer needs for 20 years!

[Home] [History Information] [Advertised Specials] [Products] [Services]

For 20 years Bits and PCs has been serving all your computer needs. Now, we invite you to join us in celebrating our 20th anniversary!

To celebrate our success we are giving away cash and prizes worth more than $10,000. Hidden throughout our Bits and PCs History pages are answers to our weekly trivia game. Find those answers and submit the trivia game of the week for a chance to win our weekly drawing. Who knows? You might be next!

For information about sales, service or store hours contact info@bitsPCs.com

Working with Tables

OBJECTIVES

Plan a table	
Create a simple table	
Span and align columns and rows	
Format table content	
Format borders	
Modify table backgrounds	
Change table dimensions	
Position page elements	

Although paragraphs are a useful way to present most Web page information, certain types of content require other formats. HTML includes extensive support for one of the most common alternate layouts: the **table**, which allows you to present information in a grid of columns and rows, creating a compact list of items and their related details. Tables are also often used as a method for laying out Web pages. Once you plan and create a table, you can align columns and rows, adjust cells so they span multiple columns or rows, and format cell data, borders, and backgrounds. You can also easily change the table size and its position on the page. Your current project at Paradise Mountain is to add an activities and events calendar with a listing of activity days and times. Formatting the activity information using a table allows Web page users to easily find information about activities that interest them.

Planning a Table

A table is a useful way to summarize many types of information, including the differences among a list of items or the results of a database search. You can also use tables to tailor Web page design by controlling element positioning. As shown in Figure F-1, table data is organized into rows and columns; a **row** is a single horizontal line of data, and a **column** is a single vertical line of data. The intersection of a row and a column is a single unit of table data called a **cell**. Many aspects of tables are customizable. Figure F-1 also shows several customizations, including table heading formatting, spans, cell alignment, background color, and a caption. Figure F-2 shows the code for the sample table. Table F-1 summarizes the HTML tags used to create a table. As you prepare to create the table for the Paradise Mountain activities page, you plan your table layout.

DETAILS

Some of the many attributes for controlling a table's appearance include:

- ### Structure and border
  You can customize a table to include exactly the number of columns and rows that your data requires. You also can modify a table's structure so that one or more cells span multiple rows or columns. By default, each cell is slightly separated from the cells that surround it. To make the boundaries between cells clearer, you can add cell borders to a table. HTML allows you to customize border color and thickness.

- ### Alignment
  Just as with standard Web page elements or paragraphs of text, you can align cell contents along the cell's right or left edges, or center it between the two edges. Additionally, you can set the vertical alignment flush with the top or bottom cell border, or centered between the two borders. The default alignment for a table cell is horizontally left aligned and vertically centered.

- ### Background
  By default, a Web page table is transparent, showing the same background image or color as the Web page. However, you can apply a custom background color to the entire table, specific rows, or individual cells.

- ### Dimensions
  In addition to customizing the number of rows and columns in the table structure, you can specify the sizes of table elements, as well as the spacing between them. You can set the entire table to a fixed width or height, or you can specify table dimensions as a percentage of the window size. You also can set the amount of blank space around the contents of each cell, as well as the amount of space between cells.

- ### Positioning
  Because tables are so flexible and customizable, Web designers have found many uses for them. Tables are commonly used to position page elements and control page layout. While the W3C recommends CSS over tables as a method of controlling element positioning, some complicated designs are easier to achieve when tables are used.

TABLE F-1: HTML table tags

tag(s)	function
`<table>...</table>`	Defines start and end of table contents
`<tr>...</tr>`	Marks contents of each table row
`<th>...</th>`	Marks contents of a table heading cell and applies table heading format
`<td>...</td>`	Marks contents of a table data cell
`<caption>...</caption>`	When coded within a table, formats text to appear as a table caption

FIGURE F-1: Table components with customizable features

Table caption

Sample Table

Column

Table heading cells

Cell B   Cell C   Cell D

Cell A spans two rows

Cell A rowspan="2"

Cell E spans two columns

Cell E: colspan="2"   Cell F

Background color (bgcolor) applied to cells

Row

Cell J valign="top"

Background color (bgcolor) applied to row

Table data cell

Cell H align="center"   Cell I, align="right"

Cell G, valign="bottom"

Cell alignment

FIGURE F-2: Sample table code

```
<style>
<!--
body, td, th    {
        color: #000000;
}
.darkbkgnd    {
        color: #CCCCCC;
        font-weight: bold;
}
-->
</style>
</head>
<body>
<table border="1" width="500" height="500" cellpadding="5" cellspacing="5">
    <caption><h2>Sample Table</h2></caption>
<tr>
    <td rowspan="2" bgcolor="#336699" width="25%" height="66%"
class="darkbkgnd" >Cell A<br />rowspan="2" </td><th height="33%"
width="25%">Cell B</td><th>Cell C</td><th>Cell D</td>
    </tr>
<tr>
    <td colspan="2" width="50%" height="33%">Cell E: colspan="2"</td><td>Cell
F</td>
    </tr>

<tr bgcolor="#CCCCCC">
<td bgcolor="#99CCFF" valign="bottom" height="33%">Cell G,
valign="bottom"</td><td align="center">Cell H align="center"</td><td
align="right">Cell I, align="right"</td><td valign="top">Cell J
valign="top"</td>
    </tr>
</table>
```

Style sheet formatting

Table caption

Rowspan in table data cell

Cell content formatting from style sheet

Opening table tag with attributes

Cell width

Bgcolor applied to row

Bgcolor applied to cell

Cell H content

Design Matters

Formatting cell contents

When working with tables it is best to avoid the use of <font>...</font> tags for formatting large areas of page content. Because browsers treat each table cell as a separate window, cell content does not inherit properties set using standard HTML formatting, such as the <font>...</font> tag outside of the table. (**Standard HTML** is HTML without the benefit of style sheets and

XHTML or DHTML enhancements.) A better method is to use CSS formatting to declare the font attributes for all table content. You can use the basefont tag to specify a formatting style for the page in order to code for **backward compatibility**—the ability to ensure that your page is displayed as expected in older browsers. In most browsers, CSS formatting overrides standard HTML formatting.

HTML

Creating a Simple Table

Tables allow you to arrange information in columns and rows, making the information easier to read and understand. However, tables require the use of several nested elements. Therefore, the code to create even a simple table is longer than most other HTML markup. Tables begin and end with `<table>...</table>`— the parent tag for all tables. Table content is contained within table cells. The two types of table cells are **table heading cells**, which are marked with `<th>...</th>`, and **table data cells**—marked with `<td>...</td>`. All table cells must be contained within a **table row**—designated by the opening and closing table row tags, `<tr>...</tr>`. The default alignment for table data cell content is left-aligned and aligned to the vertical middle. The default alignment for table heading content is horizontally aligned in the center and vertically aligned in the middle. Table heading content also appears as boldfaced type, making column or row headings stand out from the contents of the regular data cells. The Activities Center director has given you some text files with information about daily youth-centered activities. You added head and document formatting codes and think that the information will be best displayed in table format.

STEPS

1. **Start your text editor, open the file htm_F-1.txt from the place where you store your Data Files, inspect the code, then save it as youth.htm in the paradise/activities folder in the place where you store your site files**

   The file contains the youth activity information that you received, along with a transitional doctype declaration, the meta character set tag, a link to your style sheet, link tags, and the image logo tag that was added earlier. As shown in Figure F-3, the file also contains several comment tags.

2. **Click after the comment tag that reads `<!-- Start table and row 1 here -->`, press [Enter], type `<table border="1">`, then press [Enter]**

   Your code starts the table and sets a one-pixel border. You'll learn more about borders in another lesson.

3. **Type `<tr>`, click before the comment that reads `<!-- End row 1 here -->`, then type `</tr>`**

   Your code starts and ends the first row. You want to make the first row a heading row.

4. **Click below `<tr>` and before the word Day, type `<th>`, click after Day, type `</th>`, then type opening and closing table heading tags before and after the following items: Time, Activity, Location, Cost, and Notes**

   You have formatted the cells in the first table row as table heading cells.

5. **Click after each of the next Start row comments, press [Enter], press [Delete], then type `<tr>`**

6. **Click before each of the End row comments, type `</tr>`, then press [Enter]**

7. **Type `<td>` before and `</td>` after each of the words or phrases listed in Table F-2**

8. **Click before `<!-- End table here -->`, type `</table>`, save your work, start your Web browser, then preview the file youth.htm in your browser**

   As shown in Figure F-4, the data for the Sunday and Monday events appears in a table of six columns and three rows. The rest of the week's activities need to be added to the table.

9. **Open another text editor window, open the file htm_F-2.txt from the place where you store your Data Files, click before `<tr>` under the comment at the top of the page, then select and copy all of the code and text to the end of the document**

10. **Return to the youth.htm file, click in the blank line above `</table>`, paste the code, then save your work**

    Your table now lists all of the youth activity events.

FIGURE F-3: Text file with XHTML elements and comment tags

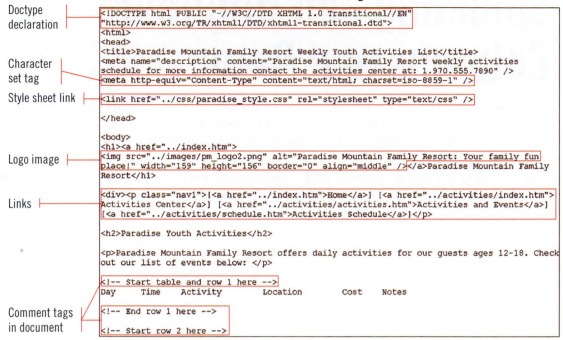

Doctype declaration

Character set tag

Style sheet link

Logo image

Links

Comment tags in document

```
<!DOCTYPE html PUBLIC "-//W3C//DTD XHTML 1.0 Transitional//EN"
"http://www.w3.org/TR/xhtml1/DTD/xhtml1-transitional.dtd">
<html>
<head>
<title>Paradise Mountain Family Resort Weekly Youth Activities List</title>
<meta name="description" content="Paradise Mountain Family Resort weekly activities
schedule for more information contact the activities center at: 1.970.555.7890" />
<meta http-equiv="Content-Type" content="text/html; charset=iso-8859-1" />
<link href="../css/paradise_style.css" rel="stylesheet" type="text/css" />

</head>

<body>
<h1><a href="../index.htm">
<img src="../images/pm_logo2.png" alt="Paradise Mountain Family Resort: Your family fun
place!" width="159" height="156" border="0" align="middle" /></a>Paradise Mountain Family
Resort</h1>

<div><p class="nav1">[<a href="../index.htm">Home</a>] [<a href="../activities/index.htm">
Activities Center</a>] [<a href="../activities/activities.htm">Activities and Events</a>]
[<a href="../activities/schedule.htm">Activities Schedule</a>]</p>

<h2>Paradise Youth Activities</h2>

<p>Paradise Mountain Family Resort offers daily activities for our guests ages 12-18. Check
out our list of events below: </p>

<!-- Start table and row 1 here -->
Day      Time     Activity        Location        Cost     Notes

<!-- End row 1 here -->

<!-- Start row 2 here -->
```

FIGURE F-4: Youth activities table code output

TABLE F-2: Opening and closing points for table cells

row	cell 1	cell 2	cell 3	cell 4	cell 5	cell 6
2	`<td>Sunday </td>`	`<td>5-7 p.m.</td>`	`<td>Build Your Own Pizza</td>`	`<td>Community Hall</td>`	`<td>$3.00 </td>`	`<td>This... another.</td>`
3	`<td>Monday </td>`	`<td>2-4 p.m. </td>`	`<td>Air Hockey Tournament</td>`	`<td>Activities Center</td>`	`<td>Free </td>`	`<td>Show... skills</td>`

Clues to Use

Using comments in tables

A useful tool in creating tables is the **comment tag**, which you can use to create statements such as (`<!-- Comment information goes here. -->`). You can insert such tags in your code to make notations and to make it easier to find specific content when you want to edit it later. Browsers do not display code or text that is contained within comment tags. Comment tags can contain one or more lines as well as other tags as long as the comment starts with `<!-`, and ends with `-->`.

UNIT F
HTML

Spanning and Aligning Columns and Rows

A basic table contains cells of data arranged in columns and rows. However, sometimes the contents of a cell apply to more than one row or column. You can mark a single cell to **span**—cover or become part of—multiple rows or columns by using attributes in the <th> or <td> tags. When used with a numeric value, the **rowspan** attribute causes a cell to span multiple rows. Likewise, the **colspan** attribute with a numeric value causes the cell to span multiple columns. The Notes column at the end of the youth activities table contains more information than the rest of the table cells. You think the content would look better positioned in a separate row that spans the width of the table below the other information for each day's event.

STEPS

1. **With your youth.htm page code open, drag to select <th>Notes</th> in row 1, then press [Delete]**

   You removed the Notes table heading because you are going to reposition the information from that column in a row located under the details for each item.

2. **Click just after <td>$3.00</td> in row 2, press [Enter], type </tr>, press [Enter] twice, then type <tr>**

   You ended the row after the cost column and started a new row, which contains the information formerly in the Notes column.

> **QUICK TIP**
>
> The process of spanning table rows is very similar to spanning columns. Instead of using the colspan attribute in a <th> or <td> tag, you use rowspan.

3. **Click after td in the opening table data tag that starts the next line of code, press [Spacebar], then type colspan="5"**

   You caused the content of the cell in the new row to span the width of your table. You did not have to code a second end table row tag because the second row used the existing </tr> tag.

4. **Repeat Steps 2 and 3 in each of the remaining rows, then save your work**

   Your code should resemble that shown in Figure F-5, which shows the code for the Monday and Tuesday events.

5. **Click the browser program button on the taskbar, then reload youth.htm**

   The information from the notes column is now formatted in a separate single-cell row that spans the width of the table. You think the dollar amounts in the fifth column would look better aligned to the right.

6. **Click the text editor program button on the taskbar to return to the youth.htm document code**

7. **Locate the opening table data tag for the row 2 cell that contains the content $3.00, click after td in the tag, press [Spacebar], then type align="right"**

8. **Repeat Step 7 to align the text for all the other cells in the Cost column, then save your work and reload the youth.htm page in the browser**

   As shown in Figure F-6, the text in the column containing the cost information is aligned to the right, enabling the decimal points in the monetary amounts to line up, but the table requires additional formatting.

FIGURE F-5: Web document containing code for cells spanning rows

```
<tr>
<td>Monday</td> <td>2-4 p.m.</td>        <td>Air Hockey Tournament</td>  <td>Activities
Center</td>        <td>Free</td>
</tr>

<tr>

<td colspan="5">Show off your air hockey skills</td>

</tr><!-- End row 3 here -->

<!-- Insert copied table rows and data below this comment -->

<tr>
<td>Tuesday</td>          <td>10 a.m. - noon</td> <td>Skateboard Instruction and
Demonstration</td>        <td>Skate Park</td>        <td>Free</td>
</tr>

<tr>

<td colspan="5">
<td>Pick up tips and tricks from some of the region's best skateboarders, then practice
what you've learned. All are welcome to watch, but helmets and permission slips are
required for guests wishing to take an active part in this event. Safety equipment is
available for rent at a nominal fee. Contact the Activities Center for more
information.</td></tr>
```

New closing and opening row tags split row

Colspan attribute extends cell to width of several cells

FIGURE F-6: Table containing Notes information in spanned rows

Notes column information moved from last column to cell spanning five columns

Right-aligned content

[Home] [Activities Center] [Activities and Events] [Activities Schedule]

Paradise Youth Activities

Paradise Mountain Family Resort offers daily activities for our guests ages 12-18. Check out our list of events below:

Day	Time	Activity	Location	Cost
Sunday	5-7 p.m.	Build Your Own Pizza	Community Hall	$3.00
This activity gives youthful guests a chance to get to know one another.				
Monday	2-4 p.m.	Air Hockey Tournament	Activities Center	Free
Show off your air hockey skills				
Tuesday	10 a.m. - noon	Skateboard Instruction and Demonstration	Skate Park	Free
Pick up tips and tricks from some of the region's best skateboarders, then practice what you've learned. All are welcome to watch, but helmets and permission slips are required for guests wishing to take an active part in this event. Safety equipment is available for rent at a nominal fee. Contact the Activities Center for more information.				
Wednesday	10 a.m. - noon	Skateboard Competition	Skate Park	Free
Pre-registration and parental permission required for all contestants. Contestants compete for resort merchandise. All contestants must wear approved safety equipment, which is available for rent at a nominal fee.				
Thursday	2-4 p.m.	Water Volleyball	Family Pool	Free
Everyone Welcome				
Friday	7 - 10 p.m.	Youth Dance	Community Hall	$2.00

Clues to Use

Aligning tables and table content

By default, all table contents are vertically centered. Table data contents are horizontally left-aligned and table heading cells are horizontally centered. You can customize the horizontal alignment of a table and its contents using an attribute common to many Web page elements—the align attribute. When set in the <tr>, <th>, and <td> tags, the align attribute determines the alignment of row or cell contents, overriding the defaults. Possible values for align are left, center, and right. When the align attribute is applied to the opening <table> tag, it affects the horizontal alignment of the entire table on the page, but does not affect the alignment of the content within the table cells. You can also control the vertical alignment of table content using the valign attribute. When applied to the <tr>, <th>, or <td> tags, the valign attribute controls the vertical placement of content within the cell. Possible vertical alignment options are top, middle and bottom. Note, however, that valign is not a supported attribute of the <table> tag.

HTML

Formatting Table Content

You can use table attributes to control the amount of space around cell content. The **cellpadding** attribute allows you to control the amount of space between the cell wall and its content, and **cellspacing** allows you to control the amount of space between table cells. You specify both attributes in the opening table tag, not in the <tr>, <td>, or <th> tags. By default, table cells take on the basefont or style sheet formatting specified for the rest of the page. When no formatting attributes are specified in the head section through CSS or the basefont tag, tables use the default browser formatting style. Tables do not take on formatting attributes specified outside of the table in the body section of a document through font or character-formatting tags. The content of your table data cells seems too close to the cell borders. In addition, the double-spaced format looks out of place in the table, so you decide to add table and style sheet formatting to make the table text more readable.

STEPS

1. Click the text editor program button on the taskbar to return to the youth.htm page code

2. Click just after border="1" in the opening table tag, press [Spacebar], type
   `cellpadding="5" cellspacing="5"`, then save your work

   The cellpadding attribute adds five pixels of space between the inner cell walls and the content for each table data and table heading cell. The cellspacing attribute adds five pixels of space between each of the table cells.

3. Click the browser program button on the taskbar, then reload the youth.htm page

   As shown in Figure F-7, the inner cell borders have expanded to five pixels in width, and additional space appears between the cell walls and the cell content.

   > **TROUBLE**
   > If you do not have a style sheet, copy the CSS folder and contents from the Unit F folder in the place where you store your Data Files.

4. Use your file management system to find your paradise_style.css style sheet in your
   paradise\css folder in the place where you save your site files, right-click your style sheet file name or icon, point to Open With on the shortcut menu, then click your text editor name

   Your style sheet opens in a separate instance of your text editor program, allowing you to keep your youth.htm page open. (If you did not complete the Unit E lessons, you may copy the css folder, which contains a modified version of the style sheet, from the Unit_F Data Files to your paradise folder in the place where you save your site files.)

5. Click just after } at the end of the body style rule, press [Enter] twice, then type the following code, pressing [Enter] after each line:

```
td, th {
        line-height: 1em;
        color: #000033;
}
```

   > **TROUBLE**
   > If your line spacing remains unchanged, make sure that you did not type a space between the line-height number (1) and "em".

6. Save your style sheet, then reload your youth.htm page in your browser

   The double line spacing has been removed from the text within the cells, as shown in Figure F-8, making it appear more compact, and the text color has been changed to a darker blue.

Expanded space
between cells
(cellspacing)

Additional space
within cells
(cellpadding)

Line formatting
changes display
of text

Clues to Use

Using CSS with tables

Prior to CSS, the only method of formatting table content was to set HTML formatting tags inside each cell. However, CSS formatting allows you to set td and th style rules to specify attributes for table cells without applying those formatting commands to each cell individually. This ability to apply style sheet formatting to table cells gives you more flexibility than ever in planning your page design.

Formatting Borders

Just as you can control the arrangement of cells in a table, you can also alter the properties of the borders between cells. By assigning a value in pixels to the **border attribute** in the `<table>` tag, you can change the thickness of the table's outside border. As you have already seen, when the border attribute is present with a value of 1 in the opening `<table>` tag, cell borders appear as lines one pixel wide. However, if the border is set equal to zero, or if the attribute is not present, cells do not display any borders. Setting a value greater than "1" causes the border to appear with a thicker line. In addition to the border attribute, the opening table tag accepts other attributes for controlling the appearance of table borders. You can set the **bordercolor** attribute to control the color of the table border. You can also set the **bordercolorlight** and **bordercolordark** attributes to apply a highlighting effect to your table borders. Table F-3 summarizes border attributes. You want to customize the look of your table by formatting the table borders.

STEPS

1. **Click the youth.htm text editor program button on the taskbar to open that instance of your text editor, click after cellspacing="5" in the opening table tag, press [Spacebar], then type `bordercolor="#99CCFF"` and save your file**
   You formatted your table borders with a light blue color.

2. **Click the browser program button on your taskbar, then reload your youth.htm file**
   The table is displayed with a light blue border surrounding the table and all of the cells. You would like to test the page with a two-color border.

3. **Click the youth.htm text editor program button on the taskbar, then click between bordercolor and the equal sign in the bordercolor attribute**

4. **Type `light` so that the attribute reads bordercolorlight="#99CCFF"**
   Bordercolorlight causes the browser to display the specified color along the top and left borders of the table and all of the table cells.

5. **Click after the closing quotation mark in the bordercolorlight attribute, press [Spacebar], then type `bordercolordark="#000033"`**
   The bordercolordark attribute causes the bottom and right edges of the table and cell borders to display the specified color. You would like to make your table borders thicker and reduce the space between cells.

6. **Click just after the 1 in table border="1", press [Backspace], then type 2**
   You increased the size of the table borders by 1 pixel.

7. **Click just after the 5 and before the closing quotation mark in the cellspacing value, press [Backspace], type 2, then save your work**
   Your code should resemble that shown in Figure F-9.

8. **Click the browser program button on the taskbar, then reload the youth.htm file in your browser**
   As shown in Figure F-10, there is less space between table cells and the table and cell borders are highlighted with a lighter color on the top and left edges and shadowed with a darker color on the bottom and right edges.

FIGURE F-9: Code for opening table tag

```
<p>Paradise Mountain Family Resort offers daily activities for our guests
ages 12-18. Check out our list of events below: </p>

<!-- Start the table and row 1 here -->

<table border="2" cellpadding="5" cellspacing="2" bordercolorlight="#99CCFF"
bordercolordark="#000033">
  <tr>
    <th>Day</th>  <th>Time</th>   <th>Activity</th>        <th>Location</th>
```

Opening table tag with border attributes

FIGURE F-10: Youth Activities table with border formatting

Light borders

Tighter cell spacing

Dark borders

TABLE F-3: Table and cell border attributes

tag	attribute	description	example
`<table>`	border	Adds borders around the table and around each cell—numeric value determines border thickness	`<table border="5">`
	bordercolor	Specifies the table border color	`<table border="2" bordercolor="#000066">`
	bordercolorlight	Specifies the color to appear on the top and left edges of table and cell borders	`<table border="2" bordercolorlight="#99CCFF">`
	bordercolordark	Specifies the color to appear on the bottom and right edges of table and cell borders	`<table border="2" bordercolorlight="#99CCFF" bordercolordark="#000033">`

Modifying Table Backgrounds

By default, table cells are transparent; the background color or image for the rest of the Web page appears as the table background. However, you can use background and bgcolor attributes in the opening `<table>`, `<tr>`, `<th>`, or `<td>` tags to assign a background image or color to a table or any part of it. You can also apply these attributes as style rules to the table, tr, th, or td selectors. As with other Web page elements, it is important to use table background color wisely and sparingly to enhance your page content, rather than overwhelm it. You want to add color to the heading and notes rows in the youth activities table to add aesthetic value and to make it easier to read.

STEPS

1. Click the paradise_style.css instance of the text editor on the taskbar

2. Click after } of the td, th style rule, press [Enter] twice, then type the following code, pressing [Enter] after each line:

```
th      {
        background-color: #6699CC;
        color: #336633;
}
```

The code near the top of your style sheet appears, as shown in Figure F-11. You set a new rule to override the style set in your td, th style rule. According to the rules of CSS proximity, the rule closest to the tag—the rule furthest down on the style sheet—takes precedence over (overrides) any other rules because it is read last. Your new rule gives all table heading cells a blue background and uses the same green color you used in your page heading. You think the notes rows should stand out so that they are easier to read.

3. Locate the nav1 class at the bottom of your style sheet, click after the } at the end of the style, press [Enter] twice, then type the following code, pressing [Enter] after each line:

```
.notesrow       {
        background-color: #CCCCFF;
        font-weight: 500;
}
```

You set a style rule to define the formatting of the notes rows of your table. The background color for each specified row will be a lighter shade of blue than the background of the heading row. Your font will be heavier. The bottom of your style sheet should resemble the code shown in Figure F-12.

4. Save your work, return to your youth.htm code, then locate the table data cell with the content that begins This activity gives...

5. Click just after colspan="5", press [Spacebar], then type `class="notesrow"`

6. Repeat Step 5 for the remaining rows to which colspan="5" has been applied

7. Save your work, click the browser program button on the taskbar, then reload your youth.htm page

As shown in Figure F-13, the header row background is a steel blue color and the notes rows are light blue.

QUICK TIP

To locate code quickly, press [Ctrl][Home] to place the insertion point at the top of the document, click Edit on the menu bar, then click Find. Type the text you are looking for in the Find what text box, then click Find Next. The text editor highlights the first instance of the text you typed. To find the next instance, click Find Next again.

Clues to Use

Adding a background image to a table

In addition to the bgcolor attribute, the most recent versions of most browser applications support the background attribute for the `<table>`, `<th>`, and `<td>` tags. You can specify the background attribute for the table in the body tag or you can use CSS to set your background image as follows:

```
background-image: url(../images/filename.gif).
```
You cannot apply a background to a table row. Because table background properties are not fully supported by all browsers, be sure to test your pages for readability in multiple browsers both with and without table background colors and images.

FIGURE F-11: Style sheet with new th and td style rules

```
body        {
            font-family: Verdana, Arial, Helvetica, sans-serif;
            font-size: 14px;
            color: #333366;
            background-color: #FFFFFF;
            line-height: 2em;
            background-image: url(../images/pm_bkgnd2.gif);
            margin-left: 0px;
            margin-top: 5px;
            margin-right: 0px;

}

td, th    {
            line-height: 1em;
            color: #000033;

}

th          {
            background-color: #6699CC;
            color: #336633;

}
```

Style rule for table data and table heading cells

New table heading style rule overrides background and text colors

FIGURE F-12: New class style rule for notes row

```
.second_bul      {
        list-style-image: url(../images/pm_bul2.png);

}

.nav1    {
        text-align: center;

}

.notesrow        {
        background-color: #CCCCFF;
        font-weight: 500;

}
```

New class rule

FIGURE F-13: Youth Activities table with style sheet formatting applied to heading and rows

Formatted table rows

Changing Table Dimensions

As with other page elements, you can customize table dimensions using the height and width attributes in the `<table>`, `<th>`, and `<td>` tags. Because all the cells in a row are displayed at the same height and all the cells in a column are displayed at the same width, you only need to set either dimension once for each row or column. Table measurements are flexible: You can specify a table width as a percentage, then set a fixed pixel width for one or more columns. This allows any columns in which no specific sizes have been set to expand or contract with the size of the browser window for a more effective design. You can also add the **nowrap attribute** to a table cell to prevent its contents from wrapping to the next line. Dimension values applied to the `<table>` tag are in relation to the browser window. Values for the `<th>` and `<td>` tags are based on the size of the table. You noticed that some page elements, including your page heading, wrap to a second line at lower resolutions or when the window is made smaller. You want to use table attributes to control these problems.

STEPS

1. **With your youth.htm page open in your browser, click the Restore Down button** ⧉ **in the upper-right corner of the browser, then, if necessary, drag the right browser border to the left until the page heading wraps to a second line**

    As shown in Figure F-14, the page heading wraps to a second line when the window size is reduced.

2. **Click the youth.htm instance of the text editor, click before `<h1>` under the opening body tag, type `<table border="0" cellpadding="0" cellspacing="0" width="800">`, then press [Enter]**

3. **Type `<tr><td nowrap>`, click after `</h1>`, type `</td></tr></table>`, then save your work**

    You used table width settings to prevent your page heading from wrapping. You would like to apply similar settings to one of the columns in your Youth Activities table.

4. **Locate the opening heading tag for the Time column in the youth activities table, click just after th, press [Spacebar], then type `nowrap width="125"`**

5. **Replace Your Name in the Modified by paragraph at the bottom of the page with your own name, update the date, save your work, then print your page code**

6. **Click the browser program button on the taskbar, reload the page, then drag the right browser border to the right and to the left**

    As Figure F-15 shows, the page heading no longer wraps, and the content of each cell in the Time column is displayed on a single line. Because all cells in a column conform to the widest cell, there is no need to set the width properties on the other cells in the column.

FIGURE F-14: Page heading and cell contents wrap in resized window

Heading wraps in resized browser window

Time cells wrap to next line

FIGURE F-15: Table attributes prevent heading and cell content from wrapping

Heading does not wrap in resized window

Time cell contents remain on one line

Design Matters

Using nested and stacked tables

You can use **nested tables**—tables that are fully contained within the cell of another table—to produce more complex page designs. You set width and height percentage values for a nested table in relation to the size of the parent cell. To gain even more control over your page layout, you can stack tables. **Stacked tables** are those in which one table ends before another begins. Stacked table sizes are not dependent upon one another, meaning that you can stack a page heading table of one width on top of a navigation table that is set at a different width. When table alignment values are also set, you can have more control over the placement of your page elements.

Positioning Page Elements

Although tables were originally developed to display data in a grid, designers have found other innovative uses for them. One of the most popular uses of tables is to create layouts that HTML does not otherwise support. For example, basic HTML codes do not allow you to position elements in specific locations in the window. However, by placing elements in a table that does not display any borders and by adding blank cells of fixed widths, you can position the table contents anywhere on the page. Now that you have experience using tables, you want to try your hand at a two-column layout. You have noticed that your resort Contact page is very long, and you think the content would fit better in two columns.

STEPS

QUICK TIP

Although most recent versions of popular browsers support new methods for placing elements, many Web page designers still prefer to use tables because they are supported by older browsers.

1. **Close any files that you have open in your text editor, open the htm_F-3.txt file in your text editor from the place where you store your Data Files, then save it as contact.htm in your paradise site folder, replacing the original file**

   The file, which contains the doctype declaration, the meta characters tag, and a link to your style sheet, replaces your original contact.htm.

2. **Click before `<h1>` under the opening body tag, type `<table border="0" cellpadding="0" cellspacing="0" width="800">`, then press [Enter]**

3. **Type `<tr><td nowrap>`, click after `</h1>`, type `</td></tr></table>`, then save your work**

   You used the table data cell settings that you used in the previous lesson to prevent the heading from wrapping when the window is resized.

4. **Click before `<h3>Reservations</h3>`, type `<table width="90%" align="center">`, press [Enter], type `<tr>`, press [Enter], then type `<td width="50%">`**

   You started creating a table that will appear at 90% of the window size, then you specified that the first cell will be 50% of that table width. The table will be centered on the page.

5. **Click before `<h3>Paradise Garden Day Spa and Fitness Center</h3>`, type `</td>`, press [Enter], then type `<td>`**

   You ended the first cell and started a second. Because the first cell has reserved 50% of the width, there is no need to specify 50% for the second cell.

6. **Click after `</p>` of the paragraph with the id "info", type `</td>`, press [Enter], type `</tr>`, press [Enter], then type `</table>`**

7. **Save your page, click the browser program button on the taskbar, then open your contact.htm page from your paradise folder in the place where you save your site files**

   As shown in Figure F-16, the content now appears in two columns, but the columns do not align at the top. In addition, some of the content in the left column seems to be crowding the content in the right column.

8. **Return to the contact.htm file in your text editor, locate the table row tag above the table data tag containing the level-three heading text of Reservations, click just after tr inside the `<tr>` tag, press [Spacebar], then type `valign="top"`**

   Because you set the vertical alignment in the row, you do not have to set it in either of the table data cells.

9. **Click just after `align="center"` in the opening table tag of the same table, press [Spacebar], type `cellpadding="10"`, update the "Page modified by" information, save your work, then reload it in the browser and print the Web page**

   As shown in Figure F-17, the cellpadding applied to the opening table tag affects both cells, and the content in the left cell no longer crowds the content in the right.

10. **Close all files and programs, then transfer your files to your remote directory**

FIGURE F-16: Web page with borderless table creates two columns

Columns 1 and 2 not aligned at top

Narrow spacing between columns

FIGURE F-17: Table content aligned and padded

Vertical alignment set in row brings content of both cells to top

Cellpadding adds extra space between columns

Practice

▼ CONCEPTS REVIEW

Name the function of each section of code indicated in Figure F-18.

FIGURE F-18

```
1   <table border="1" width="70%" cellspacing="2" cellpadding="2" align="center">                            9
2   <tr>
3   <th>Hand Care</th>
    </tr>                                                                                                    8

4   <tr>
    <td>Deluxe spa manicure (with paraffin treatment)</td><td>$40.00</td>
    </tr>                                                                                                    7

    <tr>
    <td>Deluxe spa manicure (with glycolic treatment)</td><td>$40.00</td>
    </tr>

    <tr>
5   <td>French manicure</td><td>$30.00</td>
    </tr>

    <tr>
6   <th>Foot Care</th>
    </tr>

    </table>
```

Match each statement with the term it describes.

10. Attribute to span a cell over multiple rows   a. Cell padding
11. Space between the cell content and the cell border   b. Cell spacing
12. Space between table cells   c. Rowspan
13. Descriptive information about a table   d. Width
14. Attribute to resize a table   e. Caption

Select the best answer from the list of choices.

15. **Which one of the following tag sets marks the contents of a header cell?**
    a. `<table>...</table>`
    b. `<th>...</th>`
    c. `<tr>...</tr>`
    d. `<td>...</td>`

16. **Which one of the following inserts a comment into an HTML file?**
    a. `<!--comment -->`
    b. `<comment>`
    c. `<comment />`
    d. `<*comment*>`

17. **Which one of the following attributes creates a cell that spans multiple columns?**
    a. Rowspan
    b. Colspan
    c. Cellpadding
    d. Cellspacing

18. **Which of the following changes the background color of a table element to red?**
    a. background-color: #333366;
    b. color: #333366;
    c. bkcolor: #333366;
    d. tablecolor: #333366;

19. **Which one of the following tag sets creates a table row?**
    a. `<table>…</table>`
    b. `<th>…</th>`
    c. `<tr>…</tr>`
    d. `<td>…</td>`

20. **Which one of the following tag sets marks a cell containing table data?**
    a. `<table>...</table>`
    b. `<th>...</th>`
    c. `<tr>...</tr>`
    d. `<td>...</td>`

▼ SKILLS REVIEW

1. **Plan a table.**
    a. Consider how tables can be used to present the information on the pages of the spa site. What pages should use tables?
    b. How would you structure each table?
    c. Are there any table cells that should span over rows or columns?
    d. How can borders and backgrounds be used to clearly present the table information?
    e. How wide should each table be displayed with respect to the browser window?

2. **Create a simple table.**
    a. In your text editor, open the file **htm_F-4.txt** from the drive and folder where your Data Files are stored, then save it as **hands.htm** to the paradise/spa directory where you save your site files. If you are asked whether you want to replace the file, click Yes.
    b. Copy the **bkg_spa.gif** and **spa_logo.gif** files from the drive and folder where your Data Files are stored, then paste the files to the paradise/images directory. If you are asked whether you want to replace the file, click Yes.
    c. Locate the comment in your **hands.htm** file indicating where the table begins, add the opening `<table>` tag, then delete the comment.
    d. Locate the comment in your file indicating where the table ends and add the closing `</table>` tag, then delete the comment.

e. Using Figure F-19 as a guide, create a table structure using the hand care and foot care data. Delete any `<br />` tags in the table data area, as well as the hyphens before the prices.

f. Save your work and view the **hands.htm** page in your browser.

FIGURE F-19

```
<table border="1">

<tr>
<th>Hand Care</th>
</tr>

<tr>
<td>Deluxe spa manicure (with paraffin treatment)</td><td>$40.00</td>
</tr>

<tr>
<td>Deluxe spa manicure (with glycolic treatment)</td><td>$40.00</td>
</tr>

<tr>
<td>French manicure</td><td>$30.00</td>
</tr>

<tr>
<th>Foot Care</th>
</tr>

<tr>
<td>Peppermint pedicure with foot & leg mask</td><td>$55.00</td>
</tr>

<tr>
<td>Deluxe spa pedicure (paraffin treatment)</td> <td>$60.00</td>
</tr>

<tr>
<td>Soothing foot bath with manicure</td><td>$45.00</td>
</tr>

</table>
```

3. Span and align columns and rows.

a. Span the heading Hand Care over two columns by adding `colspan="2"` to the first `<th>` tag.

b. Span the heading Foot Care over two columns by adding `colspan="2"` to the second `<th>` tag.

c. View the table changes in your browser.

d. Save your work.

4. Format table content.

a. Add one pixel between the cells in the table by adding a cellspacing attribute to the opening table tag. (*Hint*: The opening table tag should now be: `<table border="1" cellspacing="1" >`)

b. Add four pixels between the cells' content and its borders by adding a cellpadding attribute to the opening table tag. (*Hint*: The opening table tag should now be: `<table border="1" cellspacing="1" cellpadding="4">`)

c. Using your text editor, create an external style sheet named **hands_style.css** and save it in your paradise/css directory. (A link to this style sheet is already in the head section of your hands.htm file.) In your hands_style.css file, add a style to change the font color of the table text to #009900. (*Hint*: Add the following style: `td, th {color: #009900;}`)

d. Save your work.

e. Reload the **hands.htm** file in your browser to view the changes to the table.

5. Format borders.

a. In your hands.htm file, change the table border to the color #999999 by adding a bordercolor attribute to the opening table tag. (*Hint*: Add `bordercolor="#999999"` to the opening table tag.)

b. Ensure that the gray color you chose in step 5-a highlights the top and left borders of the table by adding the word **light** to the value **bordercolor**. (*Hint*: the new value should be `bordercolorlight="#999999"`.)

c. Add the color #006633 to the bottom and right borders of the table. (*Hint*: In the opening table tag, add `bordercolordark="#006633"` after bordercolorlight="#999999".)

d. Increase the table border to five pixels by changing border="1" to `border="5"` in the opening table tag.

e. Save your work.

f. View the changes to the table in your browser.

6. Modify table backgrounds.

a. In your hands_style.css style sheet, add a style of `th {background-color: #CCFFCC;}` to format the table headings with a light green color.

b. Bold the table data by adding a style to the **hands_style.css** file of `td {font-weight: bold;}`.

    c. Save your work.

    d. Open the **hands.htm** file in your browser to verify the changes to the table.

7. Change table dimensions.

    a. In your hands.htm file, change the width of your table to 600 pixels by adding `width="600"` to the end of the attribute list in the opening table tag.

    b. Locate the first appearance of `<td>$40.00 </td>` in the table section and add a width attribute of 140 pixels by adding `width="140"` inside the opening td tag.

    c. Align the contents of one of the prices by placing `align="right"` in its opening `<td>` tag.

    d. View the right-aligned price in your browser, then delete the align="right" code from the `<td>` tag.

    e. Save your work.

    f. Verify the changes to the table dimensions by viewing the **hands.htm** page in the browser.

8. Position page elements.

    a. In your hands.htm file, change the width of your table to be displayed at 80% of the window size by changing the width attribute in the opening table tag to `width="80%"`.

    b. Display the second column of the table at 30% of the total table size by changing the width="140" in the opening td tag of the second row in the table to `width="30%"`.

    c. Center the table in the browser window by adding `align="center"` to the opening table tag.

    d. Save the changes to your **hands.htm** file.

    e. Verify the table changes by viewing the **hands.htm** page in your browser.

    f. Add your name to the hands.htm and hands_style.css pages using comments at the end of the files, then save and print the pages. (*Hint*: Add `<!-- Your Name -->` to each page. In the hands.htm file, place the comment before the `</body>` tag.)

    g. Transfer the files to your remote directory.

▼ INDEPENDENT CHALLENGE 1

As you continue developing the Web site for your resort rental business, Star Vacations, you want to organize your featured resorts using a table.

    a. In your text editor, open the file **htm_F-5.txt** from the drive and folder where your Data Files are stored, then save it as **features.htm** in the vacations folder where you save your site files. If you are asked whether you want to replace the file, click Yes.

    b. Locate the comment tags indicating the place where a table will be used to organize the resort information. Enclose the resort data with opening and closing table tags, then delete the comments.

    c. Add a border of one pixel to the table.

    d. Add opening and closing `<tr>`, `<td>`, and `<th>` tags to structure the resort data, as shown in Figure F-20.

    e. Add five pixels of spacing between cells.

    f. Add 10 pixels of space between the cells' content and border.

FIGURE F-20

Resort	Location	Link
Canyon Ranch	Lenox, MA	Canyon Ranch
Arizona Biltmore	Phoenix, Arizona	Arizona Biltmore
Ojai Valley Inn and Spa	Ojai, Calfornia	Ojai Valley Inn and Spa
Banff Park Lodge	Alberta, Canada	Banff Park Lodge
Tomahawk Resort	Ontario, Canada	Tomahawk Resort

    g. Display the table at 60% of the browser window.

    h. Center the table in the browser window.

    i. Add your name to the address tag at the bottom of the page.

    j. Save your work, display the **features.htm** file in your browser to check your table, then print the file in your browser.

    k. Close all files, then transfer your completed features.htm page to your remote directory.

▼ INDEPENDENT CHALLENGE 1 (CONTINUED)

Advanced Challenge Exercises

- Add a caption of Featured Resorts to the table in your **features.htm** file.
- Save your work and display the **features.htm** file in the browser to check your caption.
- In a separate text editor window, open the file **htm_F-6.txt** from the drive and folder where your Data Files are stored, then save it as **star_style.css** in the vacations folder where you save your site files. If you are asked whether you want to replace the file, click Yes. (The star_style.css is an external style sheet for your features.htm page.)
- Add a style to the **star_style.css** file that formats table captions with Lucida Calligraphy or a serif font.
- Save your **star_style.css** file and display the **features.htm** file in your browser to check the formatting of your table caption. (You do not have to add the link to the style sheet because it was in the data file.) If you do not have the Lucida Calligraphy font on your computer, the caption will be displayed in a substituted serif font.
- Close all files, then transfer your completed pages to your remote directory.

▼ INDEPENDENT CHALLENGE 2

You will use tables along with an external style sheet to organize the water-conservation Web site you are developing for your employer, Metro Water. You decide to start by using a table to organize the links in the navigation bar.

a. In your text editor, open the **htm_F-7.txt** file from the drive and folder where your Data Files are stored, then save it as **resources.htm** in the water folder where you save your site files. If you are asked whether you want to replace the file, click Yes.

b. Replace the Add table here comment with a table structure of one row and six columns where each column is displayed as a table heading. (*Hint*: Type the code for one column, copy it, then paste it five times.)

c. Add a border of one pixel to the table.

d. Add two pixels of space between the cells' content and the border.

e. Add three pixels of space between the table's cells.

f. Add an attribute to display the table at 70% of the browser window.

g. Place each of the six links from the top navigation bar into a table heading cell, then delete the entire top navigation bar.

h. Save your file, then view the navigation table in your browser.

i. Create an external style sheet, then save it as **navstyle.css** in the water folder where you save your site files. Add styles to format the links, as shown in Figure F-21.

j. Add a link in the resources.htm file to the navstyle.css style sheet. (*Hint*: Place the following before the </head> tag:

```
<link href="navstyle.css" rel="stylesheet" type="text/css" /> )
```

FIGURE F-21

```
a:link {
        color:#0066FF;
        text-decoration:underline;
}
a:hover {
        font-weight:bold;
        color:#CC66CC;
        text-decoration:underline;
}
```

k. Refresh the **resources.htm** file in your browser and verify that the styles in the navstyle.css file have been applied to the table links.

l. Add your name as a comment to the bottom of the page, save your work, print the resources.htm and navstyle.css files, then transfer the files to the remote site.

▼ INDEPENDENT CHALLENGE 2 (CONTINUED)

Advanced Challenge Exercises

- ■ Use the search engine of your choice to research the frame attribute for the `<table>` tag.
- ■ Use the frame attribute in the table on your resources.htm file to place borders only on the left and right sides of the cells.
- ■ Save the **resources.htm** file, print it, then view the table in your browser, verifying the change in the cell borders.
- ■ Close all files, then transfer your completed pages to your remote directory.

▼ INDEPENDENT CHALLENGE 3

Tables are used to organize data and to lay out information on a Web site. You want to add tables to your Web site, but first you need to research how you can make them accessible for all users.

Go to the Online Companion for this book, locate the links for this unit, then click the link for the W3C Web Accessibility page and review the information for tables. Write one or two paragraphs answering the following questions about tables that are used to organize data:

- **a.** How can captions be used to increase accessibility?
- **b.** If a caption is not appropriate, how can you use attributes to describe the purpose of the table?
- **c.** What attribute is especially important for tables with cells that span multiple columns or rows?
- **d.** How should row and column headers be identified?
- **e.** Add your name and today's date to the top of your paper, then print it.

Use your favorite search engine to research authoring techniques to ensure HTML tables are easily adaptable for international audiences. Summarize your findings in a paragraph, add your name to the paper, then print the document.

▼ INDEPENDENT CHALLENGE 4

Now that you've used tables to organize data, you are ready to add tables to the pages on your Web site.

- **a.** Determine how tables can be used in your Web site to clearly present the pages' information. Lay out your tables on paper to determine which table properties can best present your site's information. Not all of your Web pages require tables.
- **b.** Create tables on pages where they clearly communicate information to a user.
- **c.** Add row and column spanning where appropriate.
- **d.** Format the table borders and backgrounds to clearly display the information.
- **e.** Position and align the contents of your tables appropriately.
- **f.** Save your work, then print the pages with tables in your browser.
- **g.** Close all files, then transfer your edited files to the remote location.

▼ VISUAL WORKSHOP

Work progresses on your Bits and PCs Web site, and you decide to use a table to advertise specials on hard drives. In your text editor, open the **htm_F-8.txt** file from the drive and folder where your Data Files are stored, then save it as **specials.htm** in the bitspcs folder where you save your site files. If you are asked whether you want to replace the file, click Yes. Replace the comment in the Data File with a table advertising the hard drive specials shown in Figure F-22. Your table should be displayed at a width of 70% of the browser window with a 5-pixel border. There should be two pixels between cells and four pixels around the cell content. Add your name to the bottom of the page before the e-mail link. Save your work, then print the **specials.htm** page in your browser. (*Hint*: Under the opening table tag, use a caption tag to display the text "Hard Drive Specials.".)

FIGURE F-22

Bits and PCs

[Home] [History Information] [Advertised Specials] [Products] [Services]

Hard Drive Specials

Capacity	Manufacturer	Buffer Size	RPM	Price
Internal				
160 GB	Maxtor	8 MB	7200	$49.99
250 GB	Seagate	8 MB	7200	$79.99
300 GB	Maxtor	16 MB	7200	$134.99
External				
80 GB	Western Digital	2 MB	7200	$89.99
300 GB	Maxtor	16 MB	7200	$269.99
400 GB	Seagate	8 MB	7200	$339.99

For information about sales, service or store hours contact Your Name info@bitsPCs.com

Using Forms to Control Input

OBJECTIVES

Plan a form	
Create a text field	
Add radio buttons	
Add check boxes	
Create a pull-down menu	
Add a comment box	
Add a push button	
Connect a form's back end	

In addition to letting you create informational pages for users, HTML also includes methods of making your pages interactive. The main HTML element that makes interactivity possible is a form. A **form** is a set of Web page elements with which you interact to submit a request or provide information. Forms are used for submitting credit card and shipping information for online purchases, completing surveys, and for requesting information. The management team at Paradise Mountain Family Resort wants to use a Web-based survey to find out how resort guests rate the services and activities provided by the resort. You and your Web development team are working to create a Web page form that allows guests to participate in the survey.

Planning a Form

Including a form on your Web site is a simple and straightforward way to allow site visitors to send you feedback or other information. If you are using the Web to sell products or services, forms are vital. As shown in Figure G-1, Web forms can allow users to enter information in several different ways, including predefined choices from which users can select as well as text entry areas. Most forms include several **form fields**—also called **form elements**—such as text boxes or pull-down menus that allow user input. Each field or group of fields is usually next to a **label**—text that explains what information is required in the adjacent field. Before you design your form, you must determine its purpose and the type of information you want to collect. Making those decisions first helps you decide what type of form fields to include. Choosing the right form elements can help ensure that the data you receive meets your needs. You met with Paradise Mountain Family Resort's marketing director to determine what type of information they need to collect. Now it is up to you to review the different types of HTML form fields and to select the most appropriate field for each type of information the director needs.

The types of form fields are:

• **Single-line text box**

A single-line text box is ideal for requesting limited user input, such as a first or last name, or street address. HTML allows you to specify the size of a single-line text box, as well as the maximum character length of user input you want to allow.

• **Check boxes and radio buttons**

Check boxes and radio buttons simplify Web forms by allowing users to select from a list of options. Users can select multiple check boxes, which are ideal for a set of options from which a user might choose none, one, or several—as when choosing pizza toppings. On the other hand, radio buttons limit user input to one choice from a set. Radio buttons are the best choice for a mutually exclusive set of choices, such as T-shirt size (S, M, L, or XL). Because it is difficult to account for all possible choices, it is often a good idea to provide a choice for "none" or "other."

• **Pull-down menus and scroll boxes**

Pull-down menus and scroll boxes both serve a similar function to radio buttons and check boxes: they allow users to make one or more selections from among multiple items. When your list of choices is lengthy, pull-down menus and scroll boxes conserve Web page space. A pull-down menu shows one choice by default, and displays the remaining choices after a user clicks the down arrow. By contrast, a scroll box shows a specified number of choices. Users view hidden options by scrolling through the list.

• **Multiline text areas**

Multiline text areas—often called comment boxes and check boxes—are designed to allow less-structured input by the user. Text areas allow users to make additional comments or ask questions. You can specify the dimensions of this area on the page.

• **Push buttons**

HTML includes code to create two kinds of predefined buttons that users can click to execute common form-related tasks. You can configure one of these buttons to submit the information entered by users to the appropriate processing system. The other button allows users to clear information they have entered and start over without reloading the form.

Single-line text boxes

Pull-down menu

Check boxes

Radio buttons

Textarea comment box

Push buttons

Clues to Use

Dealing with privacy issues

Surveys consistently show that many Web users are concerned that their personal information is not adequately secure when they interact on the Web. The topic of security is important when considering whether your Web site will include forms, which are often designed to collect information that people want to keep as private as possible. A Web designer is not often in a position to decide a company's policy on use of personal information collected from Web users. You can, however, make site users feel more secure by clearly communicating your organization's policy regarding use of the information you request. Nearly all Web sites that request information allow users to select options within the form that keep their information off e-mail and printed material mailing lists. Sometimes organizations want to collect additional information if users are willing to provide it. Be sure your Web page makes it clear that such fields are optional; that way, you avoid losing the business of potential customers who refuse to answer such questions.

Creating a Text Field

The text and fields that compose a Web page form are always surrounded by the `<form>...</form>` tag. Most form fields use the `<input />` tag with attributes that specify the kind of form field and any special characteristics. The required attribute for input elements is **type**. Input tags are self-closed using the cancel mark (/) at the end of the tag. To create a **text field**—also known as a single-line text box—you set the input type attribute value to "text". Text fields are useful for collecting information such as the user's name. Because most form-processing scripts use the name assigned to each form field for matching collected data with processing instructions and output display, another recommended attribute for all forms and form elements is **name.** Table G-1 explains the syntax and attributes for the `<form>...</form>` and `<input />` tags. You want to include text fields to collect guests' names. You will use tables to arrange the form elements.

The nonbreaking spaces in the form hold table cells open until you add form elements.

1. **Start your text editor program, open the file htm_G-1.txt from the place where you store your Data Files, save it using the All Files type as survey.htm in your paradise folder in the place where you save your site files, then inspect the code**
   As shown in Figure G-2, the page is set up in a table-based format and contains several comment tags, with prompts regarding the placement of your form elements. First, the form needs opening and closing form tags.

2. **Locate and select the comment `<!-- Begin Form Here -->`, press [Delete], then type**
   `<form name="survey" action="" method="post">`
   The form name value in the opening form tag identifies the form for processing purposes. To accomplish their designated purpose, forms use methods—such as post and get—and actions. **Post** is used to send information to a server, and **get** is used to retrieve information. The form **action** identifies the script or page used to process the form. Because this form will send survey information to the Marketing Department, you specified the post method. You will specify the form action later.

3. **Scroll to the bottom of the document, select the comment `<!-- End Form Here -->`, press [Delete], then type `</form>`**
   All of the form field elements must be coded between the opening and closing form tags. Notice that the opening and closing form tags surround the form table. Tables make it easy to align form fields.

4. **In the page code, locate and select the comment `<!--Label 1 -->`, press [Delete], type First name:, press [Spacebar], move to the next line, drag to select the comment `<!-- Input First name text field -->`, press [Delete], then type `<input type="text" name="fname" size="20" />`**
   You set the first form prompt label, "First Name", and its matching form field.

Be sure to type the letter "l" (for last name) and not the number "1" in the name value.

5. **Locate and select the Label 2 comment tag, press [Delete], type Last name:, move to the next line, select `<!-- Last name text field -->`, press [Delete], type `<input type="text" name="lname" size="20" />`, then save your work**
   You have created first and last name input elements for your form.

6. **Move to the bottom of the page, locate and select the comment tag `<!-- input, e-mail -->`, press [Delete], then type `<input type="text" name="email" size="100" />`**
   The text box for the e-mail address is considerably longer than the others. Your design team has created the rest of the form labels for you, but you need to insert the form fields.

7. **Save your work, start your Web browser, then open the file survey.htm in your browser**
   The text entry boxes and labels in which users can supply their first name, last name, and e-mail address appear on the Web page, as shown in Figure G-3.

8. **Click in the First name text box, type your first name, press [Tab], type your last name in the Last name text box, press [Tab], then type your e-mail address**
   Your text boxes accept input, but the form requires additional form elements.

```
<p>Dear Valued Guest, </p>
<p>Thank you for taking the time to fill out our guest satisfaction survey. Your answers
help us improve our services at Paradise Mountain Family Resort and are strictly
confidential. None of your personal information will be shared with other organizations.
<br />
 <hr />
<br /></p>
</td>
</tr>
<tr valign="top">
<td>

<!-- Begin Form Here -->
<table border="0" width="90%" id="frm_table" cellpadding="4" align="center">
  <tr valign="top">
    <td align="right" width="25%" nowrap><!-- Label 1 --> </td>
    <td width="25%"><!-- Input First name text field --> </td>
    <td align="right" width="25%" nowrap><!-- Label 2 --> </td>
    <td width="25%"><!-- Last name text field --> </td>
  </tr>
  <tr valign="top">
    <td align="center" colspan="4">Tell us about your visit<br />
    <hr />
    </td>
  </tr>
  <tr valign="top">
    <td colspan="3">At what time of year was your last visit to Paradise Mountain Family
Resort? </td>
    <td>Season: <!-- Dropdown season -->
    </td>
  </tr>

  <tr valign="top">
    <td colspan="3">During your last visit, how many people were in your party?  
```

Comments guide element placement

Nonbreaking spaces hold cells open

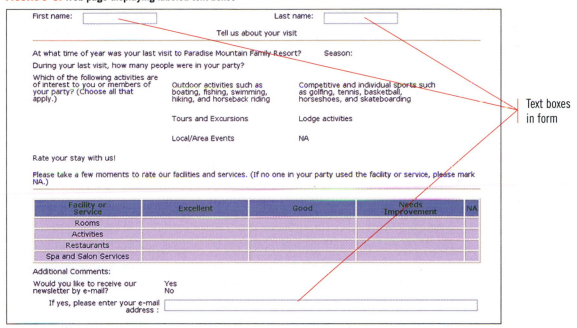

Text boxes in form

TABLE G-1: Common form field tags

tag(s)	attribute	description	example
`<form>...</form>`		Defines the form boundaries	`<form method="post">...</form>`
`<input />`	type	Specifies the type of form field to create	`<input type="text" />`
	name	Assigns a form or element name; used by scripts to reference and process forms	`<form name="survey">...</form>` `<input type="text" name="value" />`
	size	Specifies the display length (width) of the form field	`<input type="text" size="20" />`
	maxlength	Sets the largest number of characters allowed in the current form field; extra typing is ignored after this number is reached	`<input type="text" maxlength="40" />`

HTML

Adding Radio Buttons

Text boxes allow form users to enter unique bits of information. However, you can reduce the potential for user input error by providing a list of choices. This eliminates the possibility that a user will enter a selection that the form processor doesn't understand or that is not useful. HTML includes several formats for controlling user input; each format is appropriate for different situations and types of information. To create a set of options that a user can see all at once, and from which a user can make only one selection, you create radio buttons. **Radio buttons** are small white circles appearing next to explanatory text. When a user clicks a circle, it fills with black to indicate it is selected. Selecting one button in a group deselects any previously selected button. You create radio buttons using the `<input />` tag, with the type attribute set to "radio." All radio buttons in a set share the same name; however, each button uses a different value. The value of the selected button is returned by the form processor as the user's response to the question. The values you specify vary depending upon how the information will be used. You want to add radio buttons to enable survey users to choose one of several options for some questions. You will configure some button groups with numeric values so they can be processed as numbers in a spreadsheet or database.

STEPS

1. **Click the text editor program button on your taskbar, then in your text editor, locate the comment that begins** `<!-- Use the comments below`

2. **Click just after the comment** `<!-- Radio button - name, rooms; value, 3 -->`, **before the nonbreaking space** ` `, **press [Enter], press [Tab], then type** `<input type="radio" name="room" value="3" />`

    You created the first button in the first group of buttons, which you've named "room." Buttons in the same group share a common name, defining a set from which users can make only one selection. You assigned a value of 3 to your first button. The rest of the buttons in the chart need to be configured.

3. **Repeat Step 2 to create radio buttons for each of the rest of the cells in the Rooms row, then create radio buttons for each cell in the Activities, Restaurants, and Spa services rows, using the values shown in the comments**

    Your code should resemble that shown in Figure G-4. The numeric values allow you to process the collected data as numbers in a spreadsheet or database to numerically rank each resort feature.

4. **Save your work, click the browser program button on the taskbar and reload the survey.htm file, then test your ratings radio buttons by clicking several buttons in each group.**

    As shown in Figure G-5, when a radio button in a group is clicked, a black dot appears in the center. When another button is clicked, the first selection is removed. When a user submits the form, the returned value for each field is the value of the selected radio button.

    > **TROUBLE**
    >
    > If you are able to select more than one radio button in the same row, check your source code to ensure that all the buttons in the same row have the same name.

5. **Return to your code, click after the comment** `<!-- Radio Button - name, newsletter; value, Yes -->`, **press [Enter], press [Spacebar] four times, type** `<input type="radio" name="newsletter" value="Yes" checked="checked" />`, **then press [Spacebar]**

    The checked attribute signifies that the radio button should appear as selected when the page opens.

6. **Click after the comment** `<!-- Radio Button - name, newsletter; value, No -->`, **press [Enter], press [Spacebar] four times, type** `<input type="radio" name="newsletter" value="No" />`, **press [Spacebar], then save your page and view it in the browser**

    The Yes and No values you set for the newsletter radio button group allow you to sort your results by respondents who wish to receive your newsletter. As shown in Figure G-6, the Yes value for the newsletter radio button group is prechecked.

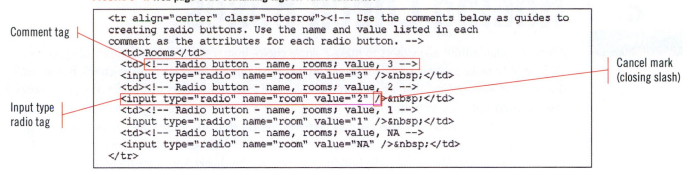

FIGURE G-4: Web page code containing tags for radio button list

Comment tag

Input type radio tag

Cancel mark (closing slash)

```
<tr align="center" class="notesrow"><!-- Use the comments below as guides to
creating radio buttons. Use the name and value listed in each
comment as the attributes for each radio button. -->
<td>Rooms</td>
<td><!-- Radio button - name, rooms; value, 3 -->
<input type="radio" name="room" value="3" /> </td>
<td><!-- Radio button - name, rooms; value, 2 -->
<input type="radio" name="room" value="2" /> </td>
<td><!-- Radio button - name, rooms; value, 1 -->
<input type="radio" name="room" value="1" /> </td>
<td><!-- Radio button - name, rooms; value, NA -->
<input type="radio" name="room" value="NA" /> </td>
</tr>
```

FIGURE G-5: Web page displaying radio button list

Mutually exclusive button choices

One button selected in each group

FIGURE G-6: Survey page with prechecked radio button

Prechecked radio button

Adding Check Boxes

Although radio buttons allow users to make a single choice from a set of options, sometimes you want to allow users to make multiple selections from a list. For situations like this, HTML offers **check boxes**, which display an array of choices that are all visible at once, and from which users may select any, all, or none. A check box appears as a small box next to its label. When a user clicks an empty check box, a check mark appears in the box; clicking a checked box removes the check mark. You create check boxes using the `<input />` tag, with the type attribute set to "checkbox." Unlike radio buttons, each check box should have a unique name. Also unlike radio buttons, you can use the checked attribute for multiple check boxes in the same section of your form to display the box with an initially checked state. If you don't specify a value attribute, the default value returned for a checked box is "On". Unchecked boxes return a value of "Off". Since the values On and Off are not very intuitive, it is a good idea to assign each check box a specific value. Paradise Mountain Family Resort offers a wide variety of activities for their guests. The Marketing Department wants to find out which activities generate the most interest. Because you want guests to be able to choose more than one option, you add the activities to the form as check box fields.

STEPS

1. **In your text editor, click after the comment tag that reads** `<!-- Checkbox name, outdoorActivities-->`**, press [Enter], press [Tab], type** `<input type="checkbox" name="outdoorActivities" value="Yes" />`**, press [Spacebar], press [Enter], then press [Tab]**

   You entered the code to create the first check box. The text following the code becomes the form label. When checked and submitted, the form returns a value of "outdoorActivities Yes". This makes it easy to sort by respondents who enjoy outdoor activities.

2. **Click after** `<!-- Checkbox name, competitiveActivities-->`**, press [Enter], press [Tab], type** `<input type="checkbox" name="competitiveActivities" value="Yes" />`**, press [Spacebar], press [Enter], then press [Tab]**

3. **Click after the comments for tours, lodge_activities, events and NA, then repeat Step 2 to create checkboxes for each of the following labels: Tours and Excursions, Lodge activities, Local/Area Events, and NA, setting each value as Yes**

   You included the "NA" option for respondents who are not interested in activities. Compare your code to that shown in Figure G-7.

4. **Save your page, then click the browser program button on the taskbar and reload the survey.htm page**

   As shown in Figure G-8, two columns of check boxes present selection options for survey users.

Design Matters

Labeling radio buttons and check boxes

The text that you enter as a label next to a radio button or a check box is just like plain text elsewhere on your Web page. Even though form fields would be meaningless to users without labels, HTML has no rules about how to label the fields. Therefore, you are free to put a label to the left or right of a field, or even above or below it. The most important guideline is to make sure it is obvious to a user which label and which field go together. From a design standpoint, it is also important to make the fields easy for users to find. By placing the check box form field in front of the label and using tables to align your content, you make it easier for the user to match form fields with their respective labels.

Comment tag with checkbox name

Checkbox with "Yes" value

```
<input type="checkbox" name="outdoorActivities" value="Yes" />
Outdoor activities such as boating,
fishing, swimming, hiking, and horseback riding </td>
<td>
<!-- Checkbox name, competitiveActivities -->
<input type="checkbox" name="competitiveActivities" value="Yes" />
Competitive and individual sports such as
golfing, tennis, basketball, horseshoes, and skateboarding</td>
</tr>

<!-- Activities Table Row 2 -->
<tr valign="top">
<td><!-- Checkbox name, tours-->
<input type="checkbox" name="tours" value="Yes" />
Tours and Excursions
</td>
<td><!-- Checkbox name, lodge_activities-->
<input type="checkbox" name="lodge_activities" value="Yes" />
Lodge activities
</td>
</tr>

<!-- Activities Table Row 3 -->
<tr>
<td><!-- Checkbox name, events-->
<input type="checkbox" name="events" value="Yes" />
Local/Area Events
</td>
<td><!-- Checkbox name, NA -->
<input type="checkbox" name="NA" value="Yes" />NA
</td>
</tr>
```

FIGURE G-8: Web page survey with check boxes

At what time of year was your last visit to Paradise Mountain Family Resort?   Season:

During your last visit, how many people were in your party?

Which of the following activities are of interest to you or members of your party? (Choose all that apply.)

Checkbox list

☐ Outdoor activities such as boating, fishing, swimming, hiking, and horseback riding

☐ Competitive and individual sports such as golfing, tennis, basketball, horseshoes, and skateboarding

☐ Tours and Excursions

☐ Lodge activities

☐ Local/Area Events

☐ NA

Creating a Pull-Down Menu

Radio buttons and check boxes lay out a group of related options so that they all are visible on the Web page. Sometimes, however, you want to save space on your Web page. You may have such an extensive set of choices that it would be impractical to include all of them in the Web page's layout. For this type of situation, HTML allows you to format your options with a more efficient form field called a pull-down menu. A **pull-down menu**—also known as a **select option box** or **drop-down list**—appears on the page like a single-line text field. However, it also contains a down-arrow button that the user clicks to open a menu of choices. In most cases, when the user clicks a choice, the list closes and the user's selection appears in the field. The pull-down menu is popular on Web page forms because it uses space efficiently and because most users are familiar with it from common operating systems and software. To create a pull-down menu, you use the `<select>...</select>` tag set to surround a list of choices. Each choice is marked with the `<option>...</option>` tag set. Table G-2 explains the common attributes used with these tags. You have identified three areas of your form that would make effective use of pull-down menus.

STEPS

1. **In your text editor, locate and select the comment tag** `<!-- Dropdown season -->`, **in the third row of your form layout table, press** [Delete], **press** [Enter], **press** [Tab], **type** `<select name="season">`, **press** [Enter], **press** [Tab], **then type**
`</select> <br /> <br />`
You typed the opening and closings tags for your drop-down list and placed two line breaks after it. The line breaks add a little extra space and prevent your form from appearing too crowded.

2. **Click just before** `</select>`, **then type the following code, pressing** [Enter] **and** [Tab] **after each line:**
```
<option value="Spring">Spring</option>
<option value="Summer">Summer</option>
<option value="Fall">Fall</option>
<option value="Winter">Winter</option>
```
Your code resembles that shown in Figure G-9. By adding a value to and closing each option, you ensure that your code works with a form-processing script.

3. **Locate and drag to select the comment tag that reads** `<!-- dropdown num_guests -->`, **press** [Enter], **press** [Tab], **type** `<select name="num_guests">`, **then press** [Enter]

4. **Press** [Tab], **then type** `</select> <br /> <br />`

5. **Click after** `<select name="num_guests">`, **press** [Enter], **press** [Tab] **twice, then type the following code, pressing** [Enter] **and** [Tab] **twice after the first and second lines**
```
<option value="1">   1   </option>
<option value="2 - 3">2 - 3 </option>
<option value="4 or more">4 or more</option>
```
Because the first option contains a single character, you insert nonbreaking spaces around it so it is easier for users to see.

6. **Save your work, then reload the** survey.htm **page in your browser**
Figure G-10 shows your form with an active pull-down menu. Unlike form element names, which are used by program code to identify form objects, option values are text strings and can contain spaces.

FIGURE G-9: Code for pull-down menu

Opening select tag

Opening option list tag

Closing select tag

Closing option list tag

```
<tr valign="top">
    <td colspan="3">At what time of year was your last visit to Paradise
Mountain Family Resort? </td>
    <td>Season: 
        <select name="season">
        <option value="Spring">Spring</option>
        <option value="Summer">Summer</option>
        <option value="Fall">Fall</option>
        <option value="Winter">Winter</option>
        </select> <br /> <br />
    </td>
</tr>
```

FIGURE G-10: Web page with active pull-down menus

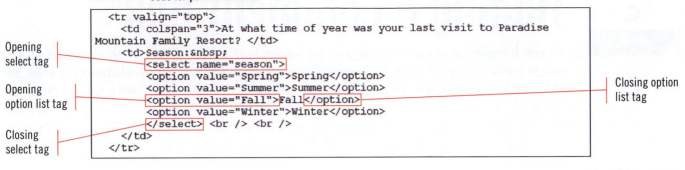

Active pull-down menu

TABLE G-2: Pull-down menu tags and attributes

tag(s)	function	attribute	description
`<select>...</select>`	Creates a list field of options in which some choices are hidden	name	Creates a field name used to reference a field for form processing
		size	Sets the number of items that appear on screen; if omitted, choices appear as a pull-down menu; if set to 2 or more, list appears as a scroll box
		multiple	Sets the number of options user may select from the list; if omitted, user may select only one list item
`<option>...</option>`	Surrounds each item in a selection list; must occur between `<select>` and `</select>` tags	value	Specifies the text to be submitted to form-processing system
		selected	Specifies the option to appear in the field text box when the Web page opens in the browser

UNIT
G
HTML

Adding a Comment Box

An effective method of ensuring that your site visitors have ample opportunity to express all of their concerns when filling out a form is to add an additional form element called a **multiline text area**, also known as a **comment box**. Comment boxes are designed to allow less-structured user input by accommodating multiple lines of user comments. To add a comment box to a page, use the `<textarea>...</textarea>` tag set. You configure the text area tag using the cols attribute for columns and the rows attributes for rows. You decide to allow users to add additional information using a comment box.

STEPS

1. In your text editor, locate the comment tag that reads `<!-- Insert textarea here -->`, drag to select the comment tag and the nonbreaking space, ` `, that follows it, press [Delete], then press [Enter]

2. Type `<textarea name="comments" rows="4" cols="40">`, then press [Enter]
   Because text area elements display content, including spaces and tabs that you type between the opening and closing tags, you decide not to space or tab after returning to the next line.

3. Type `</textarea>`, then save your page
   Your code should resemble the code shown in Figure G-11. Although you can add prompting text such as, "Type your comments here" to the content area of a comment box, you decide not to do so because if a site visitor chooses not to add a comment of his or her own, the placeholder text will be returned as the form field value.

4. Locate the code for the opening table data tag and Additional Comments label that reads: `<td colspan="2">Additional Comments: </td>`

5. Click just after colspan="2" inside the opening table data tag, press [Spacebar], then type `align="right"`
   Aligning the label content to the right brings it next to the comment box letting users know that the label belongs to the box.

6. Locate the "Page modified by" paragraph at the bottom of the page, replace Your Name with your own name, update the date text to show the current date, then save the page

7. Click the browser program button on the taskbar, then reload the survey.htm page
   As shown in Figure G-12, the comment box appears on the page and is ready for user input.

HTML G-12 USING FORMS TO CONTROL INPUT

FIGURE G-11: Code for text area comment box

```
<tr valign="top">
   <td colspan="2">Additional Comments: </td>
   <td colspan="2">
<textarea name="comments" rows="4" cols="40">
</textarea></td>
   </tr>
```

Textarea
code not
indented or
spaced

FIGURE G-12: Web page with comment box

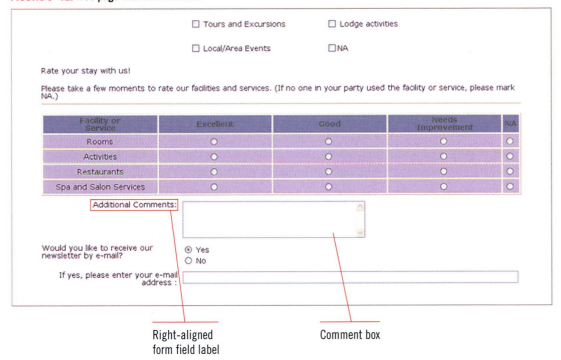

Right-aligned
form field label

Comment box

HTML

Adding a Push Button

Once users finish filling out a form, they need to submit their information to your organization for processing. To allow users to execute such tasks, HTML forms include **push buttons**, which are labeled objects that a user can click to perform a task. You create a push button using the `<input />` tag, and you specify its function using the type attribute. The most common push button types are reset, submit, and button. A **reset button** clears all the input in a form, allowing a user to start over. The **submit button** performs one of the most common form activities—submitting information for processing. Input elements of the button type use an Onclick event associated with a script in order to perform a function. For input elements with the attributes submit, reset, or button, you can use the value attribute to change the text on the button face. You want to add submit and reset buttons to your form to make it easy for your site visitors to use.

STEPS

1. **In your text editor, select the comment** `<!-- Insert Submit button here -->` **as well as the nonbreaking space, ` `, that follows it near the bottom of the document, then press [Delete]**

2. **Type** `<input type="submit" value="Complete Survey" name="submit" />`

3. **Select the comment that reads:** `<!-- Insert Reset button here -->` **as well as the nonbreaking space that follows it, then press [Delete]**

4. **Type** `<input type="reset" value="Start Over" name="reset" />`, **press [Spacebar], then save your file**

   This portion of your HTML document should resemble the code shown in Figure G-13.

5. **Click the browser program button on the taskbar, reload the page, then click the Complete Survey button**

   The browser reloads the page as shown in Figure G-14 and clears the information you entered in the form. If you have access to a server with form-processing capabilities, you can configure your form to submit information by adding the name of your processing script as the value of the form action. Check with your instructor or server administrator to find out if your server has form-processing capabilities.

6. **Close your browser and your text editor, then transfer your updated files to your remote directory**

Clues to Use

Using a graphic as a push button

The value attribute allows you to customize the text on a push button to fit its specific function on your Web pages. You can further customize a button to fit your page's overall theme by specifying a graphic to use as a button. To use a graphic as a push button, set the `<input />` tag type attribute to "image," then specify the path and name of the graphic file with the src attribute. Like other images in your Web pages, you should specify alternate text for a graphical button by using the alt attribute.

FIGURE G-13: Web page code containing tags for push buttons

Submit
button code

```
<tr valign="top">
  <td> </td>
  <td colspan="2" align="right">
    <input type="submit" value="Complete Survey" name="submit" /> </td>
  <td><input type="reset" value="Start Over" name="reset" /></td>
  </tr>
```

Reset button code

FIGURE G-14: Web page displaying push buttons

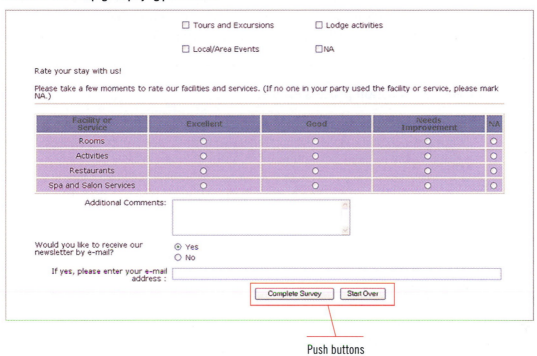

Push buttons

Using input buttons

Submit and Reset input buttons have built-in **event actions** that allow them to function without additional scripting: When clicked, the Submit button automatically sends form data to the processing file specified in the opening form tag's action attribute. The Reset button automatically clears the form without reloading the page. However, you may want your button to perform an additional action before submitting the form, such as calculating information or sending a response. In these cases, you can use button or image type input elements. Although they look very similar to Submit and Reset elements, button (type="button") and image (type="image") elements require the addition of an onClick event with a reference to an associated file, function, or processing script, as in the following example: `<input type="button" name="submit" value="Send Information" onClick="verify();" />`, where verify() is the name of a function, which is a scripted action.

HTML

Connecting a Form's Back End

Like tags to format other Web page elements such as text and graphics, the tags for creating a form only generate the Web page that users see in their browsers; that page is known as the **front end**. Once a user clicks the Submit button, however, the information entered requires processing that is not performed by the page's HTML code. When the code specifies an action in the opening form tag, clicking the submit button automatically instructs the browser to send the entered data to your Web server for processing. The programs that reside on an organization's computer system and that are responsible for processing the submitted data make up the **back end**. Figure G-15 shows the different parts of the front end and the back end and how data moves between them. Generally, Web page designers are responsible for creating the front end, and other people in an organization, such as the Web site administrator, handle the back-end tasks. However, it is important that the front-end designer work with the people responsible for the back end to ensure that the parts of the Web site that both of you create work together as expected. Table G-3 describes form attributes and values for submitting information from the server. You are meeting the Paradise Mountain Family Resort site administrator to begin coordinating your work on the submission process for the visitor survey. You can get more information on connecting to the form's back end by visiting the Student Online Companion for this text.

The form-submission process includes:

- ### Browser packaging

  When a user clicks the submit button, the browser refers to the `<form>` tag attributes for details on how to submit the information. These attributes, which are described in Table G-3, allow you to specify where the information entered in a form is sent, how the browser sends it, and in what format. Your IT Department has not yet finalized the submission requirements, but will provide you with these settings in time to test the system before the site survey page goes online.

- ### Form handler

  The border between a Web site's front end and back end is the communication between the Web server—where the HTML document is stored—and the programs that process the information collected in a form. This communication is facilitated through a form handler, and sometimes takes place using a standardized protocol known as **CGI (Common Gateway Interface)**. CGI is not a scripting language. It is instead an interface between the Web client and the processing script. Most CGI scripts are written in PERL, C++, or JavaScript. They are often compiled as executable programs with .exe or .dll extensions. Other types of form handlers are ASP (Active Server Page), JSP (Java Server Page), and PHP (Hypertext PreProcessor) scripting, which are all used extensively for making connections to database servers.

- ### Form processing and confirmation

  The final step in submitting form contents is the processing by the appropriate software. Because forms have many uses, they require different types of processing—for example, searching for information in a database, adding information to a database, or transforming in some way the data that was submitted. In any case, form submission and processing generally require an acknowledgement to the user, which confirms that the information was submitted, and which may also contain the results of the submission. For the Paradise Mountain guest survey form, your department is using a simple form handler. However, at such a time when the resort begins to accept online payment for reservations, you have made arrangements to work with a **shopping cart service**, which can bill the user's credit card for the amount of the reservation and inform the resort when the payment has cleared. The interface for one of the most popular shopping cart services, PayPal, is shown in Figure G-16. PayPal provides processing services for both businesses and individuals.

FIGURE G-15: Web page front end and back end

FIGURE G-16: PayPal services Web page

TABLE G-3: `<form>` tag attributes for submitting information

attribute	description	example
method	Indicates how the data entered by the user is submitted to the server; acceptable values are "get"—for calling information from the server—and "post"—for sending information to the server	`method="post"`
enctype	Specifies how the browser formats the user responses on the form before submitting them to the server	`enctype="text/plain"`
action	Indicates the path and name of the processing program that the server must run when the form is submitted	`action= "/cgi-bin/execmacro/input"`

HTML

Practice

▼ CONCEPTS REVIEW

Name the function of each section of code indicated in Figure G-17.

FIGURE G-17

```
1 ──  <form method="post" action="/cgi-bin/execmacro/input">                 ── 9

      <p>Select the product(s) that you would like to purchase:
      <br />
      <input type="checkbox" name="product" value="max160i" /> Maxtor Internal
      160 GB $49.99
      <input type="checkbox" name="product" value="sea250i" />Seagate Internal      ── 8
      250 GB $79.99
      <input type="checkbox" name="product" value="wed80e" />Western Digital
      External 80 GB $89.99
      <input type="checkbox" name="product" value="max300e" />Maxtor External
      300 GB $269.99
      </p>

      <br />Credit card Information:
      <br />Type:
      <select name="payment">
      <option value="visa">Visa</option>
      <option value="mc">MasterCard</option>                                      ── 7
2 ──  <option value="amx">American Express</option>
      </select>

      <br /> Number:
      <input name="num" type="text" size="25" />
      <br />Expiration date:                                                      ── 6
      <input name="exp" type="text" size="4" />

      <p>
      Choose a Shipping Method:

      <input type="radio" name="ship"  value="yes" />Ground
      <input type="radio" name="ship" value="no" />Air                           ── 5
      </p>

                                                                                 ── 4
      <p><input type="submit" value="Order" name="submit" />
      <input type="reset" value="Start Over" name="reset" /></p>                 ── 3

      </form>
```

Match each statement with the term it describes.

10. Form element that allows multiple user selections   **a.** Label
11. Form element that limits user input to one choice   **b.** Type
12. Multiline text area   **c.** Radio button
13. Descriptive text that accompanies a form field   **d.** Comment box
14. Required attribute for all input fields   **e.** Check box

Select the best answer from the list of choices.

15. **Which attribute can you use to display an item as selected in a radio button list?**
    a. Type
    b. Checked
    c. Length
    d. Order

16. **Which of the following attributes determines the number of items that appear by default in a pull-down menu?**
    a. Value
    b. Multiple
    c. Name
    d. Size

17. **Which tag(s) mark a choice in a pull-down menu?**
    a. <form>...</form>
    b. <input />
    c. <select>...</select>
    d. <option>...</option>

18. **Which attribute allows you to customize the text on a push button?**
    a. Text
    b. Type
    c. Name
    d. Value

19. **The Web page that users see in their browsers is called the Web site's:**
    a. Form
    b. Front end
    c. Back end
    d. Script

20. **The interface between the Web client and the processing script is called:**
    a. Browser packaging
    b. CGI
    c. Scripting
    d. Order processing and confirmation

▼ SKILLS REVIEW

1. **Plan a form.**
   a. Consider how a form could be used to sell spa products over the Web. What type of data would you collect on a product order form?
   b. Which form fields would you use on the form?
   c. How would you structure the form?
   d. Which types of push buttons would you place on your form?
   e. How would you connect your form's back end to a Web server?

2. **Create a text field.**
   a. In your text editor, open the file **htm_G-2.txt** from the drive and folder where your Data Files are stored, then save it as **spaproducts.htm** to the paradise/spa directory where you save your site files.
   b. Locate the comment in the file indicating where the first set of text fields begins and place an input tag of `<input type="text" name="name" size="25" />` next to the Name: label to add a field for the customer's name.
   c. In the following line next to the Address: label, place an input tag of `<input type="text" name="address" size="25" />` to add a field for the customer's address.

d. In the following line next to the City: label, place an input tag of `<input type="text" name="city" size="15" />` to add a field for the customer's city.

e. In the following line next to the State: label, place a similar text input tag assigning the name of state and a size of 2.

f. In the following line next to the Zip Code: label, place a similar text input tag assigning the name of zip and a size of 5.

g. In the following line next to the E-mail Address: label, place a similar input tag assigning the name of email and a size of 25.

h. Locate the comment in the file indicating where the second set of text fields begins, and place an input tag of `<input type="text" name="num" size="25" />` next to the Number: label to add a field for the credit card number.

i. In the following line next to the Expiration Date: label, place an input tag of: `<input type="text" name="exp" size="4" />` to add a field for the expiration date.

j. Save your file and view the form in your browser to check your work.

3. Add radio buttons.

a. Locate the comment in the file indicating where the radio buttons begin, and beneath the comment place an input tag of `<input type="radio" name="ship" value="ground" />Ground` to add a radio button choice for Ground shipping.

b. In the next line, place an input tag of `<input type="radio" name="ship" value="air" />Air` to add a radio button choice for Air shipping.

c. Save your work.

d. View the form in your browser to check your work.

4. Add check boxes.

a. Locate the comment in the file indicating where the check boxes begin, and beneath the comment place an input tag of `<input type="checkbox" name="product" value="soap" />Shea Butter Soap $12` to add a check box choice for Shea Butter Soap. Add two nonbreaking spaces by entering `  ` after the price.

b. In the next line, place an input tag of `<input type="checkbox" name="product" value="handcream" />Hand Cream $25` to add a check box choice for Hand Cream. Add two nonbreaking spaces after the price.

c. In the next line, place a similar input tag using a value of salts and a label of Bath Salts $9 to add a check box choice for Bath Salts with two nonbreaking spaces following the choice.

d. In the next line, place a similar input tag using a value of **bodycream** and a label of Body Cream $30 to add a check box choice for Body Cream.

e. Save your work

f. View the form in your browser to check your work.

5. Create a pull-down menu.

a. Locate the comment in the file indicating where the pull-down menu begins, and beneath the comment place the tag `<select name="payment">` to begin the list of choices.

b. In the next line, place an option tag of `<option value="visa">Visa</option>` to add a choice for Visa.

c. In the next line, place an option tag of `<option value="mc">MasterCard</option>` to add a choice for MasterCard.

d. In the next line, place a similar option tag for an American Express choice, using an option value of amx.

e. In the next line, place the tag `</select>` to end the list of choices.

f. Save your work.

g. View the form in your browser to check your work.

6. Add a comment box.

a. Locate the comment in the file indicating where the comment box begins, and place an opening `<textarea>` tag to start a multiline text area for customer product suggestions.

b. Add the attribute `name="newproducts"` to the opening textarea tag to give a name to the comments your customers provide in the box.

   c. Add the attribute `rows="5" cols="45"` to the opening textarea tag to create a box of five rows and 45 columns.

   d. Add the closing `</textarea>` tag to end the multiline comment area.

   e. Save your work.

   f. View the form in your browser to check your work.

7. Add a push button.

   a. Locate the comment in the file indicating where the push buttons begin, and place an `<input />` tag to start a button that can be used to submit your customer form data.

   b. Add the attribute `type="submit"` to the input tag to define the button as a submit button.

   c. Add the attribute `value="Order"` to the input tag to place the label Order on the button.

   d. Add the attribute `name="submit"` to the input tag to assign a name of submit to the button.

   e. Add an `<input />` tag to start a button that can be used to reset the form in the event that a customer would like to clear the form data.

   f. Add the attribute `type="reset"` to the input tag to define the button as a reset button.

   g. Add the attribute `value="Start Over"` to the input tag to place the label Start Over on the button.

   h. Add the attribute `name="reset"` to the input tag to assign a name of reset to the button.

   i. Delete any unnecessary blank lines in your file, then save your work.

   j. View the form in your browser to check the buttons.

8. Connect a form's back end.

   a. Locate the opening form tag in your file. What is the value of the method attribute?

   b. How will the order data entered by your customers be submitted to the server?

   c. What is the value of the action attribute in your form tag?

   d. What does this action value describe about the process the server uses to work with the form data?

   e. Delete all the comments, add a comment with your name, then print the code.

   f. Transfer the **spaproducts.htm** file to your remote directory.

▼ INDEPENDENT CHALLENGE 1

As you continue developing the Web site for your resort rental business, Star Vacations, you decide that forms can help to measure the interest of your customers in new markets. You decide to use a form to gather input about interest in Australian rentals.

   a. In your text editor, open the file **htm_G-3.txt** from the drive and folder where your Data Files are stored, then save it as **survey.htm** to the vacations folder where you save your site files.

   b. Locate the form area where the text fields are placed to collect contact information. Add an input tag to create a text field for the Zip Code label using a name of zip and a size of 5.

   c. Add the input tag to create the text field for the E-mail Address label using a name of email and a size of 25.

   d. Locate the form area where the Yes radio button is placed to collect responses from customers who are interested in Australia rentals. Under the Yes radio button option, add an input tag to create a radio button option for the No label using a name of rental and a value of no.

   e. Locate the form area where the check boxes are placed to collect locations of interest in Australia. Under the Melbourne choice, add the input tag to create a check box choice for the Perth label using a name of location and a value of perth.

   f. Under the Perth choice, add the input tag to create a check box choice for the Hayman Island label using a name of location and a value of hayman.

   g. Locate the form area where customers are asked about other locations of interest in Australia. Add a multiline text area under the comment "What other locations would you like to visit in Australia?" Assign the text area a name of newlocations, and provide space for five rows and 35 columns.

   h. Locate the form area where the pull-down menu is placed to collect length of rentals in Australia. Under the Two Weeks choice, add the option tags to create a choice for the Three Weeks label using a value of "three".

HTML

▼ INDEPENDENT CHALLENGE 1 (CONTINUED)

i. Under the Three Weeks choice, add the option tags to create a choice for the One Month label using a value of "month".

j. Locate the form area where the comment tag indicates a submit button should be placed, and add a submit button with a name of "submit" and the value Submit on the button.

k. Locate the form area where the comment tag indicates a reset button should be placed, and add a reset button with a name of "reset" and the value Start Over on the button.

l. Delete the comments from your file, add a comment line with your name, save and print the file, then display the **survey.htm** file in your browser to check your form.

m. Transfer your **survey.htm** page to your remote directory.

Advanced Challenge Exercises

- Add a size attribute with a value of two to the opening select tag to display two choices in the pull-down menu. (*Hint*: Add `size = "2"` inside the `<select>` tag.)
- Save your work and display the form in your browser to check your pull-down menu.
- Add a comment to your file describing the change in the pull-down menu.
- Transfer your form to your remote directory.

▼ INDEPENDENT CHALLENGE 2

Metro Water publishes monthly newsletters on a variety of topics related to water conservation. You will create a subscription form for Metro Water's customers to sign up for the monthly newsletters.

a. In your text editor, open the **htm_G-4.txt** file from the drive and folder where your Data Files are stored, then save it as **newsletter.htm** in the water folder where you save your site files.

b. Using the Begin form here comment, add an opening form tag with a method of "post" and an action of `/cgi-bin/execmacro/input`.

c. Locate the comment in your file indicating the area for check boxes, then use the table to the right to add check boxes with four newsletter choices. Place each choice on its own line. (*Hint*: Use a line break after each option.)

Check box labels and attributes

Label	Name	Value
Inside Conservation	newsletter	inside
Outside Conservation	newsletter	outside
Landscaping	newsletter	landscaping
Resources	newsletter	resources

d. Locate the comment in your file indicating the area for a comment box and add a multiline text area with five rows and 70 columns for customer input about future newsletters. Assign a name of "newtopics" to the text area.

e. Locate the comment in your file indicating the area for radio buttons, then use the table on the right to add radio buttons that will grant permission for future e-mail contact with your customers.

Radio button labels and attributes

Label	Name	Value
Yes	lecture	yes
No	lecture	no

f. Locate the comment in your file indicating the area for the submit and reset buttons, then use the table on the right to add buttons that will submit or reset the form data. Add the closing `</form>` tag.

Name	Value
submit	Submit
reset	Start Over

g. Delete the comments in the form, add a comment containing your name, save your file, then view the form in your browser.

h. Save your work, print the file, then transfer your **newsletter.htm** file to the remote site.

▼ INDEPENDENT CHALLENGE 2 (CONTINUED)

Advanced Challenge Exercises

- Locate the check box area and the Inside Conservation item. Add a checked attribute with a value of "checked" to the input tag of the Inside Conservation choice in the check box area to display the form with this option selected.
- Save your work and display the form in the browser comparing the check boxes to Figure G-18.
- Add a checked attribute with a value of "checked" to the No choice in the radio button area to display the form with this option selected.
- Save your work and display the form in the browser comparing the radio buttons to Figure G-19.
- Transfer your form to your remote directory.

FIGURE G-18

Select the newsletter(s) that you would like to receive:
- ☑ Inside Conservation
- ☐ Outside Conservation
- ☐ Landscaping
- ☐ Resources

FIGURE G-19

May we inform you by e-mail of local water conservation lectures?
○ Yes ◉ No

▼ INDEPENDENT CHALLENGE 3

Forms are used to interact with Web site users. You want to add forms to your Web site, but first you need to research how you can make them accessible for all users.

Go to the Student Online Companion for this book, and go to the Unit G link for the W3C Web Accessibility page and review the information for forms. Write one or two paragraphs answering the following questions about forms:

a. How can initial text in the text area tag be used to increase form accessibility?

b. How can push buttons be coded to increase their accessibility?

c. How can forms be designed to allow keyboard access between form elements?

d. Add your name and today's date to the top of your paper, then print the document.

▼ INDEPENDENT CHALLENGE 4

Now that you've used forms to collect user data, you are ready to add forms to your Web site.

a. Determine how forms can be used in your Web site to gather user information

b. Lay out your forms on paper to determine which form elements are necessary to collect user information.

c. Create the forms using your text editor.

d. Add submit and reset buttons.

e. Format your forms appropriately.

f. Add appropriate accessibility features to your forms.

g. Transfer your edited forms to the remote location.

You have created user groups for your Bits and PCs customers. You will use a form to sign up members for the four groups that you have created. Use Figure G-20 as a guide to create the form in your text editor for the user group membership. Use descriptive names for your form data. Save your form as **usergroups.htm** in the bitspcs folder where you save your site files.

FIGURE G-20

Join Bits and PCs User Groups

You will receive e-mail about upcoming meetings of the user groups. Please provide the following information:

E-mail Address: _____

Select the group(s) that you would like to join:
☐ Flash
☐ Photoshop
☐ MAC
☐ Unix

What other user groups would you be interested in joining?

```
[                                    ]
```

May we inform you by e-mail of specials at Bits and PCs?
○ Yes   ○ No

[Join] [Start Over]

Controlling Page Layout with Frames and Tables

OBJECTIVES

Understand layout tools

Create a navigation bar

Create a frameset

Target links

Format frame borders

Use nested frames

Create a structuring table

Create a template

HTML was originally designed for identifying the content of Web page elements, rather than specifying how the elements should appear in a browser. This meant that early versions of HTML provided no methods of implementing layout and readability features you usually see in print media. However, later versions of HTML allowed more readable and useful Web page layouts through the use of tables, which you learned about in Unit F, and frames. **Frames** allow you to divide the browser into multiple scrollable windows, each of which contains a separate HTML document. Tables let you create single-page, grid-based layouts that resemble frames layouts; they are easy to construct but can be difficult to maintain. Although frames can produce more flexible pages, they can be difficult to use and might not be viewable in all browsers. You are investigating the possibility of converting Paradise Mountain's site to a new design and are considering the use of frames to standardize your navigation.

Understanding Layout Tools

To successfully convey information, a visual layout must divide it into discrete sections. Although you can divide a page using such HTML elements as headings and line breaks, such a format is **linear**, meaning it limits you to stacking page elements above and below each other, and provides few options for horizontal placement. Frames and tables both let you design more effective HTML layouts by allowing you to place elements anywhere on the screen, and by providing additional means of indicating divisions between them. In a frames page, such as the one shown in Figure H-1, the page is divided into windows that users can scroll individually. Each window contains a separate HTML document. A page organized with a table, like the page shown in Figure H-2, includes the entire page contents in one HTML file. Each option is appropriate for creating different effects. As you prepare to enhance the layout of the Paradise Mountain pages, you review the principal advantages of laying out a Web site using frames and tables.

DETAILS

Some advantages of using frames or tables include:

- ### Grid positioning
  Print media designers frequently use a **grid**, a set of columns and rows, to position and group page elements. Using a grid gives a design a sense of balance, consistency, and organization. You can easily add a grid to a Web page by creating columns and rows with the HTML table tags. Frames can also create a grid structure, as each frame can serve as a separate column or row. The ability to create a layout grid is the underlying feature of tables and frames that makes them both especially valuable for page layout.

- ### Unified appearance
  As you incorporate more pages into a Web site, it becomes important to ensure that users can easily navigate the site. After following a trail of links away from the home page, a user may wish to explore another area of the site. Rather than requiring users to return to the main page, well-designed sites usually include a **site navigation bar**—a set of links to the home page and main sections of the site—that appears on every page. In the most user-friendly sites, the navigation bar and other page elements, appear in the same location on each page, giving all the site's pages a unified appearance. This predictable layout reassures users that they won't get lost, and encourages them to explore the site. You can easily achieve a unified site appearance by implementing a frames-based layout or by creating a table. You can also unify your site by creating a **template**, a Web page coded with the site's page structure and primary elements, and then using the template as the starting point for each new Web page.

- ### White space control
  Tables and frames offer effective methods of controlling white space in page borders and between page elements. This ability to control white space allows designers to create pages that are aesthetically pleasing and easy to read.

FIGURE H-1: Web page layout using frames

Right frame contains page content

Left frame contains navigation bar

Scroll bars allow frames to move independently

FIGURE H-2: Web page layout using structuring table

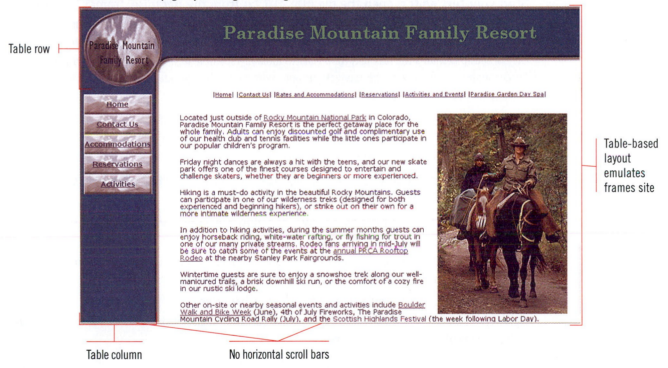

Table row

Table-based layout emulates frames site

Table column

No horizontal scroll bars

Design Matters

Exploring style sheet positioning

Although both frames and tables are powerful Web page layout tools, they were created for simpler tasks, and neither offers an exhaustive set of design options. However, Cascading Style Sheets (CSS), as you learned in Unit E, are specifically designed for Web page formatting. CSS formatting is more intuitive and effective than earlier page design methods. CSS formatting not only allows you to control multiple page elements from an external file and apply defined attributes to multiple instances of the same element; it also allows you to control page layout by specifying settings for horizontal and vertical positions. Most browsers support CSS layout, but some older browsers do not. This means that users of older browsers might not see your content in the layout you planned. On the other hand, pages that use CSS layout formatting are more effectively displayed on alternate output devices such as personal digital assistants (PDAs)—making it the layout method of choice for site designers who strive to meet federal accessibility mandates. Nevertheless, frames and tables continue to be effective Web page layout tools—especially for smaller sites.

Creating a Navigation Bar

Although you can add a simple navigation bar to any page layout, creating a grid layout provides more choices for the bar's formatting and its location on the page. You can position the bar's paragraphs or graphics at the bottom of the screen in a linear layout, but positioning the bar in the same place on each page could require adding imprecise spacing elements, such as line breaks. By contrast, when using frames or tables you can specify the exact dimensions of each component, allowing you to place it in a consistent page location. Additionally, in a grid layout you can create a vertical navigation bar, running along the left or right edge of the browser window, and include other page elements alongside it. You begin your redesign by creating a navigation bar that you can incorporate into the page layout for the Paradise Mountain site.

STEPS

1. **Using your computer's file system, locate and copy the folder named frames and all of its contents from the UnitH\Lessons folder in your Data File location, then paste it into your paradise site folder in the place where you save your site files**

   The folder contains all the Data Files you need for this unit.

2. **Start your text editor, open the file htm_H-1.txt from the paradise\frames folder in your site files location, inspect the code, then save it in the same folder as navbar.htm**

   Your new file uses a linked style sheet that one of your team members created for formatting your site documents. It also contains the link text for a vertical toolbar. Your new style sheet formats your page with a left-border graphic and formats the navigation table cells with a background button image to give them the appearance of standard buttons.

   QUICK TIP

   You can apply a background button to a table cell without the aid of style sheets by using the background attribute of the table cell.

3. **Locate the table heading cell of the row with the attribute id="vnavRow1", click before Home, type `<a href="main.htm">`, click after Home, then type `</a>`**

   You created the first link in the site navigation bar.

4. **Click before Contact Us in the next row, type `<a href="contact.htm">`, click after Us in the same row, then type `</a>`**

5. **Link the content of the next three rows as follows: Accommodations: rates.htm, Reservations: reserve.htm, Activities: activities/index.htm**

   Because you know your background image will tile if the cell content is too large, you decided to shorten the Activities and Events text. Your code appears similar to that shown in Figure H-3.

6. **Save your work, then preview your file in your browser**

   Figure H-4 shows the finished page. Using the same background graphic for all the table buttons keeps your Web page download time to a minimum.

FIGURE H-3: Web page code for navigation bar and linked style sheet code

Table heading
cell formatted
with CSS as
navigation
buttons

```
<table width="136" border="0" cellpadding="0" cellspacing="0" align="left" id="vnav">
<tr align="center" id="vnavRow1">
<th width="135" height="40" class="nav2">
<a href="main.htm">Home</a>
</th>
</tr>

<tr id="vnavRow2" align="center">
<th width="135" height="40" class="nav2">
<a href="contact.htm">Contact Us</a>
</th>
</tr>

<tr id="vnavRow3" align="center">
<th width="135" height="40" class="nav2">
<a href="rates.htm">Accommodations</a>
</th>
</tr>

<tr id="vnavRow4" align="center">
<th width="135" height="40" class="nav2">
<a href="reserve.htm">Reservations</a>
</th>
</tr>

<tr id="vnavRow5" align="center">
<th width="135" height="40" class="nav2">
<a href="activities/index.htm">Activities</a>
</th>
</tr>
</table>
```

```
.nav2    {
         background-image: url(../images/btn_pm1_blank.png);
         color: #000033;
         font-weight: 1000;

}
```

FIGURE H-4: Navigation page displayed in browser

Table cells formatted
as links with text and
background graphics

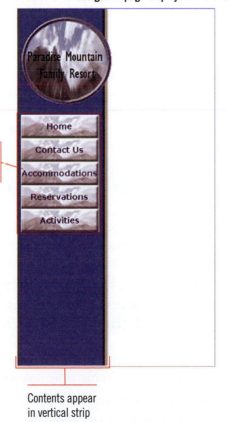

Contents appear
in vertical strip

Creating a Frameset

In a frames-based layout, the browser is divided into sections called **windows**. Each window—also called a **frame**—displays the contents of a separate HTML document. You create these individual documents with the same tags you use for standard Web pages. The document that controls the layout and organization of your frames is called a **frameset**. The total number of documents required to create a frames-based layout is equal to the number of frames plus one for the frameset. Because there must be at least two windows in a frameset, the minimum number of documents required is three. Figure H-5 shows the relationship between HTML files in a frames page. Table H-1 describes the tags and attributes required to create a frameset. 🎨 You have divided the contents of your new design into two separate HTML documents, similar to the layout design shown in Figure H-5. Each document will appear in a frame on the Paradise Mountain home page. You begin to lay out the page by creating a frameset.

STEPS

1. **In your browser, open the file main.htm from the paradise\frames folder in the place where you save your site files**

   This is the Paradise Mountain home page that will appear in the right frame of the frameset when users first open the Paradise Mountain frameset. Notice that the page background and heading elements have been stripped from the document. For the content of the left frame, you decide to use the navigation bar you created earlier.

2. **In your text editor, open the file htm_H-2.txt from your paradise\frames folder, and save it as frameset.htm in the same folder**

   The file contains the frameset DTD. You begin by entering the basic tags for your frameset document.

3. **Click in the line below the DTD, type `<html>`, press [Enter] twice, type `<head>`, press [Enter], type `<title>Paradise Mountain online</title>`, press [Enter], type `</head>`, then press [Enter] twice**

QUICK TIP

To create a frameset composed of rows instead of columns, use the rows attribute in place of cols.

4. **Type `<frameset cols="180,*" frameborder="0">`, then press [Enter] twice**

   The opening `<frameset>` tag marks the beginning of the frameset. In a frameset document, this tag replaces the standard HTML `<body>` tag. You use the cols attribute to indicate the width, in pixels, of each column. You specified the width of the first column—the navigation bar—as 180 pixels, and used an asterisk (*) for the width of the second column, indicating that it should occupy the remaining width of the browser window. You set the frameborder attribute equal to zero to remove the default border that appears between frames.

QUICK TIP

To divide a frame, you can enter a `<frameset>`. . . `</frameset>` tag in place of a `<frame>` tag, then nest `<frame>` tags within this set to specify the sources of the set's frame documents.

5. **Type `<frame src="navbar.htm" name="nav"/>`, press [Enter], type `<frame src="main.htm" name="main"/>`, press [Enter] twice, type `</frameset>`, then press [Enter] twice**

   Each frame requires a `<frame>` tag that specifies the name and location of its source file using the src attribute. It is also important to name each frame using the name attribute, so that each frame's hyperlinks work properly. It is good practice to include additional text that will appear in the window of a browser that does not support frames.

6. **Type `<noframes>`, press [Enter], type `This page was designed to be viewed with frames. You can open individual pages using the <a href="navbar.htm"> navigation bar</a>.`, press [Enter], type `</noframes>`, press [Enter] twice, then type `</html>`**

   Your alternate text provides a link to the navigation bar and ensures that users of older browsers can still access the entire site. Figure H-6 shows the completed code for the frameset Web page.

7. **Save your work, click the browser program button on the taskbar, open the file frameset.htm, then scroll the right window down using the vertical scroll bar**

   The browser displays both frames, as shown in Figure H-7. If necessary, resize the browser window. Notice that each frame includes a scrollbar, allowing you to scroll one side of the screen without moving the other side's contents.

FIGURE H-5: Frameset structure

One document contains contents of left frame

Separate document holds content of frame on right

Frameset document sets frames structure

FIGURE H-6: Frameset code

Frameset DTD

Frameset defines frame structure

Content source declared in frame tag

Noframes section provides link for site visitors without frames support

```
<!DOCTYPE html PUBLIC "-//W3C//DTD XHTML 1.0 Frameset//EN"
SYSTEM "http://www.w3.org/TR/xhtml1/DTD/xhtml1-frameset.dtd">

<html>

<head>
<title>Paradise Mountain online</title>
</head>

<frameset cols="180,*" frameborder="0">

<frame src="navbar.htm" name="nav"/>
<frame src="main.htm" name="main">

</frameset>

<noframes>
This page was designed to be viewed with frames. You can open individual
pages using the
<a href="navbar.htm">navigation bar</a>.
</noframes>

</html>
```

FIGURE H-7: Frameset in browser

Navigation frame

Main frame

Vertical scroll bar

Horizontal scroll bars

TABLE H-1: Frame tags and attributes

tag(s)	description	attributes	function
`<frameset>...</frameset>`	Marks frameset contents and describes their layout	rows	Defines number and sizes of horizontal frames to create
		cols	Defines number and sizes of vertical frames to create
		frameborder	Turns border between frames on or off; set to "0" or "no" to turn borders off
`<frame>`	Specifies a frame's source file and name	src	Defines location and filename for frame contents
		name	Defines frame name for reference by hyperlinks
`<noframes>...</noframes>`	Defines alternate page content for browsers that do not support frames; requires no attributes		

HTML

Targeting Links

When you click a link in a standard Web page, your browser usually replaces the current page with the linked one. In a page structured with frames, however, you choose the frame in which the linked page will open. This feature of frames has facilitated a popular frameset layout that fixes a page of links in one frame and displays content in another frame. When users click a link, the content of the navigation frame remains static and the content of the other frame changes. HTML offers two methods for setting the location where a linked page opens. One option is to add the target attribute to a link's `<a>` tag, and set this attribute equal to the name of the frame in which the linked page should open. You also can create a global setting for all of a page's links by adding the `<base />` tag to the page's head section and assigning the tag the appropriate target setting. Table H-2 explains target values with special behaviors. You used the `_blank` value in Unit B to open a page in a new window. 🎨 You want the navigation bar to remain visible to users as they explore the Paradise Mountain Web site. You add the `<base />` tag to the navbar.htm page's head section and apply the target attribute with a value to make the pages open in the frame on the right side of the frameset.

STEPS

1. **With the file frameset.htm open in your browser, click a link in the vertical navigation bar, then click your browser's Back button**

   When you click a link, the navigation bar is replaced by the link target file and, as shown in Figure H-8, is no longer available in the frameset. By default, a linked page opens in the same frame as the link that opened it.

2. **In your text editor, open the file navbar.htm**

3. **Locate the `</title>` tag in the head section, click after the closing >, press [Enter] twice, then type `<base target="main" />`**

   Figure H-9 shows the Web page code containing the `<base>` tag. When you created the frameset file, you assigned the name "main" to the frame on the right side of the screen. By setting the target attribute in the `<base />` tag, you allow users to click any link in the left frame—the navigation bar—to change the contents of the right frame.

4. **Save your work, click the browser program button on the taskbar, then click the Go button next to the browser Address Bar to reload the page**

   Clicking the Go button next to the Address Location box reloads the entire frameset.

5. **Click one of the link buttons in the vertical navigation bar**

   As shown in Figure H-10, the linked page opens in the main content frame, and the navigation bar remains in the left frame, allowing you to continue moving around the site.

6. **Click one of the links in the right (main) window frame**

   The page for the link you clicked opens in the right frame. Because your opening page for the right frame doesn't specify a target value for the links, the linked pages open by default in the same frame, as you intended. You want to make sure that linked pages from other sites (external links) do not appear in your frameset's content window because it could be considered a violation of copyright law.

7. **Open main.htm from your paradise\frames folder in the text editor, then locate the link for the PRCA Rooftop Rodeo, click inside the link just before >, press [Spacebar], then type `target="_blank"`**

   Because the target URL is not a page that you created, you want it to open in a new window outside of your Web site to make sure you won't violate copyright laws.

8. **Repeat Step 7 for the Boulder Walk and Bike Week, and the Scottish Highlands Festival links, then save your work and test the links in your browser**

   The linked pages open in a new window.

FIGURE H-8: Linked page replaces navigation bar content

Main frame does not change

Linked file opens in navigation frame

FIGURE H-9: Page code with base target

Base target set in head section

```
<!DOCTYPE html PUBLIC "-//W3C//DTD XHTML 1.0 Transitional//EN"
"http://www.w3.org/TR/xhtml1/DTD/xhtml1-transitional.dtd">
<html>

<head>

<title>Paradise Mountain Family Resort: Vertical Site Navigation</title>
<base target="main" />

<meta name="description" content="Paradise Mountain Family Resort
vertical site navigation />
```

FIGURE H-10: Linked file opens in main content frame

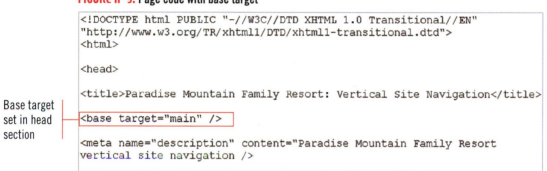

Link opens in target window

Navigation frame remains available

TABLE H-2: Special values for the target attribute

value	link behavior
_blank	Opens in new browser window
_self	Opens in current frame; this is the default setting
_parent	Replaces current frameset; use when you want external links to open with the Back button enabled
_top	Replaces contents of current browser window; use on links to your own frameset to prevent new framesets from opening within existing framesets

Formatting Frame Borders

Like most other Web page elements, frames support the attributes that change the frames' appearance in a browser. Several of these attributes are similar to those used to format tables. Although narrow borders appear between frames by default, you can use the frameborder attribute in the `<frameset>` tag to remove them or to change their appearance. Once a frameset includes borders, you can use other attributes to control border thickness and color, as well as the width of the margin between a frame's border and its contents. By default, Web page users can move the borders between frames to change the amount of the browser window that each frame occupies. If you want to make sure your layout remains fixed, you can add the noresize attribute to `<frame>` tags to ensure that the frames remain the width or height you specified in the `<frameset>` tag. Table H-3 describes several attributes available for formatting frames. You want to experiment with borders and border formats in your layout.

STEPS

1. **In your text editor, open** frameset.htm

2. **Locate the opening** `<frameset>` **tag, select the text** `frameborder="0"`, **press** [Delete], **then, if necessary, press** [Delete] **again or press** [Backspace] **to remove the extra space before the closing** >

3. **Save your work, click the** browser program button **on the taskbar, then click the** Go button **next to the browser's Address Location box to reload** frameset.htm

   Clicking the Go button reloads the frameset; however clicking the Reload button while viewing a frameset reloads the pages currently displaying in your browser. As shown in Figure H-11, the frameset appears with a border separating the two windows.

4. **Move the mouse pointer over the frame border, then click and drag to the right**

   The mouse pointer changes to a double arrow, indicating you can resize the frames. Dragging the border to the right resizes both frames.

5. **In your text editor, locate the opening** `<frameset>` **tag, click before** >, **press** [Spacebar], **then type** `frameborder="10" border="10" framespacing="10"`

   The border and framespacing attributes change the thickness of borders between frames. Because each attribute is appropriate for different browsers, you use all with the same setting to ensure your frames appear similarly to all users.

QUICK TIP

Use caution in setting the noresize attribute of your frames—this setting could cause some content to become unavailable to some users.

6. **Click directly before** > **in the first** `<frame>` **tag, press** [Spacebar], **then type** `noresize`

   Figure H-12 shows the completed code for the frameset document. Adding the noresize attribute to a `<frame>` tag prevents users from resizing that frame, as well as adjoining frames, in the browser window.

7. **Save your work, click the** browser program button, **then click the** Go button **to reload the frameset with its default pages**

   As shown in Figure H-13, the border between the two frames appears wider.

8. **Move the mouse pointer over the frame border**

   Because you added the noresize attribute to the left frame, the mouse pointer does not change to a double arrow and you cannot drag the frame border, which remains in its original location.

FIGURE H-11: Frameset windows separated by border

Border

FIGURE H-12: Page code for formatting frame borders

```
<head>
<title>Paradise Mountain online</title>

</head>
<frameset cols="180,*" frameborder="10" border="10" framespacing="10">

<frame src="navbar.htm" name="nav" noresize>
<frame src="main.htm" name="main" >

</frameset>

<noframes>
This page was designed to be viewed with frames. You can open individual
pages using the <a href="navbar.htm">navigation bar</a>
</noframes>

</html>
```

Frame borders formatted to work in most major browers

FIGURE H-13: Frames page with formatted, wider border

Wider frame border

TABLE H-3: Frame formatting attributes

tag	attribute	function	allowable values
`<frameset>`	frameborder	Determines whether or not borders appear	"0" or "no" turns off borders; "1" or another positive number or "yes" enables borders (the default setting)
	border	Specifies the space between frames	A size in pixels
	framespacing	Specifies the space between frames	A size in pixels
	bordercolor	Customizes color of lines separating frames	Hexadecimal color value or corresponding color name
`<frame>`	marginheight	Specifies space between frame contents and top and bottom borders	A size in pixels
	marginwidth	Specifies space between frame contents and left and right borders	A size in pixels
	noresize	Prevents users from changing a frame's dimensions	Requires no value; the presence of noresize enables this option
	scrolling	Controls the appearance of the frame's scrollbars	A "yes" value always includes scrollbars; "no" prevents scrollbars from appearing; when attribute is absent or set to "auto", scrollbars appear as needed

Using Nested Frames

Thus far you've worked with two-window framesets, but you can also create nested framesets that allow you to divide your browser window into multiple rows or columns or into both rows and columns. In a **nested frameset**, the <frameset> tag, with frames and framesets of its own, replaces one of the <frame> tags. You can achieve a more sophisticated layout using nested framesets. 🎨 You decide to use nested framesets to create a page layout with a heading frame, and both a left-border navigation frame and a content frame below the heading.

STEPS

1. **In your browser, open top.htm from your paradise\frames folder**

   A member of your design team created the top.htm file earlier in the design process. This file uses a top-border graphic and a corner logo graphic with a curved bottom edge.

2. **Open top.htm in your text editor and inspect the code, then close the file without making any changes**

   This file uses a table with CSS formatting to create a horizontal page heading layout that fits in a top frame.

3. **If necessary, open your frameset.htm file in your text editor and save it as frameset2.htm in your paradise\frames folder**

   The file is ready for editing and does not replace your original frameset. You want to create a frameset with three windows. The top frame serves as a page banner with a logo and heading, and spans the width of the navigation and content frames. Because the logo will be in your top frame, you want to replace navbar.htm with a version that does not contain the logo.

4. **Click before <frameset, type <frameset rows="163,*" frameborder="0" border="0" framespacing="0" noresize>, press [Enter], then type <frame src="top.htm" name="top" border="0" scrolling="no">**

5. **Locate the code for the left-border frame, click after navbar, type 2, save your work, then load frameset2.htm in your browser**

   The file navbar2.htm was created for you by a member of your design team. The combination of the top-border background and the curved logo gives the illusion of a rounded content area. The shadow effect applied to the graphics adds depth to the page appearance; however, all frame borders must be eliminated for the full effect. Also, indenting the nested frame makes your code easier to read.

6. **Return to your frameset2.htm code, click before <frameset cols="180,*", press [Spacebar] twice to indent it, then change the frameborder, border, and framespacing values in the second frameset from 10 to 0**

7. **Click before the frame tag with the src value navbar2.htm, press [Spacebar] twice, then indent the next two lines of code, ending with the </frameset> line**

   The parent <frameset> tag you added in Step 4 and 5 needs a closing tag.

8. **Click after </frameset>, press [Enter], type </frameset>, then save your work**

   You closed the parent frameset. Your code appears similar to that shown in Figure H-14.

9. **Return to your browser, open frameset2.htm from your paradise\frames folder, then click the links to test them**

   As shown in Figure H-15, your new frames-based layout appears in the browser, but the page heading from both top.htm and main.htm are visible.

10. **In your frameset2.htm file, locate the reference to main.htm and change it to main2.htm, then save your work and view it in your browser**

    Your new frameset appears without the double headings. The Home link in the main2.htm page targets frameset2.htm.

FIGURE H-14: Nested frameset code

```
<frameset rows="163,*" frameborder="0" border="0" framespacing="0"
noresize>

<frame src="top.htm" name="top" border="0" scrolling="no">

  <frameset cols="180,*" frameborder="0" border="0" framespacing="0">

  <frame src="navbar2.htm" name="nav" noresize>
  <frame src="main2.htm" name="main">

  </frameset>

</frameset>
```

Parent frameset

Nested frameset

FIGURE H-15: Nested frameset displayed in browser

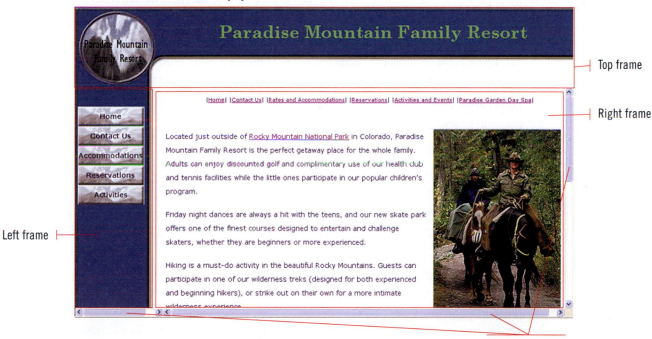

Top frame

Right frame

Left frame

Frameset scrollbars

Creating a Structuring Table

You can lay out a Web page in a grid using a **structuring table**, which allows you to include all the page elements within one large table. Structuring tables offer positioning benefits similar to frames, yet make your pages accessible to most users whose browsers don't support frames. ▰▰▰▰ You decide to try your layout in a structuring table, to compare its appearance with frames. To achieve the same effect using tables, you'll create a heading row, a vertical navigation column, and a content column. Some areas of your frames-based page are already positioned using tables. You will include these sections in your structuring table as nested tables.

STEPS

1. **In your text editor, open the file htm_H-3.txt from your paradise\frames folder in your site file location, then save it as home.htm in the same folder**

   As shown in Figure H-16, the file is a table-based layout page with placeholder text to guide you in the process of nesting tables from your frame source pages in your new document. A class called headrow, which adds a top-border background graphic, was embedded in the document and applied to the first row. The contents of your main2.htm page have already been pasted into the content cell.

2. **Click after width="100%" inside the opening table tag, press [Spacebar], then type `cellpadding="0" cellspacing="0" border="1"`**

   The design you are working to achieve is dependent upon your ability to precisely position your logo image. Setting the cellpadding and cellspacing to zero helps you achieve the effect you want. Although a borderless structuring table is usually the most effective for layout, you temporarily turn on the borders to help you quickly and easily see if any page elements are out of place. You want to place the logo graphic in the first cell of the heading row.

3. **Drag to select the text in the first cell that reads Logo goes here, press [Delete], type `<img src="images/logo_pm3.png" width="188" height="165" alt="Welcome to Paradise Mountain Resort" />`, then save your work**

   You want to copy the heading content from the top.htm file into the second cell in your home.htm file table.

4. **Open your top.htm file in a separate instance of your text editor**

5. **Click after `<!-- Heading content -->`, drag to select `<br clear="all" />` through the `</h1>`, copy the selected text, then close the file**

TROUBLE

Make sure that you do not copy the closing table data, table row, or table tags for the parent table.

6. **In your home.htm file, drag to select `top.htm content goes here`, press [Delete], paste the copied code, then save your work**

7. **Open your navbar2.htm file in a separate instance of your text editor, locate the table with the attribute `id="vnav"`, drag to select the entire table, as shown in Figure H-17, then copy the code**

TROUBLE

If your page elements don't appear as shown, make note of which elements are out of place by inspecting the grid marks in the browser, then check your code for errors.

8. **In your home.htm file, drag to select `navbar2.htm content goes here`, press [Delete], paste the code you copied in Step 7, then save your work and preview your page in your browser**

   The layout is nearly identical to the one you created with frames. The difference, as shown in Figure H-18, is that you can see the grid work of white borders, which push the logo image slightly to the right.

9. **Return to your home.htm code, locate the opening table tag just below the opening body tag, change the border value from 1 to 0, save your work, then view your page in your browser**

   The border disappears and your page closely resembles your frameset2.htm layout.

FIGURE H-16: Starting code for structuring table

Headrow class adds top border graphic

Placeholder text in table cells

```
</head>

<body>
<table width="100%">
<!-- The heading row starts below this comment -->
<tr valign="top" class="headrow">

<td width="188" height="165">Logo goes here</td>

<td nowrap>top.htm content goes here</td>
</tr>

<tr valign="top">

<td>
<!-- Begin holding table for site navigation -->
<table width="146" cellpadding="5" id="nav_holdTable">
<tr>
<td><!-- Insert site navigation table below -->
navbar2.htm content goes here

</td>
</tr>
<!-- End holding table for site navigation -->
</table>
<!-- End navigation cell -->
</td>

<!-- Content from main2.htm goes in the content cell below. -->
<td>
<p style="text-align: center; font-size: 75%;">|<a href="frameset.htm"
target="_top">Home</a>| |<a href="contact.htm">Contact Us</a>| |<a href="rates.htm">Rates
and Accommodations</a>| |<a href="reserve.htm">Reservations</a>| |<a
href="activities/index.htm">Activities and Events</a>| |<a href="../spa/index.htm"
```

FIGURE H-17: Copied code for structuring table

```
<table width="136" border="0" cellpadding="0" cellspacing="0" align="left" id="vnav">

<tr align="center" id="vnavRow1">

<th width="135" height="40" class="nav2">
<a href="main.htm">Home</a>
</th>
</tr>

<tr id="vnavRow2" align="center">
<th width="135" height="40" class="nav2">
<a href="contact.htm">Contact Us</a>
</th>
</tr>

<tr id="vnavRow3" align="center">
<th width="135" height="40" class="nav2" background="images/btn_pm1_blank.png">
<a href="rates.htm">Accommodations</a>
</th>
</tr>

<tr id="vnavRow4" align="center">
<th width="135" height="40" class="nav2" background="images/btn_pm1_blank.png">
<a href="reserve.htm">Reservations</a>
</th>
</tr>

<tr id="vnavRow5" align="center">
<th width="135" height="40" class="nav2" background="images/btn_pm1_blank.png">
<a href="activities/index.htm">Activities</a>
</th>
</tr>
</table>
```

FIGURE H-18: Web page laid out in structuring table

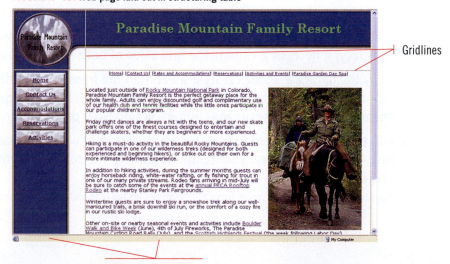

Gridlines

No individual scrollbars

HTML

Creating a Template

Once you finalize your site layout with a structuring table, it is important to implement the layout uniformly on all your Web site's pages. Rather than reentering the code for common elements for every page in your site, however, you can make your design tasks easier by creating a template. A **template** contains the Web page code for the page's structure, along with any text or other elements that appear on every page. You can create a template by removing the page-specific items from your original layout. Then you can use it as a starting point for creating additional pages. It is also good practice to add comments to the code, so that other designers using the template clearly understand where to insert their own page-specific elements. After you presented your layout sample options and explained the advantages and drawbacks of each, your Web design team decided to use your structuring table design for the Paradise Mountain site. You want to create a template from your Web page to make the team's work on the site more efficient, and to ensure that each team member implements the same layout.

STEPS

1. **In your text editor, save a copy of** home.htm **as** template.htm **in your paradise folder**

   Because you can use this template for any page in your site, you want to save it in your site root folder.

2. **Click just after** `<body>`**, press** [Enter]**, type** `<!-- Web page structuring table, two rows by two columns -->`**, then press** [Enter]

3. **Click after** `<tr valign="top" class="headrow">`**, press** [Enter]**, then type**
   `<!-- Logo image - Do not change -->`

   Figure H-19 shows the Web page code containing the first comments, some of which are from your home.htm file.

4. **Click before** `<td nowrap><br clear="all" />`**, type** `<!-- Second column - Page heading goes here  -->`**, then press** [Enter]

5. **Click before** `<tr align="center" id="vnavRow1">`**, type** `<!-- Site-standard navigation bar - Do Not Change -->`**, then press** [Enter]

6. **Click after** src=" **in the image tag for the trail_ride2.jpg image, drag to select the entire source path, press** [Delete]**, type** `file.jpg`**, click after** alt="**, select the entire alt statement, press** [Delete]**, then type** `Placeholder graphic. Insert your own image and alt statement in this tag.`

7. **Drag to select the remaining text in the content column, stopping just before** `<address style="text-align: center;">`**, press** [Delete]**, type** `<p>Insert your page text here.</p>`**, then press** [Enter] **twice**

8. **Edit the Day Spa link to remove the** ../ **so that the spa files are available from the root directory; if necessary, change the href value of both home links to** index.htm

9. **Copy the paradise_style2.css style sheet from the** frames\css **folder and paste it into the** paradise\css **folder, then copy the images from the** frames\images **folder and paste them into the** paradise\images **folder, clicking** No **if prompted to replace files**

10. **Edit the "Page modified by" paragraph as necessary with your name and today's date, save your work, preview your template and print it from your browser, then close the file and exit the program**

    Your template appears with site-standard elements and placeholder text, as shown in Figure H-20.

FIGURE H-19: Opening comments in page template code

Comment tags in template

```
<body>
<!-- Web page structuring table, two rows by two columns -->
<table width="100%" cellpadding="0" cellspacing="0" border="0">
<!-- The heading row starts below this comment -->
<tr valign="top" class="headrow">
<!-- Logo image - Do not change -->

<td width="188" height="165"><img src="images/logo_pm3.png" width="188" height="165"
alt="Welcome to Paradise Mountain Resort" /></td>

<td nowrap><br clear="all" />
<br /><br />
<h1 class="heading">Paradise Mountain Family Resort</h1></td>
</tr>

<tr valign="top">

<td>
<!-- Begin holding table for site navigation -->
<table width="146" cellpadding="5" id="nav_holdTable">
<tr>
<td><!-- Insert site navigation table below -->
<table width="136" border="0" cellpadding="0" cellspacing="0" align="left" id="vnav">

<tr align="center" id="vnavRow1">

<th width="135" height="40" class="nav2">
<a href="main.htm">Home</a>
</th>
</tr>

<tr id="vnavRow2" align="center">
<th width="135" height="40" class="nav2">
```

FIGURE H-20: Completed template

Navigation elements

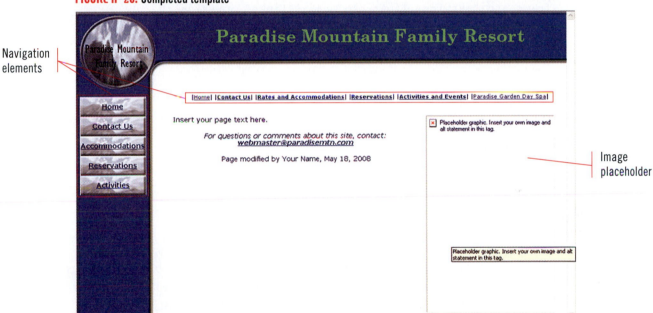

Image placeholder

Choosing between frames and tables

Frames offer several features that tables can't match, such as independently scrolling window areas and the ability to maintain site-standard information such as navigation, headings, and footers in easily updated, separate files. However, due to the fragmentation of information on a frames-based site, it is difficult to optimize such sites for search engine listings. Frames-based sites also create some of the problems they were meant to prevent. If, for example, a frame's content page is opened outside of the frameset (as can easily happen when a visitor comes across page content via a search-engine listing), that standardized information you so carefully constructed as part of your frameset is not available. Moreover, framesets are no longer part of the W3C standard. Consequently, most professional Web designers find that the advantages of tables and divisions outweigh the benefits of frames. Because all the page contents of a table or division layout are contained in one HTML file, pages constructed in this manner are easier for users to print, and they provide more accurate data for search engine indexes. Additionally, because a browser's address bar displays the name and location of the table- or division-based pages, they are more accessible to site visitors who want to bookmark them for later use.

HTML

Practice

▼ CONCEPTS REVIEW

Name the function of each section of code indicated in Figure H-21.

FIGURE H-21

```
<html>
<head>
<title>Services Information</title>

<frameset rows="160,*"  frameborder="0"  border="0"  framespacing="0"
noresize>
<frame src="top.htm" name="top"  scrolling="no" />
<frameset cols ="200,*"  frameborder="0"  border="0"
framespacing="0" >

       <frame src="services_links.htm" name="links"  noresize />

       <frame src="services_first.htm" name="main" />
</frameset>
</frameset>

<noframes>
This page was designed to be viewed with frames. You can open
individual pages using the <a href="services_links.htm">navigation
bar</a>
</noframes>

</html>
```

Match each statement with the term it best describes.

10. Navigation bar
11. Frameset
12. Frame
13. Target
14. Noresize

a. Attribute that prevents the change of a frame's dimensions
b. A set of links to the home page and main sections of a Web site that appears on every page
c. A file specifying the organization of frame files within the browser window
d. A window within a frameset that displays a separate HTML document
e. A method of setting the location where a link page opens

Select the best answer from the list of choices.

15. **In a Web page laid out with frames, each frame displays:**
    a. The contents of a separate Web document.
    b. The contents of a table cell.
    c. The contents of a table.
    d. The same Web document.

16. **Which tag would you use to create a global setting to target a different frame for all of a page's links?**
    a. `<body>`
    b. `<head>`
    c. `<base />`
    d. `<noframes>`

17. **How can the pages in a frameset be refreshed?**
    a. Click the Refresh or Reload button in the browser.
    b. Click the Go button in the browser.
    c. Hold down [Ctrl] while refreshing the frameset page.
    d. Hold down [Fn] while refreshing the frameset page.
18. **Which attribute in the frame tag defines the location for the frame contents?**
    a. cols
    b. rows
    c. src
    d. name
19. **How many HTML files would you need in order to create a frameset that displays two frames?**
    a. One
    b. Two
    c. Three
    d. Four
20. **Which tags cannot be used within `<frameset>...</frameset>` tags?**
    a. `<frame />`
    b. `<frameset>`
    c. `<body>`
    d. `<noframes>`

▼ SKILLS REVIEW

1. **Understand layout tools.**
   a. Consider how frames can be used to present the information on the pages of the spa site. How would you lay out the spa pages using frames?
   b. Which spa pages would you lay out using structuring tables?
   c. How would you include the spa logo on your pages if using tables or frames?
   d. What advantages do you see in using frames for the spa site?
   e. What advantages do you see in using structuring tables for the spa site?

2. **Create a navigation bar.**
   a. Copy the files **wraps.htm**, **packages.htm**, **salon.htm**, and **hands.htm** from the drive and folder where your Data Files are stored to the paradise/spa folder where you save your site files. If you are asked whether you want to replace the files, click Yes.
   b. Copy the file **services_style.css** from the drive and folder where your Data Files are stored to the paradise/css folder where you save your site files.
   c. Copy the **spa_logo.gif** from the drive and folder where your Data Files are stored to the paradise/images folder where you save your site files. If you are asked whether you want to replace the file, click Yes.
   d. In your text editor, open the file **htm_H-4.txt** from the drive and folder where your Data Files are stored, then save it as **services_links.htm** to the paradise/spa directory where you save your site files.
   e. Locate the comment in the file indicating where the navigation bar is placed. Add the link for the massage therapy information by placing `<a href="wraps.htm">` before Massage Therapy and `</a>` after this label in the first table row.
   f. Add the link for the spa packages by placing `<a href="packages.htm">` before Spa Packages and `</a>` after this label in the second table row.
   g. In the third table row, add a link to the salon.htm page for Aphrodite's Salon.
   h. In the fourth table row, add a link to the hands.htm page for Hand and Foot Care.
   i. Delete the comment, save your file, then open the **services_links.htm** file in your browser to view the navigation bar and test its links.

3. Create a frameset.

   a. In your text editor, open the file **htm_H-5.txt** from the drive and folder where your Data Files are stored, then save it as **servicesframes.htm** to the paradise/spa directory where you save your site files. Copy the **services_first.htm** file from the drive and folder where your Data Files are stored to your paradise/spa folder.

   b. Create a frameset with the configuration shown below in Table H-4 by inserting `<frameset cols="200,*">` under the title information.

TABLE H-4

200 pixels	Remaining browser width

   c. Specify your navigation bar, services_links.htm, as the source file with the name of links that will appear in the left frame by inserting `<frame src="services_links.htm" name="links" />` under the `<frameset>` tag.

   d. In the servicesframes.htm file, specify a source file of services_first.htm with the name `main` for the right frame by inserting `<frame src="services_first.htm" name="main" />` on the line below the first `<frame />` tag.

   e. In the servicesframes.htm file, end the frameset after the second `<frame />` tag using the `</frameset>` tag.

   f. Provide alternate page content in the servicesframes.htm file for browsers that do not support frames by adding the following before the closing `</html>` tag: `<noframes>` This page was designed to be viewed with frames. You can open individual pages using the `<a href="services_links.htm">`navigation bar`</a>` `</noframes>`.

   g. Save your work, then view the **servicesframes.htm** file in your browser.

4. Target links.

   a. If necessary, open the **services_links.htm** file in a separate instance of your text editor.

   b. Using a base tag, set a target attribute of `main` for this page so that the contents of the page's links are displayed in the right frame of the servicesframes.htm file. (*Hint*: Under the title information, add `<base target="main" />`.)

   c. Save your **services_links.htm** file.

   d. Refresh your **servicesframes.htm** file in your browser using the Go button.

   e. Check the targets for your links in the left frame to be sure their content can be displayed in the right frame, then close the services_links file.

5. Format frame borders.

   a. In the servicesframes.htm file, hide the border of the frames by adding `frameborder="0"` in the opening `<frameset>` tag.

   b. To ensure compatibility with the greatest number of browsers, add `border="0"` and `framespacing="0"` to the opening `<frameset>` tag.

   c. Prevent users from resizing the left frame by adding `noresize` in the first `<frame />` tag.

   d. Save your **servicesframes.htm** file and refresh the page in your browser.

   e. Check your work by making sure the left frame cannot be resized and that the borders do not appear.

6. Use nested frames.

   a. In your text editor, open the file **htm_H-5.txt** from the drive and folder where your Data Files are stored, then save it as **servicesframes2.htm** to the paradise/spa directory where you save your site files.

   b. Create a frameset with the configuration shown in Table H-5 by inserting `<frameset rows="160,*">` under the title information.

TABLE H-5

160 pixels
Remaining browser height

   c. Turn off the frame borders and prevent resizing of the frames by adding `frameborder="0" border="0" framespacing="0" noresize` to the `<frameset>` tag.

   d. Copy the **top.htm** file from the drive and folder where your Data Files are stored, then save it to your paradise/spa folder. In the serviceframes2.htm file, specify the top.htm page as the source file with the name `top` for the upper frame by inserting `<frame src="top.htm" name="top" />` under the `<frameset>` tag.

   e. Prevent scrollbars from being displayed in the upper frame by adding `scrolling="no"` to the `<frame />` tag.

f. Place the frame structure you created in the servicesframes.htm file in the lower frame of the servicesframes2.htm page by copying the code between the title information and the closing `</html>` tag and pasting it above the closing `</html>` tag of the servicesframes2.htm file. Your nested frame configuration is shown in Table H-6.

TABLE H-6

top.htm	
services_links.htm	services_first.htm

g. In the servicesframes2.htm file, close the first `<frameset>` tag by adding `</frameset>` after the existing closing `</frameset>` tag.

h. Save your work, then open the **servicesframes2.htm** file in your browser to view the frames. See Figure H-22.

FIGURE H-22

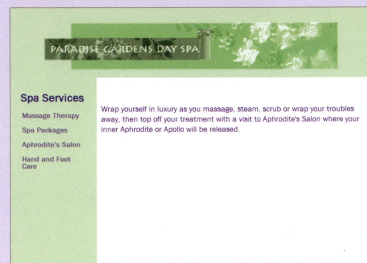

7. Create a structuring table.

a. In your text editor, open the file **htm_H-6.txt** from the drive and folder where your Data Files are stored, then save it as **servicestable.htm** to the paradise/spa directory where you save your site files.

b. Add the spa logo from the **top.htm** file to the top row of the table by opening top.htm file in your text editor, copying the code between the opening and closing `<body>` tags, then using the comment in the servicestable.htm file as a guide to paste the code in the top row of your table. Close the top.htm file.

c. Add the navigation bar to the left side of your table by opening the **services_links.htm** file in your text editor, copying the code between the opening and closing `<body>` tags, then using the comment in the servicestable.htm file as a guide to paste the code in the first cell of the second row of your table. Close the services_links.htm file.

d. Add the starting text for the table by opening the **services_first.htm** file in your text editor, copying the code between the opening and closing `<body>` tags, then using the comment in the servicestable.htm file as a guide to paste the code in the second cell of the second row of your table. Close the services_first.htm file.

e. Delete any remaining comments from your servicestable.htm file, save your work, then open the **servicestable.htm** page in your browser to check your work.

8. Create a template.

a. In your text editor, save a copy of servicestable.htm as **servicestemplate.htm** to the paradise/spa directory where you save your site files.

b. Provide information about the structure of the table by adding a comment of `<!-- Web page structuring table, two rows with lower row divided into two columns -->` under the opening `<body>` tag.

c. Provide information about the location of the logo image by adding a comment of `<!-- Logo image - Do not change -->` under the first `<tr>` tag in the body of the page.

d. Provide information about the location of the navigation bar by adding a comment of `<!-- Site navigation bar - Do Not Change -->` in the line below the second `<tr>` tag in the body of the page. In the `<td>` tag in the line below this comment, add `width="20%"` to keep the navigation bar sized appropriately when the amount of page text changes in the future.

e. Mark the area where the opening text should be placed by replacing the text in the last `<td>...</td>` tag set with `Insert your page text here`.

f. Add your name to the servicestemplate.htm file using a comment, preview the template in your browser, then save and print the page.

g. Transfer the files to your remote directory.

▼ INDEPENDENT CHALLENGE 1

As you continue developing the Web site for your resort rental business, Star Vacations, you decide to use frames to lay out your rentals page. You decide to place the navigation bar in an upper frame and the linked contents in the lower frame.

a. In your browser, open the file **rentals.htm** from the drive and folder where your Data Files are stored. View the page, then open the source code in your text editor.

b. In a separate instance of your text editor, open the file **htm_H-7.txt** from the drive and folder where your Data Files are stored, then save it as **navbar.htm** to the vacations folder where you save your site files.

c. In your rentals.htm source code, locate the Vacation Rental Listings title and the navigation bar area and paste them between the body tags in your navbar.htm file. (*Hint*: Copy everything from the rentals.htm file between the opening <body> tag and "Information coming soon!")

d. Save your **navbar.htm** file.

e. In your text editor, open the file **htm_H-7.txt** again from the drive and folder where your Data Files are stored, then save it as **open_page.htm** to the vacations folder where you save your site files.

f. Locate and copy the five lines above the closing </body> tag in your rentals.htm file, paste them between the <body> tags in your open_page.htm file, then save the **open_page.htm** file.

g. In your text editor, open the file **htm_H-8.txt** from the drive and folder where your Data Files are stored, then save it as **vacationframes.htm** to the vacations folder where you save your site files.

h. Assign navbar.htm as the source file for the top frame with a name of links and an attribute to prevent resizing the frame.

i. Assign open_page.htm as the source file for the bottom frame with a name of main.

j. Save the **vacationframes.htm** file.

k. Add a <base> tag to your navbar.htm file to set the target for the links to the lower frame and resave the **navbar.htm** file. (*Hint*: The name of the lower frame is main.)

l. Copy the files **faq.htm** and **features.htm** from the drive and folder where your Data Files are stored to the vacations folder where you save your site files. If you are asked whether you want to replace the files, click Yes. You will use these files to test the navbar.htm links.

m. Open your **vacationframes.htm** file in your browser and test the Frequently Asked Questions and Featured Resorts links.

n. Add your name to the vacationframes.htm file in a comment, then save your work and print your vacationsframes.htm file from your text editor.

o. Transfer your pages to your remote directory.

Advanced Challenge Exercises

- Refer to Table H-3 in the Format Frame Borders lesson to find the attribute that customizes the border color for a frame.
- Use the appropriate attribute to add a color of #6600FF to the first frame tag in the vacationframes.htm file.
- Save your work and display the **vacationframes.htm** file in your browser to check the border.
- Transfer your vacationframes.htm file to your remote directory.

▼ INDEPENDENT CHALLENGE 2

Metro Water publishes water conservation tips on their Web site. You will use a structuring table to lay out links for a variety of water conservation tips.

a. In your text editor, open the **htm_H-9.txt** file from the drive and folder where your Data Files are stored, then save it as **conservation_links.htm** in the water folder where you save your site files. You will use the code in this file as part of a structuring table on a Web page.

b. In your text editor, open the **htm_H-10.txt** file from the drive and folder where your Data Files are stored, then save it as **tip.htm** in the water folder where you save your site files. You will use the code in this file as part of a structuring table on a Web page.

c. In your text editor, open the **htm_H-11.txt** file from the drive and folder where your Data Files are stored, then save it as **watertable.htm** in the water folder where you save your site files.

▼ INDEPENDENT CHALLENGE 2 (CONTINUED)

d. Using the comment in the watertable.htm file that identifies the location of the structuring table and the code from the files conservation_links.htm and tip.htm, add the table elements to create the rows and columns, as shown in Table H-7.

e. Add the level three formatting, as shown in Table H-7, for the Metro Water Conservation heading. Add the attribute to set the width of the conservation_links.htm cell. Save the **watertable.htm** file and view the file in your browser to check your work.

TABLE H-7

Metro Water Conservation (Format with level-three heading)	
conservation_links.htm	tip.htm
width 40%	

f. Create a template by adding comments to mark the locations of the page heading, links, and the tip. Save your template as **watertemplate.htm**

g. Add your name to the watertemplate.htm file as a comment and print the page from your text editor.

h. Save your work and transfer your pages to the remote site.

Advanced Challenge Exercises

■ Although using tables for page layout is often preferable to using frames, many Web designers do not use tables in this way. Use your favorite search engine to research the challenges associated with using tables for Web page layout.

■ Write a paragraph citing four problems associated with page layout using tables. Include the preferred method for Web page layout.

■ Add your name and today's date to the top of your paper and print it.

▼ INDEPENDENT CHALLENGE 3

In this unit you used frames to lay out Web pages. You are considering using frames to standardize your site navigation, but first you need to research how you can make them accessible for all users.

Go to the Student Online Companion for this book, locate the link for this unit, then click the link for the W3C Web Accessibility page and review the information on frames. Write one or two paragraphs answering the following questions about frames:

1. How can titles in frames be used to increase their accessibility?
2. What information about frames is important to note in a frameset?
3. What is the best place to add descriptions of the frames in a frameset?
4. Add your name and today's date to the top of your paper, then print it.

▼ INDEPENDENT CHALLENGE 4

Now that you've used frames and structuring tables to lay out Web pages, you are ready to add them to your Web site.

a. Determine how frames and structuring tables can be used in your Web site to standardize navigation.

b. Lay out your Web pages on paper to determine which structure works best.

c. Create the frames and/or structuring tables using your text editor.

d. Create templates for the structures to use for other pages.

e. Format your frames and tables appropriately.

f. Add appropriate accessibility features to your pages.

g. Test and edit your pages, then add your name and the current date. Save and print the pages, then transfer them to the remote location.

▼ VISUAL WORKSHOP

You have created a Web page with links for the services provided by Bits and PCs. You want to use nested frames to lay out the page with a header in the top frame and two columns in the lower frame. The contents of the links in the left frame should appear in the right frame. Use Figure H-23 as a guide to create the page layout in your text editor using the data files: bitshead.htm, first.htm, and bitslinks.htm. Be sure to include a description in the frameset page for browsers that do not display the frames. Add your name as a comment in the frameset page, save your frameset page as **bitsframes.htm** in the bitspcs folder where you save your site files, then print the page.

FIGURE H-23

Bits and PCs

Services

Home Networking

Data Recovery

System Upgrades

For 20 years Bits and PCs has been serving all your computer needs. Now, we invite you to join us in celebrating our 20th anniversary!

To celebrate our success we are giving away cash and prizes worth more than $50,000. Hidden throughout our Bits and PCs History pages are answers to our weekly trivia game. Find those answers and submit the trivia game of the week for a chance to win our weekly drawing. Who knows? You might be next!

Appendix

HTML

Appendix

OBJECTIVES

Put a document on the Web
Use other FTP client programs
Increase Web site traffic
HTML tag reference
HTML browser-safe colors
HTML color names
Cascading Style Sheet reference
HTML special characters
Formatting with HTML 4.0 attributes

When you create HTML documents for use in a business setting, it is important not only to know how to construct Web pages, but also how to transfer documents and take advantage of resources on the Web. These resources include a variety of search engines and Web sites devoted to helping your business have a Web presence. You also should be aware of the variety of options available for increasing traffic to your Web site. This appendix provides useful HTML code and publishing references for you to use as you create and publish your Web pages.

Putting a Document on the Web

Crucial factors in making your site successful are availability and accessibility. Accessible Web sites are stored on a Web server (a computer that makes files available over the World Wide Web) with adequate bandwidth—data-transfer capacity—so that Web traffic can flow smoothly and quickly. It is also important that the company you choose as your hosting service provides reliable support and backup services so your site is always available. Your school or Internet service provider (ISP)—the company that provides your Internet access—may have a Web server available for your use. Free Web space is also available on many Web sites. However, free sites usually require you to display advertising banners and pop-up windows, both a source of annoyance to visitors, on your pages in exchange for the free service. Figure AP-1 shows a Web page on one such site.

DETAILS

Ensure that your site is ready for users by doing the following:

- **Establish your URL**

  When you place your Web site on a free or inexpensive Web server, the resulting URL is usually a subdirectory on the Web server's domain—for example, www.course.com/users/~torxdesign/. Such a URL is not easy for potential users to remember or to type. The alternative is to register your own domain name, such as www.thomson.com. Domain name registration involves payment of a yearly fee, in addition to paying a Web space provider to store your pages and domain name. In either case, the logistics of setting up your Web site location can take time, so begin making arrangements for a Web server well in advance of your target publishing date.

- **Submit your URL to search engines**

  Submitting your URL for inclusion in search engine databases facilitates potential users locating your site. Each search engine has different site indexing policies. You can access a list of submission instructions by clicking on the About or Businesses link, which is usually near the bottom of a search engine's home page. Figure AP-2 shows the About Google page with a link leading to instructions for submitting a URL. An alternative to submitting your own site URL is to use a search engine submission service. For a nominal fee, these service providers submit your site to a wide variety of search engines. You should be aware, however, that most of these companies use submission "robots"—special software programs that automatically submit your site to a variety of search engines on a rotating basis. Some search engines give less weight to this type of submission.

- **Test your Web pages**

  Extensively test your files using a variety of browsers, operating systems, and display conditions to weed out any errors and design problems before you publish.

- **Ensure Web server compatibility**

  Every hosting service has a list of recommended default file names. Check with your chosen hosting service for a list of recommended file names, then review your filenames to be sure they are named accordingly.

- **Verify hyperlinks**

  Confirm that the hyperlinks in your documents point to the correct filenames. As some operating systems and scripts are case sensitive, it is best practice to use all lowercase in assigning filenames. It is particularly important that all of your files be saved with lowercase extensions. Another common problem with hyperlinks is drive letters that appear in file paths. As you check your links, be sure that no drive-letter paths, such as c:\\ appear in your links. Also, be sure that hyperlinks between pages in your Web site use relative pathnames.

- **Learn the publishing procedure**

  Every Web server uses a unique system for adding new Web sites. Make sure you understand the procedure outlined by your Web space provider, and make sure you have the necessary software.

FIGURE AP-1: Pop-up windows and banners located on a free Web site

FIGURE AP-2: About Google information page

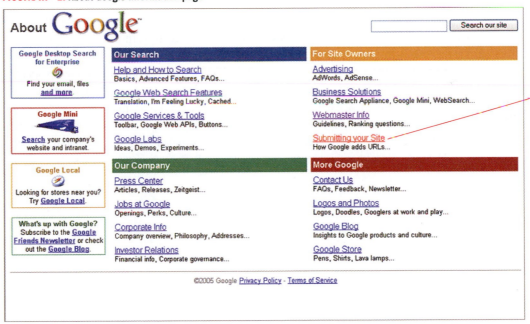

Instructions for submitting site to Google

HTML

Using Other FTP Client Programs

Unless you are using a Web development software program that comes with its own file transfer application, you need to establish a method of transferring your files to a Web server. This is usually accomplished through the use of an FTP client program. Before using any FTP client, make sure that you have a valid user ID, password, and directory path as assigned by your instructor or server administrator. If you do not have this information, make sure you get it before attempting to transfer files.

DETAILS

Two common FTP client programs are WS_FTP, which comes in both Home and Pro versions for Windows clients, and Fetch FTP for Apple Macintosh users:

- ### WS_FTP by Ipswitch

  Ipswitch's WS_FTP_Home and Pro programs are high-powered FTP clients that are easy to use and make transfers lightning fast. Figure AP-3 shows the WS_FTP interface with its daily startup tip. While the program walks the user through the install process, WS_FTP Home also supplies its own Getting Started Tutorial. When you start WS_FTP_Home for the first time, you are presented with a Welcome page that supplies a link to the tutorial. If you choose not to view the Getting Started tutorial, simply click the Next button at the bottom of the screen to continue with the setup. (You can always come back to the tutorial at a later time.) (To go directly to the tutorial, go to the Student Online Companion for this book.)

- ### Fetch FTP by Fetch Softworks

  Fetch is an FTP client program by Fetch Softworks. Fetch is designed for use with the Apple Macintosh operating system. It supports FTP and SFTP. As with other FTP clients, Fetch can be used to transfer files from your local computer to another computer on the Internet for document-sharing and Web publishing purposes. Using Fetch, you can also rename, move, delete, and change the permissions of files on a Web server. As shown in Figure AP-4, Fetch uses the graphical user interface common to programs that run on Macintosh operating systems. To view a step-by-step tutorial on using Fetch, go to the Student Online Companion for this book. If you are a student or employee at a public or accredited private school, college, university, or academy or a volunteer at a nonprofit agency, you may qualify for a fee-exempt license. Students and parents in some home-school situations might also be eligible to receive free downloads. Fetch 5.0 supports Mac OS X 10.2.4 or later. If your operating system is older than that, you can download Fetch 4.0, a previous version of Fetch that may still be available for purchase on the Fetch Softworks Web site.

FIGURE AP-3: WS_FTP Home startup screen with Tip

FIGURE AP-4: Fetch GUI windows

Increasing Web Site Traffic

Have you ever wondered why a Web site can be found by one search engine but not by another? How does a site get listed in an index? Some search engines conduct periodic—and laborious—searches of Web sites, and other search engines depend on site submissions to their indices. The key to a successful Web site is its accessibility to Web users. After all, if no users see your site, the caliber of its design is irrelevant.

DETAILS

Make sure users can access your Web pages using search engines by using these guidelines:

- ### Submit your URL to search engines

  One of the simplest steps in getting your site listed by search engines is to provide them with your URL. Most search engine Web sites contain contact information for requesting your site to be added to their index. Figure AP-5 shows the submission form for Google. Because search engine databases have size limits and must continually purge outdated information, you should resubmit your URL on a regular basis to prevent your site's removal. To maximize the number of users sent to your site, target your requests to the search engines with the most visitors. Web site audience measurement statistics are available from comScore Networks, through the comScore Media Metrix service, as shown in Figure AP-6.

- ### Use keywords

  When adding a Web page to its database, a search engine's goal is to locate terms in the page that identify the page's key concepts or focus. It adds these terms, known as **keywords**, to the index for its database. When a user conducts a search, the search engine uses these keywords to determine which URLs it provides as search results. For this reason, it is important that you optimize your page for search-engine submission by using relevant wording throughout your Web page. Because many search engines compare information listed in both the page title—the number-one comparison factor—and the meta tags with the information contained within the text of your Web site, it is important that your title and meta tags contain information your target audience is seeking and that matches your page content. Figure AP-7 shows the source code for a page that has been optimized for search-engine selection.

- ### Plan ahead

  Some search engines can take as long as three months from the time you submit your URL until the time your site is included in their index. In the intervening period, your business may have minimal Web site traffic, which can be a serious problem. If your business plan relies heavily on Web traffic, you may need to schedule the rollout of your Web site prior to the official opening of your business so that it appears in search engine databases.

- ### Make your page a high priority

  Although a search may yield hundreds of sites, most people generally look at only the first few entries in search results. You can give your page a higher priority by skillfully implementing the `<title>` and `<meta />` tags in your Web site. Some search engines look only at the text marked by these tags when indexing, or give extra weight to this text when evaluating your page's relevance to particular topics. The `<meta />` tag includes attributes that allow you to suggest to the search engines the most appropriate keywords, as well as the most appropriate description, for your Web page. Figure AP-7 shows the code for a Web page using `<meta />` tags.

FIGURE AP-5: URL submission form on the Google search engine Web site

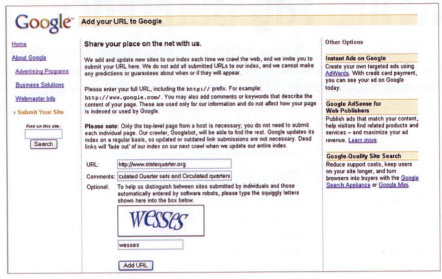

FIGURE AP-6: comScore Media Metrix: the Internet audience measurement service

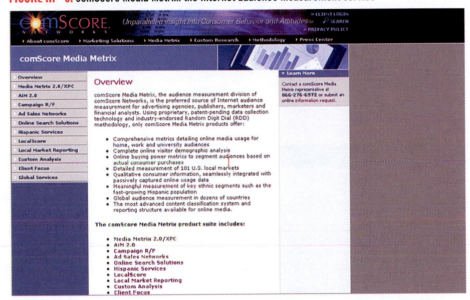

FIGURE AP-7: Web page incorporating optimized `<meta />` title and content tags

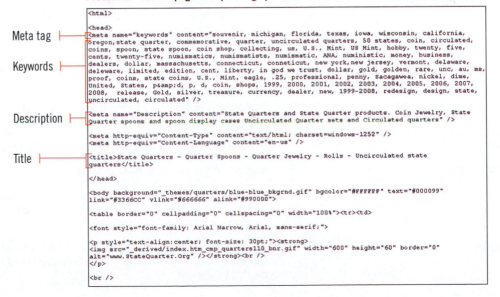

Meta tag

Keywords

Description

Title

HTML Tag Reference

The following are commonly supported HTML tags and properties. You can view more detailed information about the latest HTML specifications at the W3C Worldwide Consortium site. Additional information about browser support for different HTML tags is available at Index DOT HTML Reference. Because the World Wide Web constantly changes, you should check this information against current browser versions. (To access these sites, go to the Student Online Companion for this book.)

STEPS

Properties are of the following types:

- *Character*   A single text character
- *Color*   A recognized color name or color value
- *CGI script*   The name of a CGI script on the Web server
- *Document*   The filename or URL of the file
- *List*   List of items separated by commas, usually enclosed in double quotation marks
- *Mime-type*   A MIME data type, such as "text/css", "audio/wav", or "video/x-msvideo"
- *Options*   Limited to a specific set of values (values are shown below the property)
- *Text*   Any legal text string
- *URL*   The URL for a Web page or file
- *Value*   A number, usually an integer

TABLE AP-1: HTML tags

tags and properties		description
`<!-- -->`		Used for comments in documenting the features of your HTML code, often divided into <!-- and -->, which could be separated by several lines
`<a>...</a>`		Marks the beginning and end of a hypertext link
	`href="url"`	Indicates the target, filename, or URL to which the hypertext points
	`name="Text"`	Specifies a name for the enclosed text, allowing it to be a target of a hyperlink
	`rel="Text"`	Specifies the relationship between the current page and the link specified by the href property
	`rev="Text"`	Specifies a reverse relationship between the current page and the link specified by the href property
	`target="Text" (_blank, _top, _self, _parent)`	Specifies the default target window or frame for the hyperlink. Choices: _blank, _top, _self, _parent or the name of the window desired
	`title="Text"`	Provides a title for the document whose address is given by the href property
`<abbr>...</abbr>`		Indicates an abbreviated form (e.g., WWW, HTTP, URI, Mass., etc.)
`<acronym>...</acronym>`		Indicates an acronym (e.g., WAC, radar, etc.)
`<address>...</address>`		The <address> tag is used for information such as addresses, authorship, and so forth; the text is usually italicized and in some browsers it is indented
`<applet>...</applet>`		Supported by all Java-enabled browsers, allows designers to embed a Java applet in an HTML document; it has been deprecated in favor of the OBJECT element

tags and properties		description
\<area\>		Defines the type and coordinates of a hotspot within an image map
	`cords="Value"`	The coordinates of the hotspot; coordinates depend on the shape of the hotspot: *value 2…*
	`Rectangle`	coords=x_left, y_upper, x_right, y_lower
	`Circle`	coords=x_center, y_center, radius
	`Polygon`	coords=x1, y1, x2, y2, x3, y3, …
	`href="URL"`	Indicates the target, filename, or URL to which the hotspot points
	`shape="Option"` `(rect | circle | poly)`	The shape of the hotspot
	`target="Text"`	Specifies the default target window or frame for the hotspot
\<b\>...\</b\>		Displays the enclosed text in boldface; use the \<strong\> tag for greater accessibility
\<base /\>		Allows you to specify the URL for the HTML document; it is used by some browsers to interpret relative hyperlinks
	`href="URL"`	Specifies the URL from which all relative hyperlinks should be based
	`target="Text"`	Specifies the default target window or frame for every hyperlink in the document
\<basefont /\>		Sets the base font size (using the size attribute). Font size changes achieved with font are relative to the base font size set by basefont. If basefont is not used, the default base font size is 3. Basefont is deprecated in favor of Cascading Style Sheets.
\<bdo\>...\</bdo\>		Allows authors to turn off the bidirectional algorithm for selected fragments of text
\<bgsound /\>		Used to play a background sound clip when the page is first opened; the embed tag is preferred and leaves the user more control.
	`loop="Value"`	Specifies the number of times the sound clip should be played; loop can either be a digit or infinite
	`src="Document"`	The sound file used for the sound clip
\<big\>...\</big\>		Increases the size of the enclosed text; the exact appearance of the text depends on the browser and the default font size
\<blockquote\>... **\</blockquote\>**		Used to set off long quotes or citations, usually by indenting the enclosed text on both sides; some browsers italicize the text as well
\<body\>...\</body\>		Encloses all text, images, and other elements that the user sees on the Web page
	`Alink="Color"`	Color of activated hypertext links, which are links the user is currently clicking, but has not yet released
	`background="File"`	The graphic image file used for the Web page background
	`bgcolor="Color"`	The color of the Web page background
	`bgproperties="Fixed"`	Keeps the background image fixed so that it does not scroll with the Web page
	`leftmargin="Value"`	Indents the left margin of the page by the number of pixels specified in value
	`link="Color"`	Color of all unvisited links
	`text="Color"`	Color of all text in the document

tags and properties		description
	topmargin="Value"	Indents the top margin of the page by the number of pixels specified in value
	vlink="Color"	Color of previously visited links
 		Forces a line break in the text
	clear="Option"	Causes the next line to start at the spot where the specified margin is clear (left | right | all | none)
<button>...</button>		Buttons created with the button element function just like buttons created with the input element, but they offer richer rendering possibilities; the button element may have content
<caption>...</caption>		Encloses the table caption
	align="Option"	Specifies the alignment of the caption with respect to the table (left | right | center | top | bottom)
<center>...</center>		Horizontally centers the enclosed text or image; the center tag is deprecated in favor of Cascading Style Sheets
<cite>...</cite>		Used for citations and usually appears in italics
<code>...</code>		Used for text taken from the code for a computer program, and usually appears in a fixed width font
<col />		Allows authors to group together attribute specifications for table columns
<colgroup>...</colgroup>		Creates an explicit column group
<dd>...</dd>		Formats text to be used as relative definitions in a <dl> list
<del>		Used to markup sections of the document that have been deleted with respect to a different version of a document
<dir>...</dir>		Encloses an unordered list of <li> items, formatted in narrow columns; deprecated in favor of <ul>
	text="Option"	Specifies the type of bullet used for displaying each <li> item in the <dir> list: (circle | disc | square)
<dfn>...</dfn>		Used for the defining instance of a term, that is, the first time the term is used; the enclosed text is usually italicized
<div>...</div>		Used to set the text alignment of blocks of text or images
<dl>...</dl>		Encloses a definition list in which the <dd> definition term is left-aligned, and the <dt> relative definition is indented
<dt>		Used to format the definition term in a <dl> list
...		Used to emphasize text; the enclosed text usually appears in italics
<fieldset>...</fieldset>		Allows authors to group thematically related controls and labels
<font>...</font>		Used to control the appearance of the text it encloses; the font tag is deprecated in favor of Cascading Style Sheets

tags and properties		description
	color="Color"	The color of the enclosed text style attributes can be applied as: style="color: color;"
	face="List"	The font face of the text; multiple font faces can be specified, separated by commas; the browser tries to render the text in the order specified by the list
	size="Value"	Size of the font on a seven-point scale (1 is smallest, 7 is largest); it can be absolute or relative. Specifying size=5 sets the font size to size 5 on the scale; specifying size=+5 sets the font size 5 points larger than default tag
<form>...</form>		Marks the beginning and end of a Web page form
	action="URL"	Specifies the URL to which the contents of the form are to be sent
	Enctype="Text"	Specifies the encoding type used to submit the data to the server
	Method="Option"	Specifies the method of accessing the URL indicated in the action attribute (post | get)
	target="Text"	The frame or window that displays the form's results
<frame>...</frame>		Defines a single frame within a set of frames
	bordercolor="Color"	Specifies the color of the frame border
	Frameborder="Option"	Specifies whether the frame border is visible (yes | no)
	framespacing="Value"	Specifies the amount of space between frames, in pixels
	marginheight="Value"	Specifies the amount of space above and below the frame object and the frame borders
	Marginwidth="Value"	Specifies the amount of space to the left and right of the frame object, in pixels
	name="Text"	Label assigned to the frame
	Noresize	Prevents users from resizing the frame
	scrolling="Option"	Specifies whether scroll bars are visible (yes | no | auto); auto (the default) displays scroll bars only as needed
	src="Document"	Specifies the document or URL of the object to be displayed in the frame
<frameset>...</frameset>		Marks the beginning and the end of a set of frames
	border="Value"	The size of the borders, in pixels
	bordercolor="Value"	The color of the frame borders
	cols="List"	The size of each column in a set of frames; columns can be specified either in pixels, as a percentage of the display area, or with an asterisk (*), indicating that any remaining space be allotted to that column (for example, cols="40,25%,*")
	rows="List"	The size of each row in a set of frames; rows can be specified either in pixels, as a percentage of the display area, or with an asterisk (*), indicating that any remaining space be allotted to that column (for example, rows="40,25%,*")
<h1>...</h1> <h2>...</h2> <h3>...</h3> <h4>...</h4> <h5>...</h5> <h6>...</h6>		The six levels of text headings ranging from the largest (<h1>) to the smallest (<h6>); text headings appear in a bold face font

HTML

Appendix

HTML

tags and properties		description
`<head>...</head>`		The head element contains information about the current document, such as its title, keywords that may be useful to search engines, and other data that is not considered document content
`<hr />`		Creates a horizontal line
	`align="Option"`	The alignment of the heading (left | right | center)
	`color="Color"`	Specifies a color for the line
	`Noshade`	Removes 3D shading from the line
	`size="Value"`	The size (height) of the line in pixels
	`width="Value"`	The width (length) of the line either in pixels or as a percentage of the display area
`<head>...</head>`		Encloses code that provides information about the document
`<html>...</html>`		Indicates the beginning and end of the HTML document
`<i>...</i>`		Italicizes the enclosed text; WAI recommends the use of ... instead of <i>...</i>
`<iframe>...</iframe>`		Allows authors to insert a frame within a block of text. Inserting an inline frame within a section of text is much like inserting an object via the object element: they both allow you to insert an HTML document in the middle of another; they may both be aligned with surrounding text, etc.
`<img />`		Used to insert an inline image into the document
	`align=Option`	Specifies the alignment of the image; specifying left or right aligns the image with the left or right page margin; the other alignment options align the image with surrounding text (left | right | top | texttop | middle | absmiddle | baseline | bottom | absbottom)
	`alt="Text"`	Text to appear if the image cannot be displayed by the browser
	`border="Value"`	The size of the border around the image, in pixels
	`controls`	Display VCR-like controls under moving images; used in conjunction with the dynsrc property
	`dynsrc="Document"`	Specifies the file of a video, AVI clip, or VRML worlds displayed inside the page
	`height="Value"`	The height of the image in pixels
	`hspace="Value"`	Controls the amount of space to the left and right of the image, in pixels
	`Ismap`	Identifies the graphic as an image map; for use with server-side image maps
	`loop="Value"`	Specifies the number of times a moving image should be played; the value must be either a digit or infinite
	`lowsrc="File"`	A low-resolution version of the graphic that the browser should initially display before loading the high-resolution version
	`src="File"`	The source file of the inline image

tags and properties	description
start="Item"	Tells the browser when to start displaying a moving image file
(fileopen | mouseover)	The file is open; mouseover directs the browser to start when the mouse moves over the image
usemap="#map_name"	Identifies the graphic as an image map and specifies the name of the image map definition to use with the graphic; for use with client-side image maps
vspace="Value"	The amount of space above and below the image, in pixels
width="Value"	The width of the image in pixels
<input>...</input>	Creates an input object for use in a Web page form
align="Option" (left | right | top | texttop | middle | absmiddle | baseline | bottom | absbottom)	Specifies the alignment of an input image; similar to the align attribute with the <img /> tag
checked	Specifies that an input check box or input option button is selected
loop="Value"	Specifies the number of times a moving input image should be played; the value must be either a digit or infinite
lowsrc="file"	A low-resolution version of the input image that the browser should initially display before loading the high resolution version
maxlength="Value"	Specifies the maximum number of characters inserted into an input text box
name="Text"	The label given to the input object
size="Value"	The visible size, in characters, of an input text box
src="Document"	The source file of the graphic used for an input image object
start="Option" (fileopen | mouseover)	Tells the browser when to start displaying a moving image file; similar to the start property for the <img> tag
type="Option" (checkbox | hidden | image | password | radio | reset | submit | text | textarea)	Specifies the type of input object • checkbox creates a check box • hidden creates a hidden object • image creates an image object • password creates a text box that hides the text as the user enters it • radio creates an option button • reset creates a button that resets the form's fields when pressed • submit creates a button that submits the form when pressed • text creates a text box • textarea creates a text box with multiple line entry fields
value="Value"	Specifies the information that is initially displayed in the input object
vspace="Value"	The amount of space above and below the image, in pixels
width="Value"	The width of the input image, in pixels
<ins>...</ins>	Used to mark up sections of the document that have been inserted with respect to a different version of a document
<label>...</label>	May be used to attach information to controls

tags and properties		description
`<legend>...</legend>`		Allows authors to assign a caption to a FIELDSET; the legend improves accessibility when the FIELDSET is rendered nonvisually
`<kbd>...</kbd>`		Used to make text look as if it came from a typewriter or keyboard; text is displayed with a fixed-width font
`<li>...</li>`		Identifies list items in a <dir>, <menu>, <ol>, or <ul> list
`<link />`		Specifies the relationship between the document and other objects
	`href="URL"`	The URL of the <link> tag links the user to the specified document
	`id="Text"`	The file, URL, or text that acts as a hypertext link to another document
	`rel="URL"`	Directs the browser to link forward to the next page in the document
	`rev="URL"`	Directs the browser to go back to the previous link in the document
	`title="Text"`	The title of the document named in the link
`<map>...</map>`		Specifies information about a client-side image map (it must enclose <area> tags)
	`name="Text"`	The name of the image map
`<menu>...</menu>`		Encloses an unordered list of items, similar to a <ul> or <dir> list
`<meta />`		Used to insert information about the document that is not defined by other HTML tags and properties; it can include special instructions for the Web server to perform
	`content="Text"`	Contains information associated with the name or http-equiv attributes
	`http-equiv="Text"`	Directs the browser to request the server to perform different HTTP operations
	`name="Text"`	The type of information specified in the content attribute
`<nobr>...</nobr>`		Prevents line breaks for the enclosed text
`<noframes>...</noframes>`		Enclosing body tags to be used by browsers that do not support frames
`<noscript>...</noscript>`		The noscript element allows authors to provide alternate content when a script is not executed
`<object>...</object>`		The object element allows authors to control whether data should be rendered externally or by some program, specified by the author, that renders the data within the user agent
`<ol>...</ol>`		Encloses an ordered list of <li> items; typically, ordered lists are rendered as numbered lists
	`start="Value"`	The value of the starting number in the ordered list

tags and properties		description
	`type="Option"` `(A | a | I | i | 1)`	Specifies how ordered items are to be marked. A = upper case letters. a = lowercase letters. I = uppercase Roman numerals. i = lowercase Roman numerals. 1 = Digits. The default is 1.
`<optgroup>...</optgroup>`		The optgroup element allows authors to group choices logically
`<option>...</option>`		Used for each item in a selection list; this tag must be placed within <select> tags
	`selected`	The default or selected option in the selection list
	`value="Value"`	The value returned to the server when the user selects this option
`<p>...</p>`		Defines the beginning and ending of a paragraph of text
	`align="Option" (left` `| center | right)`	The alignment of the text in the paragraph
`<pre>...</pre>`		Retains the preformatted appearance of the text in the HTML file, including any line breaks or spaces; text is usually displayed in a fixed-width font
`<q>...</q>`		User agents should render quotation marks in a language-sensitive manner (see the lang attribute); many languages adopt different quotation styles for outer and inner (nested) quotations, which should be respected by user agents
`<samp>...</samp>`		Displays text in a fixed-width font
`<script>...</script>`		The script element places a script within a document. This element may appear any number of times in the head or body of an HTML document. The script may be defined within the contents of the script element or in an external file.
	`src="URL"`	This attribute specifies the location of an external script
	`type="Text"`	This attribute specifies the scripting language of the element's contents and overrides the default scripting language
	`language="Text"`	Deprecated. This attribute specifies the scripting language of the contents of this element. Its value is an identifier for the language, but since these identifiers are not standard, this attribute has been deprecated in favor of type.
	`defer`	When set, this boolean attribute informs the browser that the script is not going to generate any document content so the browser can continue parsing and rendering
`<select>...</select>`		Encloses a set of <option> tags for use in creating selection lists
	`multiple`	Allows the user to select multiple options from the selection list
	`name="Text"`	The name assigned to the selection list
	`size="Value"`	The number of visible items in the selection list
`<small>...</small>`		Decreases the size of the enclosed text; the exact appearance of the text depends on the browser and the default font size
`<span>...</span>`		Defines content to be inline but imposes no other presentational idioms on the content; thus, authors may use span in conjunction with style sheets
`<strike>...</strike>`		<strike> and <s> are deprecated; render strike-through style text
`<strong>...</strong>`		Used to strongly emphasize the enclosed text, usually in a bold font

Appendix

HTML

tags and properties		description
`<style>...</style>`		Contains information that identifies the style sheet in use
`<sub>...</sub>`		Displays the enclosed text as a subscript
`<sup>...</sup>`		Displays the enclosed text as a superscript
`<table>...</table>`		The HTML table model allows authors to arrange data—text, preformatted text, images, links, forms, form fields, other tables, etc.—into rows and columns of cells
	`summary="Text"`	This attribute provides a summary of the table's purpose and structure for user agents rendering to nonvisual media such as speech and Braille
	`align="Text"` `(left|center|right)`	Deprecated. This attribute specifies the position of the table with respect to the document. Permitted values: left: The table is to the left of the document center: The table is to the center of the document right: The table is to the right of the document
	`width="Value"`	This attribute specifies the desired width of the entire table and is intended for visual user agents. When the value is a percentage value, the value is relative to the user agent's available horizontal space. In the absence of any width specification, table width is determined by the user agent.
	`id, class`	document-wide identifiers
	`Lang`	language information
	`Dir`	text direction
	`Title`	element title
	`Style`	inline style information
	`bgcolor="Value" or Text`	table background color
	`frame, rules, border`	borders and rules
	`cellpadding="Value"`	cell margins
	`cellspacing="Value"`	cell margins
`<tbody>...</tbody>`		Contains the body content of a table and should be nested within the <table> tags and after the table header and table footer elements
`<td>...</td>`		Cell data is contained within the <td> tags nested within <tr> tags and the <tbody> and <table> tags
	`scope="Scope-name"`	This attribute specifies the set of data cells for which the current header cell provides header information
	`abbr="Text"`	This attribute should be used to provide an abbreviated form of the cell's content
	`axis="cdata"`	This attribute may be used to place a cell into conceptual categories that can be considered to form axes in an n-dimensional space
	`headers="idrefs"`	The list of header cells that provide header information for the current data cell

HTML AP-16 APPENDIX

tags and properties		description
	rowspan="Number"	This attribute specifies the number of rows spanned by the current cell. The default value of this attribute is one ("1"). The value zero ("0") means that the cell spans all rows from the current row to the last row of the table section (thead, tbody, or tfoot) in which the cell is defined.
	colspan="Number"	This attribute specifies the number of columns spanned by the current cell. The default value of this attribute is one ("1"). The value zero ("0") means that the cell spans all columns from the current column to the last column of the column group (COLGROUP) in which the cell is defined.
	Nowrap	Deprecated. When present, this Boolean attribute tells visual user agents to disable automatic text wrapping for this cell. Style sheets should be used instead of this attribute to achieve wrapping effects. Note: If used carelessly, this attribute may result in excessively wide cells.
	width="Length"	Deprecated; this attribute supplies user agents with a recommended cell width
	height="Length"	Deprecated; this attribute supplies user agents with a recommended cell height
<textarea>...</textarea>		Creates a text box
	cols="Value"	The height of the text box in characters
	name="Text"	The name assigned to the text box
	rows="Value"	The width of the text box in characters
	wrap="Option" (off | virtual | physical)	Specifies how text should be wrapped within the text box. off turns off text wrapping. virtual wraps the text, but sends the text to the server as a single line. physical wraps the text and sends the text to the server as it appears in the text box.
<tfoot>...</tfoot>		TFOOT must appear before TBODY within a TABLE definition so that user agents can render the foot before receiving all of the (potentially numerous) rows of data
<th>...</th>		Defines a cell that contains header information
<thead>...</thead>		Defines a table header grouping that contains replicating table heading information. Must contain at least one table row grouping.
<title>...</title>		Used to specify the text that appears in the Web browser's title bar
<tr>...</tr>		Acts as a container for a row of table cells (<td> or <th>)
<tt>...</tt>		Displays text in a fixed width, teletype style font
<u>...</u>		Underlines the enclosed text, should be avoided because it confuses users with hypertext, which is typically underlined
<ul>...</ul>		Encloses an unordered list of <li> items; typically, unordered lists are rendered as bulleted lists
	Type="Option" (circle | disk | square)	Specifies the type of bullet used for displaying each <li> element in the <ul> list
<var>...</var>		Used for text that represents a variable, and usually appears in italics

HTML Browser-Safe Colors

The following list of 216 hexadecimal color values is supported by all Web browsers. To view these colors, you must have a video card and monitor capable of displaying up to 256 colors. These colors were designed to be displayed the same in all browsers when rendered using their hexadecimal triplet code.

TABLE AP-2: Browser-safe colors

Color Code	RGB Values	Color Sample	Color Code	RGB Values	Color Sample
#FFFFFF	255,255,255		#FF00CC	255,000,204	
#FFFFCC	255,255,204		#FF0099	255,000,153	
#FFFF99	255,255,153		#FF0066	255,000,102	
#FFFF66	255,255,102		#FF0033	255,000,051	
#FFFF33	255,255,51		#FF0000	255,000,000	
#FFFF00	255,255,000		#CCFFFF	204,255,255	
#FFCCFF	255,204,255		#CCFFCC	204,255,204	
#FFCCCC	255,204,204		#CCFF99	204,255,153	
FFCC99	255,204,153		#CCFF66	204,255,102	
#FFCC66	255,204,102		#CCFF33	204,255,051	
#FFCC33	255,204,051		#CCFF00	204,255,000	
#FFCC00	255,204,000		#CCCCFF	204,204,255	
#FF99FF	255,153,255		#CCCCCC	204,204,204	
#FF99CC	255,153,204		#CCCC99	204,204,153	
#FFCC99	255,153,153		#CCCC66	204,204,102	
#FF9966	255,153,102		#CCCC33	204,204,051	
#FF9933	255,153,051		#CCCC00	204,204,000	
#FF9900	255,153,000		#CC99FF	204,153,255	
#FF66FF	255,102,255		#CC99CC	204,153,204	
#FF66CC	255,102,204		#CC9999	204,153,153	
#FF6699	255,102,153		#CC9966	204,153,102	
#FF6666	255,102,102		#CC9933	204,153,051	
#FF6633	255,102,051		#CC9900	204,153,000	
#FF6600	255,102,000		#CC66FF	204,102,255	
#FF33FF	255,051,255		#CC66CC	204,102,204	
#FF33CC	255,051,204		#CC6699	204,102,153	
#FF3399	255,051,153		#CC6666	204,102,102	
#FF3366	255,051,102		#CC6633	204,102,051	
#FF3333	255,051,051		#CC6600	204,102,000	
#FF3300	255,051,000		#CC33FF	204,051,255	
#FF00FF	255,000,255		#CC33CC	204,051,204	

Color Code	RGB Values	Color Sample	Color Code	RGB Values	Color Sample
#CC3399	204,051,153		#993300	153,051,000	
#CC3366	204,051,102		#9900FF	153,000,255	
#CC3333	204,051,051		#9900CC	153,000,204	
#CC3300	204,051,000		#990066	153,000,102	
#CC00FF	204,000,255		#990033	153,000,051	
#CC00CC	204,000,204		#990000	153,000,000	
#CC0099	204,000,153		#66FFFF	102,255,255	
#CC0066	204,000,102		#66FFCC	102,255,204	
#CC0033	204,000,051		#66FF99	102,255,153	
#CC0000	204,000,000		#66FF66	102,255,102	
#99FFFF	153,255,255		#66FF33	102,255,051	
#99FFCC	153,255,204		#66FF00	102,255,000	
#99FF99	153,255,153		#66CCFF	102,204,255	
#99FF66	153,255,102		#66CCCC	102,204,204	
#99FF33	153,255,051		#66CC99	102,204,153	
#99FF00	153,255,000		#66CC66	102,204,102	
#99CCFF	153,204,255		#66CC33	102,204,051	
#99CCCC	153,204,204		#66CC00	102,204,000	
#99CC99	153,204,153		#6699FF	102,253,255	
#99CC66	153,204,102		#6699CC	102,253,204	
#99CC33	153,204,051		#669999	102,253,153	
#99CC00	153,204,000		#669966	102,253,102	
#9999FF	153,153,255		#669933	102,253,051	
#9999CC	153,153,204		#669900	102,253,000	
#999999	153,153,153		#6666FF	102,102,255	
#999966	153,153,102		#6666CC	102,102,204	
#999933	153,153,051		#666699	102,102,153	
#999900	153,153,000		#666666	102,102,102	
#9966FF	153,102,255		#666633	102,102,051	
#9966CC	153,102,204		#666600	102,102,000	
#996699	153,102,153		#6633FF	102,051,255	
#996666	153,102,102		#6633CC	102,051,204	
#996633	153,102,051		#663399	102,051,153	
#996600	153,102,000		#663366	102,051,102	
#9933FF	153,051,255		#663333	102,051,051	
#9933CC	153,051,204		#663300	102,051,000	
#993399	153,051,153		#6600FF	102,000,255	
#993366	153,051,102		#6600CC	102,000,204	

Color Code	RGB Values	Color Sample	Color Code	RGB Values	Color Sample
#993333	153,051,153		#660099	102,000,153	
#660066	102,000,102		#333300	051,051,000	
#660033	102,000,051		#3300FF	051,000,255	
#660000	102,000,000		#3300CC	051,000,204	
#33FFFF	051,255,255		#330099	051,000,153	
#33FFCC	051,255,204		#330066	051,000,102	
#33FF99	051,255,153		#330033	051,000,051	
#33FF66	051,255,102		#330000	051,000,000	
#33FF33	051,255,051		#00FFFFFF	000,255,255	
#33FF00	051,255,000		#00FFCC	000,255,204	
#33CCFF	051,204,255		#00FF99	000,255,153	
#33CCCC	051,204,204		#00FF66	000,255,102	
#33CC99	051,204,153		#00FF33	000,255,051	
#33CC66	051,204,102		#00FF00	000,255,000	
#33CC33	051,204,051		#00CCFF	000,204,255	
#33CC00	051,204,000		#00CCCC	000,204,204	
#3399FF	051,153,255		#00CC99	000,204,153	
#3399CC	051,153,204		#00CC66	000,204,102	
#339999	051,153,153		#00CC33	000,204,051	
#339966	051,153,102		#00CC00	000,204,000	
#339933	051,153,051		#0099FF	000,153,255	
#339900	051,153,000		#0099CC	000,153,204	
#3366FF	051,102,255		#009999	000,153,153	
#3366CC	051,102,204		#009966	000,153,102	
#336699	051,102,153		#009933	000,153,051	
#336666	051,102,102		#009900	000,153,000	
#336633	051,102,051		#0066FF	000,102,255	
#336600	051,102,000		#0066CC	000,102,204	
#3333FF	051,051,255		#006699	000,102,153	
#3333CC	051,051,204		#006666	000,102,102	
#333399	051,051,153		#006633	000,102,051	
#333366	051,051,102		#006600	000,102,000	

Color Code	RGB Values	Color Sample	Color Code	RGB Values	Color Sample
#333333	051,051,051		#0033FF	000,051,255	
#0033CC	000,051,204		#0000CC	000,000,204	
#003399	000,051,153		#000099	000,000,153	
#003366	000,051,102		#000066	000,000,102	
#003333	000,051,051		#000033	000,000,051	
#003300	000,051,000		#000000	000,000,000	
#0000FF	000,000,255				

HTML Color Names

The following is a list of extended color names and their corresponding hexadecimal triplets supported by most Web browsers. To view these colors, you must have a video card and monitor capable of displaying up to 256 colors. As with other aspects of Web page design, you should test these color names on a variety of browsers before committing to their use. Different browsers may render these colors differently or not at all.

TABLE AP-3: HTML extended color names

color name	value	RGB	preview	color name	value	RGB	preview
aliceblue	#F0F8FE	240,248,254,		darkpurple	#871F78	135,031,120,	
antiquewhite	#FAEBD7	250,235,215,		darksalmon	#E9967A	233,150,122,	
aqua	#00FFFF	000,255,255,		darkslateblue	#6B238E	107,035,142,	
aquamarine	#70DB93	112,219,147,		darkslategray	#2F4F4F	047,079,079,	
azure	#F0FFFF	240,255,255,		darktan	#97694F	151,105,079,	
beige	#F5F5DC	245,245,220,		darkturquoise	#7093DB	112,147,219,	
black	#000000	000,000,000,		darkviolet	#9400D3	094,000,211,	
blue	#0000FF	000,000,255,		darkwood	#855E42	133,094,066,	
blueviolet	#9F5F9F	159,095,159,		dimgray	#545454	084,084,084,	
brass	#B5A642	181,166,066,		dustyrose	#856363	133,099,099,	
brightgold	#D9D919	217,217,025,		feldspar	#D19275	209,174,117,	
bronze	#8C7853	140,120,083,		firebrick	#8E2323	142,035,035,	
brown	#A52A2A	165,042,042,		forestgreen	#238E23	035,142,035,	
cadetblue	#5F9F9F	095,159,159,		gold	#CD7F32	205,127,050,	
chocolate	#D2691E	210,105,030,		goldenrod	#DBDB70	219,219,112,	
coolcopper	#D98719	217,135,025,		gray	#C0C0C0	192,192,192	
copper	#B87333	184,115,051,		green	#00FF00	000,255,000,	
coral	#FF7F50	255,127,080,		greencopper	#527F76	082,127,118,	
crimson	#DC143C	220,020,060,		greenyellow	#93DB70	147,219,112,	
cyan	#00FFFF	000,255,255,		hotpink	#FF69B4	255,105,B4	
darkblue	#00008B	000,000,139,		huntergreen	#215E21	033,094,033,	
darkbrown	#5C4033	092,064,051,		indianred	#4E2F2F	078,047,047,	
darkcyan	#008B8B	000,139,139,		indigo	#4B0082	075,000,130,	
darkgoldenrod	#B8860B	184,134,011,		ivory	#FFFFF0	255,255,240,	
darkgray	#A9A9A9	169,169,169,		khaki	#9F9F5F	159,159,095,	
darkgreen	#006400	000,100,000,		lavender	#E6E6FA	230,230,205	
darkkhaki	#BDB76B	189,183,107,		lightblue	#C0D9D9	192,217,217,	
darkmagenta	#8B008B	139,000,139,		lightcoral	#F08080	240,128,128,	
darkolivegreen	#4F4F2F	079,079,047,		lightcyan	#E0FFFF	224,255,255,	
darkorange	#FF8C00	255,140,000,		lightgray	#A8A8A8	068,068,068,	
darkorchid	#9932CD	102,050,205,		lightgreen	#90EE90	144,238,144,	

color name	value	RGB	preview	color name	value	RGB	preview
lightpink	#FFB6C1	255,182,193,		pink	#BC8F8F	188,143,143,	
lightsteelblue	#8FBDBD	143,189,189,		plum	#EAADEA	234,173,234,	
lightwood	#E9C2A6	233,194,166,		powderblue	#B0E0E6	176,224,230,	
lime	#00FF00	000,255,000,		purple	#800080	128,000,128,	
limegreen	#32CD32	050,205,050,		quartz	#D9D9F3	217,217,F3	
magenta	#FF00FF	255,000,255,		red	#FF0000	255,000,000,	
mandarinorange	#E47833	228,120,051,		richblue	#5959AB	089,089,171,	
maroon	#8E236B	142,035,107,		royalblue	#4169E1	065,105,225,	
medium aquamarine	#32CD99	050,205,102,		saddlebrown	#8B4513	139,069,13	
mediumblue	#3232CD	050,050,205,		salmon	#6F4242	111,066,066,	
medium forestgreen	#6B8E23	107,142,035,		sandybrown	#F4A460	244,164,096	
medium goldenrod	#EAEAAE	234,234,174,		scarlet	#8C1717	140,023,023	
mediumorchid	#9370DB	147,112,219,		seagreen	#238E68	035,142,68	
mediumseagreen	#426F42	066,111,066,		sienna	#8E6B23	142,107,035,	
mediumslateblue	#7F00FF	127,000,255,		silver	#E6E8FA	230,232,250	
medium springgreen	#7FFF00	127,255,000,		skyblue	#3299CC	050,102,204,	
medium turquoise	#70DBDB	112,219,219,		slateblue	#007FFF	000,127,255,	
mediumvioletred	#DB7093	219,112,147,		snow	#FFFAFA	255,250,250,	
mediumwood	#A68064	166,128,100,		spicypink	#FF1CAE	255,028,174,	
midnightblue	#2F2F4F	047,047,079,		springgreen	#00FF7F	000,255,127,	
mintcream	#F5FFFA	245,255,250,		steelblue	#236B8E	035,107,142,	
mistyrose	#FFE4E1	255,228,225,		summersky	#38B0DE	056,176,222	
navyblue	#23238E	035,035,142,		tan	#DB9370	219,147,112,	
neonblue	#4D4DFF	077,077,255,		teal	#008080	000,128,128,	
neonpink	#FF6EC7	255,110,199,		thistle	#D8BFD8	216,191,216,	
newmidnightblue	#00009C	000,000,156,		tomato	#FF6347	255,099,071,	
newtan	#EBC79E	235,199,158,		turquoise	#ADEAEA	173,234,234,	
oldgold	#CFB53B	207,181,059,		verydarkbrown	#5C4033	092,064,051,	
olive	#808000	128,128,000,		verydarkgray	#CDCDCD	205,205,205,	
orange	#FF7F00	255,127,000,		violet	#4F2F4F	079,047,079,	
orangered	#FF2400	255,036,000,		violetred	#CC3299	204,050,102,	
orchid	#DB70DB	219,112,219,		wheat	#D8D8BF	216,216,191,	
palegoldenrod	#EEE8AA	238,232,170		white	#FFFFFF	255,255,255,	
palegreen	#8FBC8F	143,188,143,		yellow	#FFFF00	255,255,000,	
paleturquoise	#AFEEEE	175,238,238,		yellowgreen	#99CC32	102,204,050,	

HTML

Appendix

HTML

Cascading Style Sheet Reference

The following are CSS1 fourth-generation browser supported styles. CSS formatting can be applied inline as part of the style attribute (`<tag style="text-align: center;">`), or embedded within the head section in the `<style>...</style>` tag. In actual use in styles, semicolons should appear at the end of each style value.

TABLE AP-4: CSS1 fourth-generation browser supported styles

property	explanation/syntax	example
Font properties		
font-style	*normal*	`{font-style: italic;}`
	oblique (similar to italic, but created manually rather than using italic typeface)	
	italic	
font-variant	*normal* (default)	`{font-variant: small-caps;}`
	small-caps	
font-weight	*extra-light*	`{font-weight: extra-bold;}`
	demi-light	
	light	
	medium	
	bold	
	demi-bold	
	extra-bold	
font-size	A number with a unit abbreviation	`{font-size: 16pt;}`
	• Points (*pt*)	
	• Pixels (*px*)	
	• Inches (*in*)	
	• Centimeters (*cm*)	
	• Percentage of default point size (%)	
	• Multiple of width of *m* character in current font family (*em*)	
line-height	Sets distance between baselines of two adjacent elements; specify multiplication factor for font size as a value (such as 1.2), percentage (120%), or measurement (1.2em)	`{line-height: 1.2;}`
font-family	Any combination of the following, in order of preference: • Specific typeface name (*times new roman*) • General type family (*times*) • Font type (*sans-serif*)	`{font-family: "times new roman", times, garamond, serif;}`

property	explanation/syntax	example
font	Shorthand for setting all six font-related attributes at once; no commas, except between font-family settings; order: font-style, font-variant, font-weight, font-size, line-height, font-family	`{font: italic small-caps extra-bold 16pt 0.75in "times new roman", times, garamond, serif;}`
text-decoration	• *none*	`{text-decoration: italic;}`
	• *underline*	
	• *italic*	
	• *line-through*	
Color and background properties		
color	Hexadecimal or keyword color equivalent for element color	`{color: #99cc66;}`
background-color	Hexadecimal or keyword color equivalent for background color	`{background-color: #000066;}`
background-image	• *none*	`{background-image: url(me.jpg);}`
	• *url(url)*	
background-repeat	Specifies if and how background image is repeated	`{background-repeat: repeat-x;}`
	• *repeat* (tiles over entire background)	
	• *repeat-x* (repeats in single band horizontally)	
	• *repeat-y* (repeats in single band vertically)	
	• *no-repeat* (single image only)	
background-attachment	• *scroll* (image scrolls with foreground)	
	• *fixed* (image remains fixed as foreground scrolls)	`{background-attachment: fixed;}`
background-position	Specifies initial position of background image; coordinates (in percent) match point at those coordinates on image with those coordinates on background	`{background-position: 100% 100%;}`
background	Shorthand for setting all five background attributes at once; no commas; order: background-color, background-image, background-repeat, background-attachment, background-position	`{background: #000066 url(me.jpg) repeat-x fixed 100% 100%;}`
Text properties		
word-spacing	Specifies additional width to insert between words (default=normal); may be negative	`{word-spacing: 0.4em;}`
letter-spacing	Specifies additional width to insert between words (default=normal); may be negative	`{letter-spacing: 0.1em;}`
text-decoration	• *underline* • *overline* • *line-through* • *none* (default)	`{text-decoration: underline;}`

property	explanation/syntax	example
vertical-align	• *baseline* • *sub* • *super* • *top* • *text-top* • *middle* • *bottom* • *text-bottom* • Percentage value; positive and negative numbers possible; specifies percentage of the element's line-height property in relation to the parent baseline	{vertical-align: super;}
text-transform	• *capitalize* capitalizes first character of each word • *uppercase* capitalizes all letters • *lowercase* makes all letters lowercase • *none*	{text-transform: capitalize;}
text-align	• *left* • *right* • *center* • *justify*	{text-align: center;}
text-indent	Positive and negative numbers possible, specifies indentation of first line, in an exact measurement, or a percentage of parent element width	{text-indent: 3em;}
line-height	Sets distance between baselines of two adjacent elements; specify multiplication factor for font size, as a value (such as 1.2), percentage (120%), or measurement (1.2em)	{line-height: 1.2;}
Box properties		
margin-top	Sets element's top margin as measurement or percentage of parent element width	{margin-top: 2%;}
margin-right	Sets element's right margin as measurement or percentage of parent element width	{margin-right: 2em;}
margin-bottom	sets element's bottom margin as measurement or percentage of parent element width	{margin-bottom: 2%;}
margin-left	sets element's left margin as measurement or percentage of parent element width	{margin-right: 2em;}
margin	Shorthand property for specifying margin-top, margin-right, margin-bottom, and margin-left properties; order: top, right, bottom, left; if only one value given, applies to all four; if one or two values missing, missing value copied from opposite side	{margin 2% 2em;}
padding-top	Sets an element's top padding, as measurement or percentage of parent element width	{padding-top: 0.3em;}
padding-right	Sets an element's right padding, as measurement or percentage of parent element width	{padding-right: 20%;}

property	explanation/syntax	example
padding-bottom	Sets an element's bottom padding, as measurement or percentage of parent element width	`{padding-bottom: 0.3em;}`
padding-left	Sets an element's left padding, as measurement or percentage of parent element width	`{padding-left: 20%;}`
padding	Shorthand property for specifying padding-top, padding-right, padding-bottom, and padding-left properties; order: top, right, bottom, left; if only one value given, applies to all four; if one or two values missing, missing value copied from opposite side	`{padding: 0.3em 20% 0.2em;}`
border-top-width; border-right-width; border-bottom-width; border-left-width;	• thin • medium • thick • measurement	`{border-top-width: 2pt;}`
border-width	Shorthand property for specifying all four border thicknesses; order: top, right, bottom, left; if only one value given, applies to all four; if one or two values missing, missing value copied from opposite side	`{border-width: 3em;}`
border-style	Can specify between one and four styles, with same organization as border-width above • *none* • *dotted* • *dashed* • *solid* • *double* • *groove* • *ridge* • *inset* • *outset*	`{border-style: groove;}`
border-color	Hexadecimal or keyword color equivalent for element color; can specify between one and four colors, with same organization as border-width above	`{border-color: navy red red;}`
border-top border-right border-bottom border-left	Shorthand properties for setting each border's width, style, and color	`{border-bottom: thick solid red;}`
border	Shorthand property for setting same width, color, and style on all four borders of an element	`{border: thin inset green;}`
width	Element width, as a length or percentage; negative values are allowed (default=auto)	`{width: 200px;}`
height	Element height, as a length or percentage, negative values are allowed (default=auto)	`{height: 50%;}`
float	Moves element to left or right and wraps text on opposite side	`{float: left;}`
clear	Specifies if an element allows floating elements around it, or should be moved clear of them • *none* • *left* • *right* • *both*	`{clear: both;}`

HTML

property	explanation/syntax	example
Classification properties		
display	• *block* • *inline* • *list-item* • *none*	{display: inline;}
white-space	• *normal* white space collapsed • *pre* formatted like HTML PRE element • *nowrap* wrapping triggered only by elements	{white-space: nowrap;}
list-style-type	Specifies marker style for list items • *disc* • *circle* • *square* • *decimal* • *lower-roman* • *upper-roman* • *lower-alpha* • *upper-alpha* • *none*	{list-style-type: lower-alpha;}
list-style-image	Specifies an image to use as a list item marker	{list-style-image: url(reddot.jpg);}
list-style-position	• *inside* less space between marker and item • *outside* more space between marker and item (default)	{list-style-position: inside;}
list-style	Shorthand property for setting list-style-type, list-style-image, and list-style-position	{list-style: lower-alpha url(reddot.jpg) inside;}

HTML Special Characters

The following table lists a portion of the HTML extended character set, also known as the ISO Latin-1 Character set. Characters in this table can be entered either by code number or code name. For example, to insert the registered trademark symbol ((r)) you use either &reg or &#174.

Although code names can be easier to remember and type than code numbers, not all code names are recognized by all browsers. Some older browsers that support only the HTML 2.0 standard do not recognize the code name "&times," for instance. Code names that may not be recognized by older browsers are marked with an asterisk. If you are planning to use these symbols in your document, you may want to use the code number instead of the code name.

TABLE AP-5: HTML special characters

character	code	code name	description
	&#00; – &#08;		Unused
	&#09;		Tab
	&#10;		Line feed
	&#11; – &#31;		Unused
	&#32;		Space
!	&#33;		Exclamation point
"	&#34;	&quot;	Double quotation mark
#	&#35;		Pound sign
$	&#36;		Dollar sign
%	&#37;		Percent sign
&	&#38;	&amp;	Ampersand
'	&#39;		Apostrophe
(	&#40;		Left parenthesis
)	&#41;		Right parenthesis
*	&#42;		Asterisk
+	&#43;		Plus sign
,	&#44;		Comma
-	&#45;		Hyphen
.	&#46;		Period
/	&#47;		Forward slash
0–9	0 – 9		Numbers 0–9
:	&#58;		Colon
;	&#59;		Semicolon
<	&#60;	&lt;	Less than sign
=	&#61;		Equal sign
>	&#62;	&gt;	Greater than sign
?	&#63;		Question mark
@	&#64;		Commercial at

character	code	code name	description
A–Z	A – Z		Letters A–Z
[	&#91;		Left square bracket
\	&#92;		Back slash
]	&#93;		Right square bracket
^	&#94;		Caret
_	&#95;		Horizontal bar
`	&#96;		Grave accent
a–z	a – z		Letters a–z
{	&#123;		Left curly brace
|	|		Vertical bar
}	&#125;		Right curly brace
~	&#126;		Tilde
	&#127; – 		Unused
‚	&#130;		Low single comma quotation mark
ƒ	&#131;		Function sign
„	&#132;		Low double comma quotation mark
…	&#133;		Ellipses
†	&#134;		Dagger
‡	&#135;		Double dagger
ˆ	&#136;		Circumflex accent
‰	&#137;		Per mile sign
Sˇ	&#138;		Capital S with hacek
<	&#139;		Left single angle quotation mark
Œ	&#140;		Capital OE ligature
	 – 		Unused
'	&#145;		Single beginning quotation mark
'	&#146;		Single ending quotation mark
"	&#147;		Double beginning quotation mark
"	&#148;		Double ending quotation mark
•	&#149;		Middle dot
–	&#150;		En dash
—	&#151;		Em dash
~	&#152;		Tilde

character	code	code name	description
™	&#153;	&trade;	Trademark symbol
sˇ	&#154;		Small s with hacek
›	&#155;		Right single angle quotation mark
œ	&#156;		Small oe ligature
	 – ž		Unused
Ÿ	&#159;		Capital Y with umlaut
			Nonbreaking space
¡	&#161;	&iexcl;	Inverted exclamation point
¢	&#162;	&cent;	Cent symbol
£	&#163;	&pound;	Pound sterling
¤	&#164;	&curren;	General currency symbol
¥	&#165;	&yen;	Yen sign
‖	&#166;	&brvbar;	Broken vertical bar
§	&#167;	&sect;	Section sign
¨	&#168;	&uml;	Umlaut
©	&#169;	&copy;	Copyright symbol
ª	&#170;	&ordf;	Feminine ordinal
«	&#171;	&laquo;	Left angle quotation mark
¬	&#172;	&not;	Not sign
-	&#173;	&shy;	Soft hyphen
®	&#174;	&reg;	Registered trademark
¯	&#175;	&macr;	Macron
°	&#176;	&deg;	Degree sign
±	&#177;	&plusmn;	Plus/minus symbol
2	&#178;	&sup2;	Superscript 2
3	&#179;	&sup3;	Superscript 3
´	&#180;	&acute;	Acute accent
µ	&#181;	&micro;	Micro symbol
¶	&#182;	&para;	Paragraph sign
·	&#183;	&middot;	Middle dot
ç	&#184;	&cedil;	Cedilla
1	&#185;	&sup1;	Superscript 1
º	&#186;	&ordm;	Masculine ordinal
»	&#187;	&raquo;	Right angle quotation mark
¼	&#188;	&frac14;	Fraction one-quarter
½	&#189;	&frac12;	Fraction one-half
¾	&#190;	&frac34;	Fraction three-quarters
¿	&#191;	&iquest;	Inverted question mark

Formatting with HTML 4.0 Attributes

Before styles came into common use, font formatting was applied using a different set of values within the `<font>` `</font>` tag. HTML was not originally designed as a formatting language, but Web users started to demand that Web pages have formatting similar to that found in print media. To accommodate this demand, formatting attributes such as face, color, and size were developed. These were not efficient because they had to be applied in multiple locations on a page, and formatting with these tags was necessarily limited. For example, there was no control of line spacing and there were only seven size formats. In spite of the fact that HTML 4.0 attributes have been deprecated by the W3C, there are still millions of Web pages that use them, so it's a good idea to become familiar with them so you can recognize them and edit them if necessary.

attribute	value	function	examples
face	typeface name	Changes font typeface; may list several alternate fonts in order of preference	`<font face="Arial, Helvetica, sans serif">`This text appears in the Arial or Helvetica typeface. If neither Arial or Helvetica are available on the system, the default sans serif font will be displayed`</font>`
color	#hexadecimal color value	Changes text color; color can be specified as any six-digit value with digits from 0 (zero) to 9 and A through F	`<font color="#000066">`This text appears in navy blue.`</font>`
color	color name	Changes text color identified by a standard color name	`font color="navy">`This text also appears in navy blue`</font>`
size	numeric value from 1 through 7	Changes text size according to its HTML number value: 1, 6 point; 2, 10 point; 3, (default size) 12 point; 4, 14 point; 5, 18 point; 6, 24 point; 7, 36 point	`<font size="7">`This text appears in the largest size available.`</font>`
size	+# (1 to 4) –# (1 or 2)	When paired with a number 1 through 4, changes font size to the numeric equivalent of font default size (3) plus the number specified When paired with a number 1 or 2, changes the font size to the numeric equivalent of the font default size (3) minus the number specified	`<font size="+1">`This text appears one size larger than the default text—equivalent to a font size 4`</font>` `<font size="+3">`This text is equivalent to a font size 7`</font>`
size	–# (1 or 2)	When paired with a number, reduces font size by the numeric equivalent of the default font size minus the number	`<font size="-1">`This text appears one size smaller than the default text—equivalent to a size 2`</font>`

Project Files List

Unit	File supplied on Data Disk		Location file is used in unit
A	htm_a-1.rtf		Lessons
A	htm_a-2.rtf		Skills Review
B	contact.htm **activities** folder containing index.htm		Lessons
B	hands.htm packages.htm salon.htm services.htm thermacore.htm **spa** folder containing index.htm		Skills Review
B	faq.htm features.htm rentals.htm **listing** folder containing index.htm		Independent Challenge 1
B	outside.htm inside.htm saver.htm **irrigation** folder containing index.htm htm_B-1.txt		Independent Challenge 2
C	htm_C-1.txt htm_C-2.txt htm_C-3.txt		Lessons
	htm_C-4.txt htm_C-5.txt		Independent Challenge 1 Independent Challenge 1 (ACE)
	htm_C-6.txt		Visual Workshop

D	htm_D-1.txt
	paradise/media folder containing:
	  clear.gif (used as spacer for
	  bg_samples page)
	  trail_ride1.jpg
	  trail_ride2.jpg
	  pm_logo1.jpg
	  pm_logo2.png
	  pm_bkgnd.gif
	  bed2.jpg
	  frontroom.jpg
	  masterbath.jpg
	  bath2.jpg
	  floorplan2bedroom.gif
	  kitchen.jpg
	  masterbedroom.jpg
		paradise/images/samples folder containing:
		  bkg_samples.htm
		  heather_bkg.htm
		  blu_heather_bkg.htm
		  background.htm
		  pm_bkgnd.htm
		  LB_PlamsThatch3.htm
		  heather_bkg.jpg
		  pm_bkgnd1.jpg
		  blu_heather_bkg.jpg
		  LB_PlamsThatch3.jpg
		
		paradise/media folder containing:
		  paradise.wmv
			Lessons

D	htm_D-2.txt
	htm_D-3.txt
	
	spa folder containing:
	  wraps.htm
	  imagemap.txt
	  hands.htm
	
	spa/media folder containing:
	  spa.wmv
		paradise/images folder containing:
		  bkg_spa.gif
		  pedi.jpg
		  spa_logo.gif
		  spa_nav.gif
			Skills Review

Unit	File supplied on Data Disk		Location file is used in unit
D	htm_D-4.txt **vacations/images folder containing:** bkg_vaca.gif Map.gif resort.jpg	**vacations folder containing:** eu.htm ak.htm hi.htm map.txt	Independent Challenge 1
D	**vacations_ace/media/folder containing:** islandseas.wav		Independent Challenge 1 (ACE)
D	htm_D-5.txt **water/media folder containing:** conserve.wav	**water folder containing:** saver.htm **water/images/folder containing:** mw.gif	Independent Challenge 2
D	**water/images folder containing:** water_bg1.jpg water_bg2.jpg waterHead2.gif		Independent Challenge 2 (ACE)
D	**bitspcs/images folder containing:** apple.gif apple.bg.gif woz-jobsbyLuckow.jpg	**bitspcs/media folder containing:** apple.wav	Visual Workshop
E	pm_bkgnd2.gif pm_bul1.png pm_bul2.png htm_E-1.txt htm_E-2.txt		Lessons
E	htm_E-3.txt	**paradise/images folder containing:** bkg_pillar_green1.gif spa_logo.gif	Skills Review
E	htm_E-4.txt		Independent Challenge 1
E	htm_E-5.txt		Independent Challenge 2
E	htm_E-6.txt		Visual Workshop
F	htm_F-1.txt htm_F-2.txt htm_F-3.txt		Lessons
F	htm_F-4.txt	**paradise/images folder containing:** bkg_spa.gif spa_logo.gif	Skills Review
F	htm_F-5.txt htm_F-6.txt		Independent Challenge 1 Independent Challenge 1 (ACE)
F	htm_F-7.txt		Independent Challenge 2
F	htm_F-8.txt		Visual Workshop
G	htm_G-1.txt		Lessons
G	htm_G-2.txt		Skills Review
G	htm_G-3.txt		Independent Challenge 1
G	htm_G-4.txt		Independent Challenge 2

Unit	File supplied on Data Disk	Location file is used in unit
H	htm_H-1.txt htm_H-2.txt htm_H-3.txt	Lessons

H	wraps.htm
	packages.htm
	salon.htm
	hands.htm
	services_style.css
	
	paradise/images folder containing:
	    spa_logo.gif
	    htm_H-4.txt
	    htm_H-5.txt
	    top.htm
	    htm_H-6.txt
	    services_first.htm
		Skills Review

H	htm_H-7.txt
	    rentals.htm
	htm_H-8.txt
	    faq.htm
	    features.htm
		Independent Challenge 1

H	htm_H-9.txt htm_H-10.txt htm_H-11.txt	Independent Challenge 2
H	bitshead.htm first.htm bitslink.htm	Visual Workshop

Glossary

_blank   Attribute to open the link in new browser window; can be used with non-frames pages.

_parent   Attribute to cause the link to replace the content of the current frameset; use _blank or _parent for links to pages outside of a frameset.

_self   Attribute to open the link in current frame; this is the default setting.

_top   Attribute to cause the link to replace the contents of current browser window; always use when creating links from a content page back to the main frameset.

Absolute link   Link that includes the target page's full Web site location and directory information (for example, <a href="http://www.course.com/sl/default.htm">); most useful to reference a specific page on a different Web site. *See also* Relative link.

Absolute URL   Complete URL including the protocol (http://), server name, domain name, path, and filename of the file to open.

Action   Attribute to indicate the path and name of the processing program that the server must run when the form is submitted.

Active link   State of a link in the process of being clicked; also, the state of a link as a site visitor clicks the Back button to return to the page after link is clicked. The highlighted link color is red by default in some browsers, purple by default in others.

Active link attributes   Attributes that must often be set to make active links readable against a background graphic or color.

Active white space   Planned white space that serves a purpose in page design.

Add-on   Small program you can download from the Web for free to extend a browser's capabilities; required for viewing some multimedia formats, including Flash animation.

Alignment   The horizontal placement of text or graphics on the page.

Alignment attribute options   Alternative ways of horizontally aligning Web elements, including left, right, center, and, justify.

Alt attribute   Also known as an alt statement, an attribute that causes alternative text to display or when the mouse pointer rests over the graphic in the browser if for any reason the image does not appear; used by screen readers to describe graphics or graphic links.

Anchor tag   In code, a tag that surrounds information users click to navigate to another location; also called a link tag.

Animated GIF   GIF file that combines two or more images into a single file to give the illusion of movement or to display banner images.

Attributes   Extra settings available in most HTML tags that allow you to add to or change a tag's default features.

Attribute string   Series of attributes applied to the same opening element tag.

Back end   Programs that reside on an organization's computer system and that are responsible for processing the data submitted from forms. *See also* Front end.

Background images   Pictures or colors that appear behind text or other graphics on a Web page; stored as separate GIF, JPG, or PNG files usually in the site's images directory.

Backward compatibility   The ability to ensure that your page is displayed as expected in older browsers.

Bandwidth   Data transfer capacity of a Web user's Internet connection.

Basefont tag <basefont />   HTML tag that sets the font for an entire page. W3C has recently deprecated it in favor of newer formatting methods; however, literally millions of pages on the Web still use this tag to format Web pages.

Baseline   The imaginary line on which text or graphics vertically align, not counting the extenders.

bgcolor attribute   Attribute to specify a background color using a color name value or its hexadecimal equivalent, such as #FFFFFF, which represents the color white.

Block-level Tags   Tags that control sections of page content, such as <blockquote> and <address>.

Blockquote tag <blockquote>...</blockquote>   The tag set that alters the default white space on either side of the affected text.

Body section   Web page section, enclosed in <body>...</body> tags, that contains the page content, such as heading and paragraph elements.

Boldfaced text   Text with a heavier (thicker) line stroke than the default text for a typeface; can be applied to text using the ... or ... tags. The latter is recommended because text readers and visual browsers recognize it.

Border   Box surrounding a displayed HTML element such as an image. Also an attribute that allows you to set the size of an element's border; when used with frames, specifies the space between frames.

Bordercolor Attribute to set the border color of a table.

Bordercolordark Attribute to define the color of the bottom and right edges of a table.

Bordercolorlight Attribute to define the color of the top and left edges of a table.

Broadband Internet connection technologies that allow faster downloads than traditional dial-up modems.

Brochure sites Web sites that display information similar to that found in a printed brochure; not designed to sell a product, but may contain links to sites where products and services are sold.

Browser *See* Web browser.

Browser packaging The appearance of the form and of the page from which it is displayed.

Business e-commerce sites Web sites that contain catalog information and order-processing elements such as shopping carts.

Business sites Web sites that contain an organization's product information, mission statement, and contact information.

Cable modem A broadband connection device that allows for faster data transmission that dial-up connection.

Call A piece of code that specifies the name and location of an external object that will be pulled into a Web page.

Cascade *See* Cascading Style Sheets (CSS).

Cascading Style Sheets (CSS) Web page formatting method that uses rules you create and apply to your Web pages; cascade refers to the ability to apply multiple styles to the same document. Can be applied at the tag level as inline attributes of almost any HMTL tag, at the page level in an embedded style sheet, or externally from a linked style sheet.

Case-sensitive Describes a language or system that treats capital and lower-case versions of the same letter as different characters.

Cell In a table, the intersection of a row and a column.

Cellpadding In a table, an attribute that allows you to control the amount of space between the cell wall and its content.

Cellspacing In a table, an attribute that allows you to control the amount of space between table cells.

CGI (Common Gateway Interface) An interface between the Web client and the processing script; most CGI scripts are written in PERL, C++, or JavaScript.

Character kerning The space between letters within a word.

Character set Defined list of characters recognized by hardware and software; most Web documents use the ISO-8859-1 character set.

Check box Input form field that appears as a small box, each of which displays a single choice among an array of choices that are all visible at once and from which users may select any, all, or none; when a user clicks an empty check box, a check mark appears in the box; clicking a checked box removes the check mark.

Child elements Code elements within a parent tag set. *See also* Parent element.

Click event When a site visitor clicks a link or other object on the page.

Code *See* Source code.

Coded line breaks Line breaks that are forced using the HTML line break tag <br/>.

Color depth The number of bits per pixel that can be displayed on a computer screen. The more bits per pixel in an image, the more colors it can display.

Colspan Attribute to cause a cell to span multiple columns. *See also* Rowspan.

Column A single vertical line of data.

Comment box A form area in which site visitors can enter text; designer specifies the maximum number of characters the box can contain. *See also* Multiline text area.

Comment tag A tag such as (<!-- Comment information goes here. -->, used to make notations and to make it easier to find specific content in your source code; not visible in browser windows.

Content-specific links Links from keywords in your Web page content area to quality external resources

Coords Pixel coordinates that describe the boundaries of the hot spot in an image map, such as coords="94, 205, 0, 205, 0, 42, 132, 137".

Crop Cut unnecessary elements from graphics to optimize images.

CSS *See* Cascading Style Sheets.

CSS class selector rules Named sets of formatting instructions that allow you to define a specific-purpose style in the style sheet and that can be triggered in the document code; the selector name is preceded by a period (.) known as a flag that identifies the rule as a class rule.

CSS declaration Code containing one or more properties and values that describe the CSS style.

CSS selector Code that specifies the element to which a CSS style is applied.

CSS style rule Instructions that describe the formatting of XHML elements; composed of a selector and a declaration. *See also* CSS style selector and CSS style declaration.

Declaration In a style rule, one or more properties and values that describe the style; a colon follows each declaration property and a semicolon follows each declaration property value.

Decoration Formatting enhancements used to emphasize text or block elements including bold text, underline, overline, and box frames.

Description Located in the head section of an HTML document, a metatag that provides a description of your Web page content; useful for supplying search engines with a preferred site description to appear under the results page link.

DHTML Dynamic Hypertext Markup Language, a Web technology that enables a Web page to react to user input without sending requests to the Web server.

Dimension Width and height of an HTML/XHTML element as displayed on a page.

Division Block-level elements often used to treat several block-level elements as one unit.

Division tag <div>...</div> Block-level tag that uses attributes to affect changes in sections of text and to control page output.

Document Type Definition (DTD) Also called a doctype declaration, a tag in the first line of source code to tell the browser what type of XHTML the page is written in, so it can interpret the code.

Dot-slash notation A combination of dots and forward slashes that serve as path designators from one folder to another up and down the directory tree.

Download time The amount of time it takes for a Web page and its files to transfer from their location on the Web to a user's browser.

Drop-down list Expanding form field that allows users to select one or more choices out of several options. *See also* Pull-down menu.

Drop-down menu *See* Drop-down list and Pull-down menu.

DSL Digital Service Line, a high bandwidth connection to the Internet often described as broadband.

E

Em The height and width of the lowercase letter "m" of a chosen font family.

E-mail links Code instructions that give users the ability to click a link that automatically opens an e-mail message; they use the mailto protocol with an e-mail address as the href attribute value.

Embed tag <embed /> Tag used to embed sound or video files to display as Web page content. Requires the source (src) attribute, which specifies the path to the media file used on the Web page.

Embedded media Sound or video files that are displayed as part of a Web page to make the files available to site visitors. Can be used for wav, avi, mpg, and mp3 files.

Emphasized text ... Marks text as emphasized; interpreted by browsers as italic. Interpretable by different Web interfaces; use instead of <i>...</i>.

Enctype Attribute to specify how a browser formats the user responses on a form before submitting to the server.

Extensible Hypertext Markup Language (XHTML) A revision of HTML that transforms the language into a rigorous system in line with related programming languages used for other applications.

Extensible Markup Language (XML) A sister language to HTML, used to deliver reusable data from many databases and multiple platforms in a clear format. This language is case-sensitive and all elements in such documents must be closed.

Extension-specific A characteristic of some file transfer programs, which require that files transferred have specific file extensions.

External style sheets Separate files, saved with a .css extension, that are linked to documents to which their defined styles are applied.

External Web files Files that are hosted on another server or Web site than the site currently being accessed.

F

File type The format in which files are saved—also called file format. Choosing the right format can affect file size and function. Supported Web image formats include JPEG (jpg) and PNG (png).

File Transfer Protocol (FTP) One of the most common methods of transferring files to a server, usually using an FTP client program. *See also* FTP Client and Secure File Transfer Protocol.

flag The period (.) character that precedes a class selector.

Font A complete set of characters, including letters, numbers and special characters, in a particular size and style of type.

Font stack A list of acceptable fonts included as part of the font-family style or font attribute string for the <font> or <basefont> tag.

Form A set of Web page elements with which users interact to submit a request or provide information.

Form element *See* Form field.

Form field A form input area such as a text box, radio button, or pull-down menu that allows user input.

Form handler Program that facilitates communication between the form's front end and back end.

Form label Text entered next to a radio button or a check box that describes the option's function.

Frame A single window in a multiple-window layout that displays the contents of a separate HTML document.

Frameborder Attribute that specifies the border size in a frameset.

Frames Layout method that divides the browser into multiple scrollable windows, each of which contains a separate HTML document.

Frameset Layout control document that specifies the placement and source content of each frame within a frames-based layout; contains one document for each frame and one document (the frameset) as the frames-placement control.

Framespacing Attribute that specifies the space between frames.

Freeware Software you can download from the Internet without charge.

Front end The Web page containing the form that users see in their browsers and from which they submit or request information. *See also* Back end.

FTP Client A program that allows users to transfer files to a server without using command-line instructions, such as InternetSoft FTP Commander or Ipswitch WS_FTP.

FTP Commander An FTP client program created by InternetSoft that lets you transfer files between a local computer and a Web server.

Flash animation A highly compressed multimedia presentation created with proprietary technology from Macromedia Inc. Can be used as a movie file or for as animated navigation elements.

Formatting A powerful tool for visually organizing the content on your Web pages, making it easier for users to identify valuable content and to navigate your site.

Frames A method of displaying page information in several windows simultaneously.

Full-page tile A square image that repeats until the entire page background is filled; usually associated with the background attribute or background style.

G

Get Method.

GIF A proprietary graphic format by CompuServ/Unisys that supports 1-bit transparency and is used for line art and animations; requires a licensing fee in some cases.

Graphical user interface (GUI) A technology that allows users to interact with a computer using icons, folders, pictures, and buttons.

Grid positioning A series of columns and rows used to position and group page elements; gives a design a sense of balance, consistency, and organization.

Hand-coding Creating Web pages by entering the HTML tags yourself, rather than using software to automatically generate code based on a design.

Head *See* Head section.

Head section The portion of a Web page that includes identifying and descriptive information, such as meta tags with the page description and keywords.

height Attribute that specifies the vertical measurement of an HTML/XHTML element in pixels.

Hexadecimal equivalent The six-digit number used to describe the color of a Web page element, such as #FFFF00, which represents yellow.

Hexadecimal triplet Six-digit number to describe a color; named because it is comprised of three pairs of numbers, one for the red value, one for the green value, and one for the blue value. *See also* Hexadecimal equivalent.

Hexadecimal A numbering system based on 16 digits (0 – 9 and A – F). *See also* Hexadecimal equivalent.

Hierarchical structure Organization of information into content sections, from general at the top to more specific beneath it; often used for organizing large sites or sites with potential for fast growth.

High-bandwidth High-speed Internet connections such as T1, T3, DS1, OC1, DSL, and cable modems.

Hot spot A linked area within an image map; defined with a coordinate system that uses the x – y axis of an image. *See also* Image map.

Hover event When the site visitor rests the mouse pointer over a link or other page object.

href The required attribute for a link tag; stands for hypertext reference.

href value In a link tag, the file name and path of the link target location.

hspace Attribute to define, in pixels, the amount of space between the left and right sides of a multimedia element and the surrounding text.

HTML document A text file made up of text and HTML instructions that a browser displays as a Web page.

HTML file *See* HTML document.

Hyperlink *See* Link.

Hyperlinking The ability to jump from one content point to another by clicking hypertext links. *See also* Link.

Hypertext links *See* Link.

Hypertext Markup Language (HTML) The language upon which all Web pages are based.

ID An identifier for any HTML element that can serve as an anchor point for jump links.

Image file extensions The three or four characters that follow the dot (.) in an image file name, such as jpg, jpeg, gif, and png.

Image map Graphic that has different areas linked to different Web files. Each of these mapped areas is a hot spot. *See also* Hot spot.

Import To bring in Web page content from another location, such as a word processing document.

Improved compression The shrinking of audio and video file sizes.

Inline images Graphics that are displayed as content on a page.

Inline style A style applied as an attribute.

Input element Type of form field that, depending upon its type attribute value, can be a radio button, checkbox, text field, push button, reset button, or submit button.

Internal links Links to pages on the same Web site.

International Organization for Standardization (ISO) International organization that helps set standards for Web documents and networks.

Internet The global network of computers that includes the World Wide Web.

Internet Protocol Address Also called an IP address, a four-part numeric address that makes it possible for Web users to find information stored on a particular server.

IP address *See* Internet Protocol Address.

ISDN Integrated Services Digital Network, a high bandwidth connection to the Internet or other networks.

JPEG *See* JPG.

JPG (or JPEG) Photographs and other images with a variable compression that allows tradeoff between better image quality and smaller file size.

Jump links Links that allow users to move from a link to a specific point on that page or on another page. Also called menu links.

Keywords Terms in a Web page that identify the page's key concepts or focus; a search engine uses these to determine ranking when adding a Web page to its database.

Line spacing In page text, the amount of white space between lines.

Linear A Web site structure in which pages are organized in "book style," with one page leading into the next. Also describes a Web page layout that limits stacking of page elements above and below each other, and provides few options for horizontal placement.

Linear layout A layout method in which elements are stacked above and below each other, providing few options for horizontal placement.

Link A specially-formatted Web page object that the user can click to open a different Web file or to move to a specified location on the current Web page or to a specified location on another Web page.

Link states On a Web page, the four possible ways a link can appear, depending on how they have been used; the four link states are normal, visited, hover, and active.

Link tag *See* Anchor tag.

Link titles ScreenTips (pop-up text balloons) that appear when site visitors rest the mouse pointer over a link in which a link title has been specified; useful as accessibility tools for sight-impaired users.

Linked images Graphics that Web page users click to link to another location; by default, linked images display a one-pixel border in the color of linked text on the page.

Logical formatting Formatting tags that indicate an element's specific role and enable the formatting to be heard via text readers as well as seen in visual browsers. *See also* Physical formatting.

Macromedia Flash animation Animation created using the Macromedia Flash program; requires the Flash player program to be installed on the Web page user's computer for viewing.

Magic targets Link targets that begin with an underscore character, usually used in sites that use frames (sites that display parts of the page in several windows simultaneously); useful for opening linked files in a new window from any page.

Margin Added space around an element.

Mark up Add HTML tags to source code so pages can be viewed using a browser.

Markup Tags surrounding page content that tell the browser how to interpret and display Web page information.

Menu links *See* Jump links.

Meta tags Placed in the head section of an HTML document, tags that provide additional information to help search engines identify and describe your page content, such as the description and keywords metatags.

Method Attribute indicate how data entered by the user is submitted to the server; acceptable values are "get"—for calling information from the server—and "post"—for sending information to the server.

middle When set, causes image middle to line up with the vertical middle of text line between baseline and text top.

Multimedia The integration of sound and/or video with Web page text and graphics.

Multiline text area A large form field designed to allow less-structured, paragraph-length user input, allowing users to make additional comments or ask questions. *See also* comment box.

Name Required attribute for HTML objects such as form fields that are accessed by a script or that submit information; defines the data field to which information is submitted or identifies the object that is accessed by the script.

Navigation bar A set of links arranged in either a horizontal or vertical display. Top-level navigation bars usually contain links to the home page and main section pages of a Web site, and usually appear on every page; can be text- or graphic-based page element with links to other pages.

Nested Frames Framesets placed within framesets; allows for both horizontal and vertical frames within the same window.

Nested list A list that is wholly contained within another list. The opening list tag of a nested list appears before the closing list tag of the parent list.

Nested tables Tables that are fully contained within the cell of another table; often used to produce more complex page designs.

Nested tags In Web page code, tags that are fully contained within another tag.

Net structure Sketch of the relationship of pages within a Web site.

Network A group of interconnected computers that can be used to share files and to communicate with one another. Networks can be local, (LAN), organization-based (Intranet), or worldwide. The largest worldwide network is the Internet.

Non-linear content Information that does not need to be read in a particular order, such as on the World Wide Web.

Noresize Attribute that prevents frames from being resized in the browser window.

Nowrap attribute Attribute that prevents table cell content from wrapping to the next line.

Object tag set <object>...</object> Used for implementing scripts on a Web page. Also used for implementing Java applets and Flash or other multimedia. When used with Flash, embeds a call to the download site for the Flash player making it easy for users to obtain and install the program.

Open tag Tags that do not have corresponding closing elements, such as the line break tag <br />.

Optimize To adjust an object's resolution, dimension, file type, and color depth to create the smallest file size possible for Web delivery.

Ordered list A list in which each item is automatically numbered or lettered. *See also* Unordered list.

Padding Added space within an element, such as a table cell.

Page-level formatting tags Tags such as ..., ... and <font>...</font> that apply formatting at the page level by applying formatting codes directly to text or other elements within the body section of a document. Most have been deprecated by the W3C in favor of style-sheet formatting.

Page title In the head section of an HTML document, the name of a page, enclosed in the <title>...</title> tags.

Paragraph tag *See* Paragraph tag set.

Paragraph tag set <p> ... </p> Marks paragraph text within the body of an HTML document.

Parent element A tag set in which another tag is nested.

Passive white space White space that serves no purpose and that can be distracting to the site user.

Personal digital assistant (PDA) Handheld device used for scheduling and other purposes, on which Web page information can be displayed.

Personal sites Web sites that can be used to communicate with friends or family, post professional résumés or portfolios, or honor a favorite public figure.

Physical formats Formats that can only be recognized visually; not recognized by text readers and other accessibility devices. *See also* Logical formatting.

Pipe A character (|) often used as a dividing element between adjacent sets of linked text in a text- based horizontal navigation bar.

Pixels Adapted from the term "pixel element," single points of light that make up the display on a computer screen; abbreviated as "px."

Placeholder File containing text explaining that a target page is incomplete; serves as a link target for an unfinished Web page. Also, a set of text elements or graphics that represent page content not yet developed.

Platform The unique characteristics of a Web user's computer system, including browser brand, browser version, operating system, and screen resolution.

PNG A Web-compatible graphic format developed by Microsoft; supports 32-bit (gradient) transparency and can be used for line art as well as for photographs.

Post *See* Method.

Posture A characteristic of type that refers to its angle on the page, such as italic.

Properties An object's qualities such as size, location, color, or type.

Public support sites Web sites that contain downloadable user manuals, forms, and software drivers. Can also be part of a company intranet that enables users to upload and download company documents and to access shared databases.

Publicly accessible Web site A site that is hosted on an Internet server and does not require log-in permission for file viewing.

Pull-down menu Expanding form field that allows users to select one or more choices out of several options; also known as a select option box or drop-down list, appears on the page as a single-line text field with a down-arrow button the user clicks to open a menu of choices. *See also* Drop-down menu and Scroll box.

Push button A labeled form object that a user clicks to perform a task; created using the <input /> tag. *See also* Submit button and Reset button.

Radio button Input form field of the type "radio" that appears as a small white circle, usually next to explanatory text; allows users to select one of several choices. Fills with black when selected.

Relative link Link that includes only information about the target page's location relative to the current Web page (for example, <a href="justice.htm">); useful for referencing other pages in a site, typing the entire path to each page. *See also* Absolute link.

Reset button An input object of the type "reset"; when clicked, erases form information without sending it. *See also* Push button and Reset button.

Resolution A monitor's screen display dimensions (width by height), in pixels; for example, 800 × 600.

Root element In well-formed HTML code, element names contained within the opening and closing html tags.

Root folder Top-level folder for a Web site; contains all Web site files.

Row In a table, a single horizontal line of data.

Rowspan Attribute to cause a cell to span multiple rows *See also* Colspan.

Sans serif fonts Literally means "without serifs;" fonts in this group do not have decorative tails. *See also* Serif font.

Script A list of commands that run automatically on a Web page to provide extra information or to track user movements.

Scroll box Expanding form field that allows users to select one or more choices out of several options. *See also* Drop-down menu and Pull-down menu.

Scrolling Attribute to control the appearance of the frame's scrollbars; a "yes" value always includes scrollbars, and "no" prevents scrollbars from appearing. When attribute is absent or set to "auto", scrollbars appear only as needed.

Seamless Applied to images, indicating that the end user cannot tell where one repetition of the image ends and the next begins.

Secure File Transfer Protocol A method of transferring files to a server that also includes encryption for addition security.

Select option box *See* Pull-down menu.

Selector In a style declaration, specifies the element to which a style is applied.

Serif fonts Fonts with small "tails" called serifs at the ends of the lines that make up each letter. *See also* Sans serif font.

Server *See* Web server.

Shopping cart service Service provider that provides order processing, billing, and credit card services.

Single-line text box Form input field that allows users to enter a limited number of alphanumeric characters such as first or last name, street address, or e-mail address; designer can specify the size and maximum number of characters permitted.

Site navigation bar *See* Navigation bar.

Site storyboard A sketch of a Web site's organization and structure.

Source *See* source code.

Source code The text and HTML code that make up a Web document.

Span In a table, to cover or become part of multiple rows or columns.

Sponsored links Links that site owners have paid search engines to place at the top of their list of found references.

Stacked tables One or more tables in which the code for one table ends before the code for another begins; not dependent upon one another for width, height, or placement.

Stacked tags In Web page code, tags that are closed before the next tag begins or are opened after the previous tag has ended.

State The condition of a link that indicates how it has been or will be used, such as active, visited, or hovered.

Storyboard *See* Storyboard layout sketch.

Storyboard layout sketch Drawing that shows the desired arrangement of the major elements you want to include in your Web page.

Storyboarding Planning Web page or Web site design by sketching the elements you want to include and how you want them arranged.

Streaming Multimedia Technology A method of transferring data that allows it to be processed in a steady, continuous stream, allowing the browser or plug-in to start displaying the data before the entire file has been transmitted.

Structuring table A grid-based page layout upon which a page template is based.

Style sheets Files composed of one or more CSS rules that dictate the way page content appears; can be embedded within a document's head section to control page formatting, or saved as separate files to control formatting for multiple pages. *See also* Cascading style sheets.

Submit button An input object with the type "submit"; when clicked, submits information for processing. *See also* Push button and Reset button.

Syntax The language rules and structures of a programming language such as XHTML.

T-1 and T-3 connections Dedicated phone line technologies that are actually bundles of copper phone lines; T-1 bundles 24 individual lines, and T-3 bundles 67 lines, each of which supports 64 Kbps of file-transfer capacity.

Table A grid-based layout of columns and rows; used to control page layout or display data.

Table data tag (<td>...</td>) In a table, indicates a table data cell, the most basic data unit in a table.

Table heading tag (<th>...</th>) In a table, identifies table heading content; its content is horizontally centered and bold.

Tag Each HTML instruction in an HTML document.

Tag set A pair of opening and closing HTML tags, such as <style> </style>, that surround a page element.

Target The Web page that opens when a user clicks a link.

Target audience Product users to whom a product or Web page designer will aim their product.

Template Document containing the Web page code for a page's structure, along with any text or elements that appear on every page; used as a basis for designing pages to ensure consistency within a site.

Template A document containing Web page code for the structure and common elements of all the pages in a Web site.

Text attribute Sets the text color for a Web page.

Text box An input element that allows users to input a short line of text. *See also* Single-line text box.

Text image A graphic showing text; best used sparingly to implement formats that HTML cannot reliably create.

Text jumping Common to graphic-heavy pages; text on a page begins to load and then must "jump" out of the way to make room for an image that appears later in the page-load process.

Tile Repeat an image across and down the page to fill the background.

Type Required attribute for input form fields; defines the way a form field appears in a form and the type of data a form field accepts.

Type selectors Also called tag selectors, specifies elements by their names and applies the CSS rule to all tags of the same name.

Typeface A series of fonts such as Times Bold, Times Italic, and Times New Roman, which are different fonts in the same family.

Uniform Resource Locator (URL) A Web site address consisting of the hypertext transfer protocol (http:), the Web server name (usually www), and the domain name, such as course.com.

Unordered list A list in which a bullet character, instead of a number or letter, designates each list item. *See also* Ordered list.

Upload Transfer, such as files to a Web server.

URL *See* Uniform Resource Locator.

User ID A unique identifying number assigned to a server user by a system administrator that, along with a password, grants the server user permission to transfer files to that server.

Value An attribute modifier that specifies or changes a tag's behavior or function.

vlink Visited link.

vspace An HTML attribute that sets the amount of vertical space in pixels between the surrounding text and the top and bottom of an inline image, media player, or object.

Web browser A software program, installed on a user's computer, that allows users to view Web page.

Web page A file containing text and HTML markup that is saved with an appropriate extensions such as, .htm, .html, .shtml, .dhtml, .asp, .jsp, etc. Also known as a Web document.

Web server A computer permanently connected to the Internet, usually by means of lines reserved for that purpose, that stores published Web documents for delivery to client computers.

Web site A group of related Web pages published to a Web server.

Webcasting Media programming delivered over the Internet, rather than through air waves.

Weight A characteristic of type appearance, such as boldfaced.

White space Any empty area in a Web page layout.

White space Any empty area on a page; not necessarily white.

Word spacing The amount of space between words.

World Wide Web (Web, WWW) Information contained on the vast network of interconnected computers known as the Internet. Information on the Web is divided up into sites and files.

Write access Permission to transfer files to a server or update files in a directory.

XHTML *See* Extensible Hypertext Markup Language.

XHTML Frameset XHTML document that uses frames to partition the browser window into two or more windows.

XHTML Strict XHTML document that contains no layout or formatting markup and that uses only CSS to apply formatting effects.

XHTML Transitional XHTML document that takes advantage of CSS but might contain markup adjustments, such as bgcolor or text and link attributes in the body tag, to make pages backward compatible.

XML *See* Extensible Markup Language.

Index